EPICUREAN JUSTICE

The ancient Greek philosopher Epicurus and his followers advanced a sophisticated theory of justice that occupied a middle position between Plato and Aristotle, on the one hand, and some Sophists, on the other. They held that justice is neither fully natural nor fully conventional, that there is a robust virtue of justice, and that it is always better to be just than to be unjust, but it is not always better to obey the laws. In this book, the first English-language monograph on the topic, Jan Maximilian Robitzsch draws on a range of sources including papyrological evidence to give a comprehensive account of Epicurean justice. He shows how it relates to Epicurean philosophy as a whole and discusses to what extent it can be seen to anticipate modern positions such as contractarianism and legal positivism.

JAN MAXIMILIAN ROBITZSCH is a senior researcher in the Department of Philosophy, University of Greifswald. He is the coeditor of *Speeches for the Dead: Essays on Plato's Menexenus* (2018) and the author of a number of articles in journals including *Ancient Philosophy*, *Apeiron*, and *Classical Quarterly*.

EPICUREAN JUSTICE

Nature, Agreement, and Virtue

JAN MAXIMILIAN ROBITZSCH
University of Greifswald

Shaftesbury Road, Cambridge CB2 8EA, United Kingdom

One Liberty Plaza, 20th Floor, New York, NY 10006, USA

477 Williamstown Road, Port Melbourne, VIC 3207, Australia

314–321, 3rd Floor, Plot 3, Splendor Forum, Jasola District Centre, New Delhi – 110025, India

103 Penang Road, #05–06/07, Visioncrest Commercial, Singapore 238467

Cambridge University Press is part of Cambridge University Press & Assessment, a department of the University of Cambridge.

We share the University's mission to contribute to society through the pursuit of education, learning and research at the highest international levels of excellence.

www.cambridge.org
Information on this title: www.cambridge.org/9781009429443

DOI: 10.1017/9781009429436

© Jan Maximilian Robitzsch 2024

This publication is in copyright. Subject to statutory exception and to the provisions of relevant collective licensing agreements, no reproduction of any part may take place without the written permission of Cambridge University Press & Assessment.

First published 2024
First paperback edition 2025

A catalogue record for this publication is available from the British Library

ISBN 978-1-009-42946-7 Hardback
ISBN 978-1-009-42944-3 Paperback

Cambridge University Press & Assessment has no responsibility for the persistence or accuracy of URLs for external or third-party internet websites referred to in this publication and does not guarantee that any content on such websites is, or will remain, accurate or appropriate.

Für
Christine Weber-Robitzsch
und
Lutz-Henning Robitzsch

Contents

Acknowledgments		*page* ix
	Introduction	1
1	The Origin of Justice	14
	1.1 The Structure of Lucretius' Account of the Development of Political Communities	16
	1.2 The Original State	19
	1.3 The *Phusis* Phase	25
	1.4 The *Logismos* Phase	37
	1.5 Epicurean Social Contract Theory	46
2	Contractual Justice	49
	2.1 The Naturally Just: *Nomos* Grounded in *Phusis*	49
	2.2 Benefit, Harm, and Security: Agreements and Their Role in Epicurean Philosophy	55
	2.3 The Parties of Epicurean Agreements	65
3	Aretaic Justice	80
	3.1 The Epicurean Virtues	81
	3.2 Justice as an Epicurean Virtue	89
	3.3 Two Kinds of Justice?	94
4	Moral Psychology	98
	4.1 Plutarch's Account of the Sage Violating a Law	99
	4.2 Moral Psychology and Justice	100
	4.3 The Importance of a Just Law	104
	4.4 Objections and Replies	112
5	Justice and Law	118
	5.1 Natural Law and Legal Positivism	119
	5.2 The Epicureans on the Relationship between Justice and Law	124

6	Ethical Naturalism	128
	6.1 The Ontology of the Moral: Justice as a Property	130
	6.2 Moral Epistemology	141
7	Conclusion	161

Appendix A Oikeōsis   165
Appendix B Cicero, the Epicureans, and the Ring of Gyges   171
Bibliography   175
Index Locorum   194
General Index   198

Acknowledgments

In writing this book on Epicurean justice, I have accumulated debts of gratitude. First and foremost, I would like to thank Susan Sauvé Meyer, Alexander Guerrero, Phillip Mitsis, and the late Charles Kahn for their conversations about and feedback on my ideas, which have made me a better researcher and saved me from many errors. Andreas Kamp first suggested to me that I should take a look at the Epicureans, and I am grateful to him for this suggestion. I had many conversations about the Epicureans and ancient philosophy more generally with many people, but I am especially thankful to Andreas Avgousti, Aditi Chaturvedi, Rex Mixon, Hal Parker, and Clerk Shaw.

I presented parts of various chapters at different professional meetings and universities. It is not possible to enumerate all of these talks here, but I am grateful to the audience members and commentators on each of these occasions for their suggestions for improvement. The two anonymous readers for Cambridge University Press helped me improve the typescript. I thank them for the time they took to read my work and to provide me with detailed comments. The same is also true of the preliminary studies on various aspects of Epicurean thought that shaped my thinking about the Epicurean justice: I am grateful to all referees for urging me to express my ideas more clearly and cogently.

Finally, I would like to thank my wife Caitlin Butler, who both has been very supportive of my decision to be an academic and has regularly reminded me that there are other important things in life besides work. And I would like to dedicate this book to my parents Christine Weber-Robitzsch and Lutz-Henning Robitzsch, without whose continued support in every imaginable way I would never be writing these lines.

Introduction

One of the greatest and best-known debates in ancient Greece is the so-called *nomos-phusis* debate that has its origins in the fifth century BCE.[1] As a first approximation, this debate is a precursor of the modern, perhaps more familiar nature-nurture debate, which deals with the issue of which features in human beings are genetically and which are culturally determined. The verb "*nomizō*" in Greek means to think, believe, or practice. Consequently, things thought, believed, or practiced by human beings are in this debate said to be "by convention" (*nomōi*). Likewise, "*nomoi*" are "culturally determined" human conventions, customs, or laws. "*Phusis*," by contrast, is usually translated as "nature," in the sense of an essential and permanent entity, and so what is "by nature (*phusei*)" is the opposite of what is by convention.

It would be a mistake, though, to leave it at this characterization of the *nomos-phusis* debate since it oversimplifies what is really at stake. The reason is that the words "*nomos*" and "*phusis*" were used in a variety of different ways in different contexts in the Classical and Hellenistic periods. For instance, they were used in regard to such different subject matters as language, perception, or cultural norms as discussions in Plato's *Cratylus* and *Theaetetus* or Herodotus' *Histories* III.38 make clear. In these contexts, the pair *nomos/phusis* can be fittingly translated by the pairs prescriptive/descriptive, appearance/reality, artificial/natural, or contingent-accidental/necessary, since the terms are respectively used to draw normative, epistemological, ontological, and modal distinctions.[2] This makes it difficult

---

[1] See above all Heinimann 1945; Pohlenz 1953; Guthrie 2003 [1971], 55–134; Kerferd 1981, 111–30; and McKirahan 2010, 405–26.

[2] McKirahan 2010, 407. The debate on justice includes normative, epistemological, and ontological aspects that are not always neatly distinguished. This plurality of aspects is also on display in third-century BCE Epicurean Polystratus' treatise *On Irrational Contempt for Common Conceptions* (cols. XXI.17–XXIX.1 Indelli), which we will examine in the following chapters.

to distill one single issue that the *nomos-phusis* debate is about and so to characterize the debate as a whole accurately.

In regard to justice, the *nomos-phusis* debate is particularly interesting and rich, as many thinkers weighed in on the question of whether justice is natural or artificial, that is, exists as part of the fabric of the world or was only created by human beings. The debate is especially clearly on display in Plato's (428/7–348/7 BCE) *Republic*, where not only the conventional *nomos* view of justice is vividly canvassed but also the rivaling *phusis* account.

After hot-headed Thrasymachus has been dismissed in book I, Glaucon steps to the fore. The fictional incarnation of Plato's brother, as the Devil's advocate, challenges Socrates, the main speaker of the dialogue and – on the most common reading – spokesperson for Plato, with an account of justice that can be said to be a prototype of the *nomos* view:

Πεφυκέναι γὰρ δή φασιν τὸ μὲν ἀδικεῖν ἀγαθόν, τὸ δὲ ἀδικεῖσθαι κακόν, πλέονι δὲ κακῷ ὑπερβάλλειν τὸ ἀδικεῖσθαι ἢ ἀγαθῷ τὸ ἀδικεῖν, ὥστ' ἐπειδὰν ἀλλήλους ἀδικῶσί τε καὶ ἀδικῶνται καὶ ἀμφοτέρων γεύωνται, τοῖς μὴ δυναμένοις τὸ μὲν ἐκφεύγειν τὸ δὲ αἱρεῖν δοκεῖ λυσιτελεῖν συνθέσθαι ἀλλήλοις μήτ' ἀδικεῖν μήτ' ἀδικεῖσθαι· καὶ ἐντεῦθεν δὴ ἄρξασθαι νόμους τίθεσθαι καὶ συνθήκας αὑτῶν, καὶ ὀνομάσαι τὸ ὑπὸ τοῦ νόμου ἐπίταγμα νόμιμόν τε καὶ δίκαιον· καὶ εἶναι δὴ ταύτην γένεσίν τε καὶ οὐσίαν δικαιοσύνης, μεταξὺ οὖσαν τοῦ μὲν ἀρίστου ὄντος, ἐὰν ἀδικῶν μὴ διδῷ δίκην, τοῦ δὲ κακίστου, ἐὰν ἀδικούμενος τιμωρεῖσθαι ἀδύνατος ᾖ· τὸ δὲ δίκαιον ἐν μέσῳ ὂν τούτων ἀμφοτέρων ἀγαπᾶσθαι οὐχ ὡς ἀγαθόν, ἀλλ' ὡς ἀρρωστίᾳ τοῦ ἀδικεῖν τιμώμενον· ἐπεὶ τὸν δυνάμενον αὐτὸ ποιεῖν καὶ ὡς ἀληθῶς ἄνδρα οὐδ' ἂν ἑνί ποτε συνθέσθαι τὸ μήτε ἀδικεῖν μήτε ἀδικεῖσθαι· μαίνεσθαι γὰρ ἄν. ἡ μὲν οὖν δὴ φύσις δικαιοσύνης, ὦ Σώκρατες, αὕτη τε καὶ τοιαύτη, καὶ ἐξ ὧν πέφυκε τοιαῦτα, ὡς ὁ λόγος.

They say that to do injustice is naturally good and to suffer injustice bad, but that the badness of suffering it so far exceeds the goodness of doing it that those who have done and suffered injustice and tasted both, but who lack the power to do it and avoid suffering it, decide that it is profitable to come to an agreement with each other neither to do injustice nor to suffer it. As a result, they begin to make laws and agreements with one another, and what the law commands they call lawful and just. This, they say, is the origin and essence of justice. It is intermediate between the best and the worst. The best is to do injustice without paying the penalty; the worst is to suffer it without being able to take revenge. Justice is a mean between these two extremes. People value it not as a good but because they are too weak to do injustice with impunity. Someone who has the power to do this, however, and is a true man would not make an agreement with anyone not to do injustice in order not to suffer it. For him that would be madness. This is the nature of justice, according to the argument, Socrates, and these are its natural origins.[3]

What makes the account that Glaucon outlines a *nomos* account is that justice is explicitly described as the result of an agreement (*suntheke*) and so said to exist only because the agreement exists. Put differently, the account that Glaucon advances emphasizes the completely conventional or artificial nature of justice, that is, that justice is the product of people having weighed advantages and disadvantages of being just at a certain point in time and having determined what is just as a kind of compromise between two undesirable extremes, the goodness of doing injustices and the badness of suffering them. In short, the account that Glaucon proposes prima facie amounts to a kind of social contract theory, a doctrine that is typically associated with early modern authors such as Thomas Hobbes and John Locke, among others.[4]

The obvious follow-up to such a conception of justice is to further probe the proponent of such a doctrine as to whether there are situations in which it is really better to be unjust rather than to be just. After all, if justice is merely conventional, as on the *nomos* view, it seems to follow that if the circumstances change (and one might not suffer the badness of suffering injustice), it may be better not to perform actions that had been previously agreed upon as just. The famous Ring of Gyges story that Glaucon relates shortly after the passage quoted above precisely addresses this issue:[5] a shepherd finds a ring that gives him the power to become invisible. This allows him to commit whatever deeds he wishes without being noticed and held accountable by his fellow human beings. Thus, in such a situation, does an agent have reasons to be just? And again: Is it better for him to be just rather than to be unjust? It seems that the conventional account of justice will simply claim that agents do not always have to be just as it is unclear that this would bring the agent more advantages than can be obtained by committing injustices. This is even more the case insofar as there is no robust virtue of justice on this view that could guarantee just behavior in the absence of the agreements that determine what is just.

---

[3] Plato, *Republic* II.358e–359b. Trans. Grube, modified.
[4] On social contract theory in antiquity, see Kaerst 1909; Guthrie 2003 [1971]: 135–47; Kahn 1981; Müller 1985; and Sprute 1989. On the history of social contract theory in general, see Gough 1957.
[5] Plato, *Republic* 359c–360d. See Appendix B on how the Epicureans engage with this thought experiment.

Unfortunately, Glaucon does not name the source for the account of justice he advances, but there is some evidence that similar views were held among Pre-Socratic thinkers and Sophists.[6] Antiphon (fifth century BCE), in particular, defends a position that in some ways resembles the account Glaucon outlines, although Antiphon's view is less radical insofar as he claims only that the *laws* (not justice) are the products of agreements in light of what is beneficial:[7]

Δικα[ιοσ]ύνη [δ' οὖ]ν τὰ τῆς πόλεως νόμιμα, [ἐν ἧι] ἂν πολι[τεύ]ηταί τις, μὴ [παρ]αβαίνειν. χρῶιτ' ἂν οὖν ἄνθρωπος μάλιστα ἑαυτῶι ξυμφ[ε]ρόντως δικαιο[σ]ύνηι, εἰ μετὰ μὲν μαρτύρων τοὺς νόμους μεγάλους ἄγοι, μονούμενος δὲ μαρτύρων τὰ τῆς φύσεως· τὰ μὲν γὰρ τῶν νόμων [ἐπίθ]ετα, τὰ δὲ [τῆς] φύσεως ἀ[ναγ]καῖα· καὶ τὰ [μὲν] τῶν νό[μω]ν ὁμολογη[θέντ]α οὐ φύν[τα ἐστί]ν, τὰ δὲ [τῆς φύσ]εως [φύντα οὐχ] ὁμολογηθ[έ]ντα [[ο]υχ [ο]μολογηθεντα]]. τὰ οὖν νόμιμα παραβαίνων ἐὰν λάθηι τοὺς ὁμολογήσαντας καὶ αἰσχύνης καὶ ζημίας ἀπήλλακται· μὴ λαθὼν δ' οὔ· τῶν δὲ τῆι φύσει ξυμφύτων ἐάν τι παρὰ τὸ δυνατὸν βιάζηται, ἐάν τε πάντας ἀνθρώπους λάθηι, οὐδὲν ἔλαττον τὸ κακόν, ἐάν τε πάντες ἴδωσιν, οὐδὲν μεῖζον· οὐ γὰρ διὰ δόξαν βλάπτεται, ἀλλὰ δι' ἀλήθειαν.

So justice is not to transgress the laws of the city in which one is a citizen. Thus a man would use justice in a way most advantageous to himself, if, in the presence of witnesses, he held the laws in esteem, whereas when he was alone, he valued the works of nature. For the works of law are fictitious, whereas those of nature are necessary; and the works of law, being conventional are not natural while those of nature, being natural, are not conventional. Thus one who transgresses the laws, if he eludes those who agree on them, also escapes shame and punishment, but if not, he does not. But if he undertakes to violate what is possible of things innate in nature, even if he eludes all men, the evil that results is no less; even if all observe, it is no more. For he is harmed, not because of opinion, but in truth.[8]

In this passage, Antiphon also maintains that the *laws* can be broken if they no longer serve their purpose. On a *nomos* account then, one might say that it is not only not always better to be just, but it is also not always better to obey the law. As a result, it is perhaps hardly surprising that the defenders of a conventional account, like Antiphon, were seen as

---

[6] For some discussion, see Horkey 2021.
[7] Since justice is not a product of an agreement for Antiphon, Guthrie 2003 [1971], 107–13, describes Antiphon as a defender of *phusis*.
[8] DK 80 B 44 (= *POxy.* XI 1364). Trans. Graham, modified.

advancing ideas that are corrosive to the foundations of morality and of the political community as such.[9]

In short, we can sum up the conventional theory of justice by the three claims that were just discussed:

(1) Justice is the result of a convention of some kind.
(2) It is not always better to be just than to be unjust (and there is no robust virtue of justice).
(3) It is not always better to obey the laws than not to obey them.

Now, as is well known, Socrates offers a detailed response to Glaucon in the *Republic*, one meant to rebut the conventional account of justice.[10] This account is a version of the *phusis* or nature account of justice. Recall that on the conventional view, justice arises only through the agreements that people make, and that prior to these agreements, there is simply no justice. Against this, the response of the *Republic* insists that, from a metaethical perspective, there are not only sensible particulars of justice but also a Form of justice.[11] What Forms precisely are, of course, is a matter of great debate in scholarship, but for present purposes, it is perhaps sufficient to note that they are the most real constituents of the world.[12] Furthermore, in contrast to the particular objects of the sensible world, they do not experience change.[13] This latter feature is especially important because it also means that Forms do not come into existence and go out of existence. Instead, they are stable models, according to which particular things, which partake in them, come to be.[14] Accordingly, Socrates counters the conventional account's first claim that justice is conventional by insisting that there is a Form of justice and that this Form is not a product of what people have agreed on contingently at a certain point in time.

In regard to the second claim of the conventional account, according to which agents are not always required to be just and there is no virtue of justice, Socrates famously proposes the analogy between a city-state and an individual as a heuristic device, since there is a continuity between the justice of a city-state and justice of an individual, on his view. Socrates

---

[9] See also the accounts of the law in the sophists Thrasymachus and Callicles in Plato's *Republic* and *Gorgias*. These accounts advance a similar conception of laws as Antiphon does. For Thrasymachus and Callicles, the laws are either artificial constraints or merely instruments of the powerful to receive what they are owed.
[10] Discussions of the main argument of the *Republic* are, for instance, found in White 1979; Annas 1981; Kraut 1992; and Pappas 1995.
[11] See, for instance, Plato, *Republic* V.479e.   [12] Plato, *Phaedrus* 247c.
[13] See, for instance, Plato, *Republic* V.479e and *Symposium* 211b.
[14] On participation, see, for instance, Plato, *Phaedo* 74a–75b and 100c–e.

suggests that the interlocutors should investigate justice in an imaginary city-state (*polis*) first because it is easier to spot there. Building the imaginary city-state, the interlocutors quickly decide that three classes are needed to create a well-functioning whole: a ruling-political class (the guardians), a ruling-policing class (the auxiliaries), and a product-manufacturing class (the artisans). And drawing on what later becomes the standard list of four virtues (wisdom, courage, temperance, and justice), Socrates sets out to identify justice as the virtue that all citizens ought to possess individually to make the state function: every class of citizens has a clearly delineated scope of work and should perform this work and not perform the work in the scope of another class. On the level of the city-state, then, according to the argument of the *Republic*, it is an injustice if a cobbler, an artisan, performs the work of a politician, a member of the ruling-political class, or if a soldier, a member of the auxiliary class, is made to perform the functions of a member of the product-producing class, say, a baker. This will lead to turmoil and stasis in the city-state.

Having identified justice in the city-state, Socrates and his interlocutors turn to the human soul. Socrates argues for its tripartite structure, consisting of rational, spirited, and appetitive parts, with analogous functions as the classes of the city-state. He then again draws on the previously identified virtues, and the interlocutors decide, in analogy to the first part of the argument, that justice is to be understood as each part of the soul performing its own function: The function of the rational part is to make decisions and so rule. The function of the spirited part is to be the driving force for action. And the function of the appetitive part is to desire objects to be pursued. On the level of the individual, the greatest injustice thus occurs when some part of the soul diverts from the function for which it was intended. Perhaps the clearest example is the case of the tyrannical person, whose appetitive part is in charge, that is, performs the function of the ruling, rational part of the soul. The result is the same as in the political case: turmoil and stasis. This, according to Socrates, gives us the reason to be just: no one wants to live a life full of mental distress.

Since people want to be free of mental distress all of the time, not merely some of the time, they have a good reason to think that being just is better than being unjust all of the time. It is hard to see how exceptions to this rule could be justified. The *virtue* of justice, understood as a stable disposition of character, accordingly plays a key role in the *Republic*, while it did not play a role in the conventional account of justice, which emphasized agreements as the means to create stability in society in place of a robust virtue of justice. Instead of the claim of the conventional account that it is not always better to be just, then, Socrates maintains with the help of the analogy between the city-state and the individual that it is indeed always better to be just.

Given the above, it is difficult to see how an agent could justify the claim that the law should not be obeyed on the account of the *Republic*, either. First, a violation of the law, no matter how minor, could create mental distress, and in real life, it is not at all certain that an agent could escape detection after violating a law. More importantly, however, Socrates himself offers a series of reasons for obeying the law in another dialogue, the *Crito*: even when he has been condemned to death by the city-state of Athens that has wronged him, Socrates argues that he has overriding, principled reasons to obey the laws of the city-state and so accept the verdict and the penalty that was established for him. In short, then, on the *phusis* view, one should always abide by the law, which contradicts the third claim advanced by the conventional account of justice, namely, that it is *not* always better to obey the laws than not to obey them.

In what is perhaps the most famous account of justice in Greco-Roman antiquity beside the *Republic*, the fifth book of the *Nicomachean Ethics*, Aristotle (384–322 BCE) offers a conception of justice that is of the same type as the *phusis* account Socrates advances in the *Republic*.[15] While Aristotle famously rejects the Platonic theory of Forms, he nevertheless argues for a kind of ethical naturalism.[16] Justice does not arise as the result of agreements, but is the same everywhere regardless of whatever laws are in place:

> Τοῦ δὲ πολιτικοῦ δικαίου τὸ μὲν φυσικόν ἐστι τὸ δὲ νομικόν, φυσικὸν μὲν τὸ πανταχοῦ τὴν αὐτὴν ἔχον δύναμιν, καὶ οὐ τῷ δοκεῖν ἢ μή, νομικὸν δὲ ὃ ἐξ ἀρχῆς μὲν οὐδὲν διαφέρει οὕτως ἢ ἄλλως, ὅταν δὲ θῶνται, διαφέρει, οἷον τὸ μνᾶς λυτροῦσθαι, ἢ τὸ αἶγα θύειν ἀλλὰ μὴ δύο πρόβατα, ἔτι ὅσα ἐπὶ τῶν καθ' ἕκαστα νομοθετοῦσιν, οἷον τὸ θύειν Βρασίδᾳ, καὶ τὰ ψηφισματώδη.

> Of the politically just, one part is natural, the other part is legal. The natural part is that which has the same force everywhere and does not seem this or that to someone. The legal part, by contrast, is that which from the beginning does not differ in one way or another, but when it has been laid down, it differs, for instance, the release on the receipt of a ransom of a mina, or the sacrificing of a goat but not two sheep, and further the laws

---

[15] See, for instance, Kraut 2002, 98–177; Young 2006; and Polansky 2014.
[16] On ethical naturalism, see also the discussion in Chapter 6.

that are passed in regard to particular cases, for instance, sacrificing to Brasidas, and the provisions of decrees.[17]

Furthermore, in addition to the political and legal forms of justice just mentioned, Aristotle distinguishes a kind of personal justice in his account. This latter kind of justice is part of his theory of virtues. This theory is quite complex in itself, and it is an open question among scholars whether Aristotle succeeded in extending his general account of the virtues to justice as well; a full review, in any case, of these ideas would require a separate monograph. Suffice it to say that Aristotle ranks justice among the moral virtues, that is, dispositions of character that agents ought to cultivate through habituation and that are essential to leading a good life.[18] Given this tight connection between justice and the good life, it is difficult to see how Aristotle could advocate for anything but the thesis that it is always better to be just. Similarly, Aristotle stresses the importance of good and just laws and political institutions for the cultivation of personal justice, making it difficult to see how he could advocate for anything but the importance of obeying the law.

Given the Socratic/Platonic view canvassed above and the (very brief) discussion of Aristotle's view, we can sum up the natural account of justice by the following three claims that contrast with the *nomos* account that Glaucon advances:

(1) Justice is natural (not merely the product of an agreement that people made).
(2) It is always better to be just (and there is a robust virtue of justice).
(3) It is always better to obey the law.

While the accounts of justice thus far discussed are the best known, they certainly do not exhaust the theoretical space. In fact, Epicurus of Samos (341–270 BCE) and his followers during the Hellenistic period[19] defend an alternative view of justice that is less well known. In many ways, the Epicurean view contrasts with the Platonic and Aristotelian way of thinking about justice, while also differing from the conventional account of

---

[17] *Nicomachean Ethics*, V.7.1134b18–24. Trans. mine.
[18] For Aristotle, justice, like all the virtues, is expressed by the choice of a "mean" (*meson*) that is in between "extremes" (*akra*), that is, between the extremes of being wronged oneself and wronging someone else. Justice extends to both the allotment of shares (distributive justice) as well as the correction of wrongs (retributive justice).
[19] On the school in general, see Erler 1994 and Clay 1998.

justice that is associated with Sophists.[20] This account will be the subject of this book.

In addition to his empiricism, atomism, and hedonism, Epicurus is known as a defender of a kind of social contract theory. Since social contract theory in general is associated with the *nomos* account of justice, that is, a kind of conventionalism, it would prima facie seem that the Epicurean account of justice would also be a kind of conventionalism. Such an inference would be incorrect, though. The Epicureans argue for a kind of naturalism when it comes to justice insofar as on their view justice is dependent on what is beneficial, which is itself not the subject of an agreement but is a matter of nature. Nevertheless, agreements also play a key role in their account, as that which codifies what is beneficial as just in a particular place at a particular time, and so the Epicurean view also highlights the conventional nature of justice. In short, Epicurus offers a kind of middle position when it comes to the ancient *nomos-phusis* debate.

Given their qualified commitment to nature in regard to the first claim, one could think that the Epicureans endorse the second and third claims of the *phusis* account that were identified above, that is, that it is always better to be just and that it is always better to obey the law. However, the Epicureans again split the difference between the two camps of the debate. They side with the defenders of *phusis* insofar as they maintain that it is always better to be just than to be unjust and introduce a robust virtue of justice. Such a move is very unusual insofar as social contract theory more generally is not supplemented by a theory of the virtues. Yet the Epicureans do not go so far as to claim that it is also better to abide by *the law* all the time; here, they side with the *nomos* camp, acknowledging that an agent's allegiance to be just trumps his allegiance to obey the law and thus that there is no absolute obligation to obey. What results, then, is an interesting middle position, a real alternative to other, better-known accounts of justice in antiquity, that of the Sophists, on the one hand, and that of classical authors such as Plato and Aristotle, on the other hand.

---

[20] Given what we know about Epicurus' dependence on Democritus (fifth century BCE) in other areas of his philosophy, one would also expect dependence in practical philosophy. Unfortunately, though, we are poorly informed about Democritus' thought in regard to ethics and politics and so it is difficult to say what influence Democritus had on Epicurean doctrines. For Democritean ethical and political ideas, see especially Vlastos 1945; Vlastos 1946; Paneris 1977; Kahn 1985; Procopé 1989; Procopé 1990; Annas 2016 [2002]; and Robitzsch forthcoming a. For some discussion of the influence of Democritus and other Sophists on the Epicurean practical philosophy, see Müller 1972; Huby 1978; Müller 1980; Müller 1984; and Warren 2002.

However, the Epicurean account of justice not only is unusual in its own time but also is interestingly different from modern approaches. First, the Epicurean account is certainly part of the social contract tradition, but its strong commitment to human nature and ultimately its specific kind of naturalism set it apart from other accounts of this tradition. Second, while the conventional nature of agreements, especially in regard to the laws, make the Epicurean account seem like a precursor of a kind of modern-day legal positivism, it is also clear that in contradistinction to the opinion of modern legal positivists, the law cannot be investigated separately from morality on the Epicurean view.

A major challenge in researching into the Epicurean account of justice is that it has to be reconstructed from a variety of different sources of greatly varying quality. This noticeably contrasts with Plato's and Aristotle's work on justice, which is found in complete treatises such as the *Republic* or the *Nicomachean Ethics* and so can be largely found in one place, even if occasional references to other works are necessary to develop a fuller understanding. For instance, there are collections of Epicurean maxims, such as the *Principal Doctrines* (*Kuriai Doxai*; *KD* in what follows),[21] eight of whose forty maxims are dedicated to justice, which lack any kind of context that would facilitate the interpretation, and protreptic treatises like the ethical *Letter to Menoeceus*, which, largely devoid of technical terminology, is primarily aimed at neophytes. Difficult technical works like the books of Epicurus' main work *On Nature* that are preserved only on severely damaged papyri are also relevant for the investigation of Epicurean justice. The same is also true of the testimonia in non-Epicurean authors like Cicero (106–43 BCE) and Plutarch (c. 46–120 CE), who in their reports are hostile to Epicurean ideas. Epicurus' own works that – as far as we can tell from a list of works he is supposed to have written – were explicitly dedicated to the topic of justice have not come down to us.[22] However, there are also comments relevant for this study that can be found in the works of Epicurus' students and successors as

---

[21] On *Kuriai Doxai* in general, see Erler 1994, 80–2; and Essler 2016. It is unclear whether all maxims can be safely ascribed to Epicurus himself, although most commentators at least tacitly assume this. Such an interpretive hypothesis is strengthened by what we know about the *Vatican Sayings* (*Sententia Vaticana* or *Gnomologicum Vaticanum Epicureum*; *SV* in what follows), a different collection of ethical maxims, which can be ascribed to different Epicurean authors. See Usener 1888. Nevertheless, attempts to attribute some of the *Principal Doctrines* to certain other authors have not found much approval. For instance, Karl Krohn's suggestion that the eight doctrines that deal with justice and law ought to be ascribed to Epicurus' student Hermarchus (1921, 6–11, following Diels 1916, 50) has been thoroughly refuted (Philippson 1923, 4–9).

[22] Diogenes Laërtius, *Lives of Eminent Philosophers* X.28.

heads of the Epicurean school (the Garden): Hermarchus (c. 325–250 BCE) and Polystratus (third century BCE), and the later Epicureans such as Philodemus (c. 110–30 BCE), Lucretius (first century BCE), and Diogenes of Oenoanda (second century CE). Since the works of these authors, with the exception of Lucretius' *On the Nature of Things*, are preserved only in a fragmentary state, they present special interpretive challenges. In addition, making use of such later authors will raise some questions about doctrinal continuity in the Epicurean school over an almost 500-year period and so add to the other interpretive challenges facing the study of Epicurean thought.[23] In short, then, in virtue of the extant sources, the study of Epicurean justice must necessarily to a higher degree be a reconstruction than discussions of Platonic or Aristotelean justice are.

Although the challenges in discussing Epicurean justice are significant, so is the payoff in working out such a theory: it recovers a line of thinking about justice that is significantly distinct from better-known paradigms. Chapter 1 investigates the origin of Epicurean justice by offering a close reading of Epicurean accounts of the development of communal life. The goal of this chapter is to point out how these accounts can be understood as a kind of social contract theory and how it also differs from such theories as well as how natural and conventional features are intertwined in Epicureanism. In accordance with early modern theories of the social contract, which offer the relevant framework for understanding the Epicurean view, the Epicureans roughly distinguish between three separate phases of social development: (1) an original state, in which human beings live dispersed; (2) a *phusis* phase of cultural development, in which human beings come together to form communities; and (3) a *logismos* phase of cultural development, in which human beings form legal and political states. These phases correspond to different degrees of the establishment and understanding of justice and the law, with law being considered as an extension of the initial agreements that bring about justice. Neither justice nor laws exist in the original state, while the first phase of development features justice without laws and the second phase features both justice and laws. On this account, justice is understood to be natural insofar as it codifies a benefit, but also conventional insofar as it arises at a particular point in time and is dependent on what is beneficial. This, again, amounts to a middle position in the ancient *nomos-phusis* debate. Furthermore, the

---

[23] For some discussion of the problem of doctrinal development within the Epicurean school, see the essays in Fish and Sanders 2011.

Epicureans also advance an account of justice that – *pace* other social contract theories – rejects a complete conventionalism in regard to justice. Accordingly, the account is not Hobbesian (even if, historically, Hobbes drew on Epicurean ideas to develop his thought), as some commentators have argued, but much closer to ideas espoused by Jean-Jacques Rousseau.

After discussing the origins of justice and law, Chapter 2 focuses on the basic features of Epicurean contractarianism. The aim of this chapter is to complement and complete the argument of the previous chapter by focusing on three claims and discussing Epicurean material on justice and the social contract outside Lucretius. The first part of this chapter discusses the relationship of justice and benefit on the Epicurean view in more detail. The second part then determines the role of Epicurean agreements within Epicurean philosophy and describes their content. It argues that justice is beneficial to obtaining security, which in turn contributes to the highest good in life according to the Epicureans – freedom from mental distress (*ataraxia*) and bodily pain (*aponia*) – and that Epicurean agreements do not entail duties that go beyond providing security (for instance, those that pertain to the equal distribution of resources). The third and last part of this chapter then investigates how non-contracting parties are covered by agreements. The Epicureans defend an indirect duty view, which means that at least to some extent the interests of animals, children, and women can be taken into account when it comes to questions of justice.

After having characterized Epicurean justice from the perspective of the *nomos-phusis* debate and having argued that justice is both natural and artificial on the Epicurean view, the next two chapters turn to justice understood as a virtue and the questions of whether agents ought to be just and to obey the law. After providing some background on the Epicurean theory of the virtues in general and discussing the virtue of justice in particular, Chapter 3 focuses on the question of how contractual justice and aretaic justice are related to each other. It argues that contractual justice provides the conditions for aretaic justice in Epicurean theory, but that the former is a necessary precondition for the latter. While it is possible, for the Epicureans, to live in a just society without laws (which are a form of contractual justice), it is not possible to live in a just society without agreements.

Chapter 4 discusses the implications of the discussion of the virtue of justice for moral psychology, that is, the questions of whether it is always better to be just and to obey the law. While, on the Epicurean view, typical agents obey the laws, not because they are just, but because they fear the punishments attached to the laws, one may wonder whether this is also true of ideal agents such as sages. This question was supposedly raised by Epicurus himself, and his answer was allegedly that "the unqualified predication is not free from difficulty." Chapter 4 unpacks this answer, arguing that while a sage would never commit an injustice according to the Epicurean view, he would violate a law if this law is unjust. On the reading offered, then, Epicurean agents are not required to obey the law for its own sake, but rather only if obeying the law yields a benefit.

Since Chapter 4 shows clearly that, on the Epicurean view, what is lawful and what is just may come apart and that the Epicureans emphasize the conventional features of the law, some scholars have understood the Epicurean view as a kind of legal positivism. Chapter 5 therefore takes up the question of how to classify the Epicurean theory of law in terms of the vocabulary of modern analytic philosophy of law, referring to debates on the nature of law, that is, the relationship between morality and legality. After offering a sketch of the intellectual landscape by discussing two theses that are commonly used to distinguish natural law theory and legal positivism, the chapter will conclude that Epicurean theory is most similar to a kind of natural law theory from a modern perspective.

Chapter 6, finally, takes a step back to work out the metaethical foundations of the Epicurean conception of justice. From a more contemporary metaethical perspective, the Epicureans defend a theory that we would call "naturalistic." Since "naturalism" is a contested category among modern philosophers, the chapter will consider different definitions of naturalism and foray into Epicurean ontology and epistemology to establish the thesis that the Epicurean theory of justice is naturalistic in alignment with more modern understandings of the term insofar as it understands justice as an accidental property that is investigated in the same general way that other natural properties are investigated. An upshot of this approach will be to show clearly how Epicurean ideas on justice relate to other parts of Epicurean philosophy, in particular, physics and canonic, that is, ontology and epistemology.

CHAPTER I

The Origin of Justice

The Epicureans defend a kind of social contract theory and so endorse the following three claims that other ancient social contract theorists also endorse:[1]

(1) There is an original condition of mankind, in which human beings do not yet live in a community.

(2) There is some deficiency associated with the original condition that makes it necessary for human beings to unite and hence to form a community.

(3) Human beings form a community by means of agreements (*sunthēkai/ foedera*) and so remedy the deficiency of the original condition.

Furthermore, the Epicureans clearly distinguish between a *pactum unionis* and a *pactum subiectionis* in their theory. By the former, agents make agreements with each other to form communities (explaining the creation of justice), and by the latter agents make agreements with a ruler to form legal and political states (explaining the creation of the laws). This makes their theory quite complex, even if the focus of their theorizing lies on the agreements of the first kind that leads to the creation of justice.

This chapter provides a detailed account of the Epicurean social contract by focusing on the creation of justice and law. It shows that (1) agreements stand at the center of the Epicurean account, (2) both justice and law are historical products, and (3) human beings are not by nature social and political beings. As a result, the Epicureans side with defenders of *nomos* in the *nomos-phusis* debate. However, the chapter will also demonstrate that the Epicurean account of justice importantly depends on the common good or what is beneficial to everyone. In the end, then, a commitment to what is beneficial is at the heart of the process of cultural development that

---

[1] Kahn 1981, 93.

makes life in groups, on the one hand, and political and legal communities, on the other hand, possible and necessary. As a result of this, it would be incorrect to view the Epicureans only as defenders of *nomos*, but one should note that on their view, *nomos* is importantly constrained by certain natural features, that is, *phusis*.

By showing what kind of social contract theory the Epicureans defend, the chapter also aims at refuting some common beliefs about the Epicurean social contract. For instance, the Epicurean account is sometimes characterized as Hobbesian.[2] However, this chapter will argue that such a reading would be mistaken (even if Hobbes himself drew on Epicurean texts to develop his ideas). If the Epicurean account is to be assimilated to a modern position, the ideas of Jean-Jacques Rousseau are a much better fit.

Epicurus' own ideas on how human communities came to be, which were perhaps found in book XII of *On Nature*, have unfortunately not come down to us.[3] Fortunately, though, the Roman Epicurean Lucretius' account, which is probably closely modeled on Epicurus' own version, can be found at *On the Nature of Things* V.925–1457.[4] This text will be the principal source in this chapter. Writing roughly 200 years after Epicurus and addressing a Roman audience, for whom Epicurean ideas are a bitter pill to swallow,[5] Lucretius likely adapts his account to the needs of his audience, thus making it necessary for the reader to be cautious of potential idiosyncrasies in comparison to orthodox Epicureanism. Accordingly, we are fortunate to have an (albeit severely) truncated Epicurean account of the development of political communities that is ascribed to the second head of the Garden, Hermarchus, which will at times serve as a counterpart to the Lucretian description and help to distill a unified account of how Epicurean justice and law come to be.[6]

---

[2] See, for instance, Perelli 1967, 166–71; and Spinelli 2019, 389–90, *pace* Robitzsch 2017.
[3] See Long and Sedley 1987, II.151. The Epicurean story is only one of many; *Kulturentstehungslehre* was a flourishing genre in antiquity. See above all Lovejoy and Boas 1965 [1935] as well as the studies by Cole 1990 [1967]; Spoerri 1959; and Gatz 1967. A helpful overview of the different themes in prehistory and accounts of the Golden Age are found in Campbell 2002b, 20–32; and Campbell 2003, 336–53 (= appendix B).
[4] For an attempt to reconstruct the contents of Epicurus' *On Nature* and relate it to Lucretius' *On the Nature of Things*, see Sedley 1998b. On the relationship between Lucretius and Epicurus, see also Boyancé 1963; Clay 1998, 55–74; and Schrijvers 1999, 167–82.
[5] Lucretius, *On the Nature of Things* I.936–50 and IV.1–25.
[6] Fr. 34 Longo Auricchio (= Porphyry, *On Abstinence* I.7–12). Porphyry describes Hermarchus' text, which is generally thought to be an excerpt from his great work *Against Empedocles*, as a "great genealogy [*genealogian makran*]" (ibid., I.7.1; see also Longo Auricchio 1988, 126–7; and Gallo 1985). On Hermarchus, see above all the editions of Krohn and Longo Auricchio as well as the comments in Erler 1994, 227–34; Obbink 1988; and Vander Waerdt 1988. For similarities between Lucretius and Hermarchus' account, see the discussions in Müller 1972, 74–7; and Müller 1987.

The following discussion will begin with some observations on the structure of Lucretius' *Kulturentstehungslehre* (1.1). These observations will then structure the following three sections of this chapter, each of which will be devoted to a distinct part or phase of cultural development according to the Epicureans, corresponding to different phases of the development of justice and law (Sections 1.2–1.4). The final section of the chapter will then turn to the question of how Epicurean social contract theory as a whole is to be understood (Section 1.5).

1.1 The Structure of Lucretius' Account of the Development of Political Communities

As many scholars have pointed out, Lucretius' *Kulturentstehungslehre* does not proceed in a strict chronological way. Lucretius describes the development of prehistoric communities and then contrasts it with modern society, leaving out certain intermediate steps of this development and jumping back and forth between prehistoric times and the modern age. In addition to the much-discussed remarks on fire, which are out of order,[7] a good example for this is the discussion of the domestication of animals.[8] It precedes Lucretius' prehistory proper and is discussed in the context of the survival of different species instead of being discussed later in the text in the context of human beings first forming communities. These oddities in Lucretius' presentation of events may be due to the circumstances of the work's composition. One of the few things we know about Lucretius' life is that he died before finishing the poem as a whole. Since book V is one of the last books, the oddities in the text could thus be explained by Lucretius' premature death.[9] Some scholars thus argue that certain parts of the text should be transposed to restore the real order of Lucretius' thought or even that the poem contains two separate cultural histories: one that is more developed and one that is a less polished draft included by a conscientious editor.[10]

While some later passages might not fit perfectly into a neat schema, the majority of scholars now agree that the section of the poem that deals with

---

[7] See Westphalen 1957, 67–74; as well as the reply in Manuwald 1980, 34–7.
[8] Lucretius, *On the Nature of Things* V.855–77.
[9] On this reading, perhaps *On the Nature of Things* could also be the product of an unknown ancient editor. The Church Father Jerome even suggests Cicero. See Eusebius, *Hieronymus' Chronicle* 149 Helm.
[10] This thesis is found in Merlan 1950. For criticism, see Westphalen 1957, 122–3; Perelli 1967, 271–2; and Manuwald 1980, 9–15.

1.1 Structure of Lucretius' Account of Political Communities

the creation of human communities can be roughly divided into three parts. These parts correspond to three stages of the development of human social life on the Epicurean view.[11] In the first part of his cultural history, Lucretius describes human beings and their primitive nature in their original condition or state (V.925–1010). In the second and third part, he expounds how civilization comes into being, distinguishing between two distinct phases of communal development (V.1011–104 and V.1105–457).

As Bernd Manuwald has suggested, this division is based on an important methodological distinction in Epicurean philosophy, which is most succinctly expressed in the *Letter to Herodotus*. The passage in question is in part corrupt, as the angle brackets in the below translation make clear, but the main point that is emphasized in the text is nonetheless sufficiently clear. According to Epicurus, who does not make an empirical claim here, but presents an inference to the best explanation, any process of cultural development really consisted of two distinct processes:

> Ἀλλὰ μὴν ὑποληπτέον καὶ τὴν φύσιν πολλὰ καὶ παντοῖα ὑπὸ αὐτῶν τῶν πραγμάτων διδαχθῆναί τε καὶ ἀναγκασθῆναι· τὸν δὲ λογισμὸν τὰ ὑπὸ ταύτης παρεγγυηθέντα ὕστερον ἐξακριβοῦν καὶ προσεξευρίσκειν ἐν μὲν τισὶ θᾶττον, ἐν δὲ τισὶ βραδύτερον καὶ ἐν μὲν τισὶ περιόδοις καὶ χρόνοις [ἀπὸ τῶν ἀπὸ τοῦ ἀπείρου] ... ἐν δὲ τισὶ καὶ ἐλάττους.

> Further, one must suppose that [human] nature was taught a large number of different lessons just by the facts themselves, and compelled [by them]; and that reasoning later made more precise what was handed over to it [by nature] and made additional discoveries – more quickly among some peoples, and more slowly among others and in some periods of time <making greater advances> and in others smaller ones.[12]

In other words, the first development is due to nature (*phusis*) and proceeds from the things themselves (*hupo autōn tōn pragmatōn*). The idea here is that things themselves make certain developments possible or indeed necessary while they preclude others. An example of this is the human larynx.[13] Although human beings did not develop a larynx in order to produce sounds and they were not designed to produce sounds, humans, in the course of time, start making more systematic sounds because of certain impressions (*phantasmata*) or feelings (*pathē*) they have. Human beings thus slowly learn to use this organ by a process that is

---

[11] See the discussion of the structure of Lucretius' *Kulturentstehungslehre* in Manuwald 1980, 8–40, whose proposal is adopted here. For a reply to Manuwald, see Sallmann 1986.
[12] *Letter to Herodotus* 75. Trans. Inwood and Gerson.   [13] Ibid., 75–6.

gradual, but not systematic. However, the continual use of the natural capacities kicks off the development of what will later become language. In order for this to happen, though, a process of reasoning (*logismos*) is needed.[14] This second development is distinct from the first.[15] During this process, reasoning perfects what was started by nature – more quickly in some cases, more slowly in others. Reasoning intervenes after nature has already made a beginning. In this case, human reasoning adds linguistic conventions by systematizing the random sounds that were produced during the *phusis* phase. Furthermore, it helps posit (*tethēnai*) and fix meanings to get rid of ambiguities and facilitate communication.[16]

The distinction between a *phusis*-development and a *logismos*-development in any developmental process yields three distinct stages of Lucretius' *Kulturentstehungslehre*:

(1) *an original state* or condition of humanity, during which no development has yet taken place
(2) *a phusis phase*, during which the development of natural human capacities takes place as a result of a necessary and natural process (*phusis*-development)
(3) *a logismos phase*, during which human reasoning perfects the process of development that nature started (*logismos*-development).

This distinction is especially relevant for the questions about justice because the three stages of cultural development correspond to different degrees of knowledge and implementation of justice and the law. As we will see, justice and law do not yet exist, and human beings have no understanding of justice and laws in the original state. In the *phusis* phase, by contrast, human beings gain an understanding of the common good,

---

[14] Referring to Diogenes Laërtius, *Lives of Eminent Philosophers* X.32 and 39, Detel writes that "[f]ür die logischen Beziehungen zwischen empirischen und theoretischen Sätzen verwendet Epikur selber den Terminus 'λόγισμος'" (1975, 29, fn. 23).
[15] In accordance with Manuwald (1980, 20–1), the two processes of cultural development are here understood to be successive chronological periods overall, although surely, there might be some overlap between them. For an alternative view, see Furley 1978, 11.
[16] On the Epicurean account of language formation, see Atherton 2009 [2005] as well as Taylor 2020, 15–42. For a discussion of the parallelism between the evolution of language and the evolution of justice, see especially Müller 1972, 93–7. Müller is right that one ought to be careful in drawing connections between the discussions of justice and language in Epicurus (see also Pigeaud 1984, 141; and Alberti 1995, 170–1 and fn. 18); not all readers have been careful enough (see, for instance, Long and Sedley 1987, II.137; Cole 1990 [1967], 73; and Vander Waerdt 1988, 91–2, fn. 21). Likewise, however, Müller may be overemphasizing the difference between the account of language and the account of justice and thereby losing sight of the commonalities in the two accounts.

and they implement this understanding by means of reciprocal agreements, which determine what is just. However, at this point in societal development, there are no laws. Finally, in the *logismos* phase, after some failed attempts to create political and legal states, the understanding of the common good is codified into laws. As a result, a human community at this stage will have not only reciprocal agreements that correspond to moral norms but also political and juridical institutions.[17] In short, then, justice and law come to be in separate, albeit related, processes.

In the next sections, let us turn to each of the three phases of development that were just distinguished and discuss them in detail in light of their significance for justice and law, especially in light of the question of whether justice and law come to be by nature or by convention on the Epicurean view.

1.2 The Original State

Book V of *On the Nature of Things* as a whole discusses the creation of the world on the basis of non-teleological principles, without the intervention of the divine. Prior to the discussion of human communities proper, Lucretius describes human beings as they were before they lived in communities. We can call this state of humanity as a whole prior to the emergence of communal life the "original state," that is, the original condition of humankind in the sense of the state of nature of early modern theories of the social contract, not in the sense of a political or legal state that precedes the present-day political or legal state. The following analysis of the original state will make clear (1) that human beings are originally self-sufficient beings, that is, not social or political beings by nature and (2) that human beings lack the requisite ethical and political knowledge about what is good for everyone to live together with others in the original state and that justice and law do not yet exist at this point in time.

Inferring to the best explanation, Lucretius reasons that in order to have survived during the phase of pre-political existence, human beings must have been physically enduring. They must have had strong bones and sinews and have been resilient to heat and cold as well as to different kinds

---

[17] Hermarchus' account, as it is preserved in Porphyry, seems to be restricted to the second phase of cultural development. It deals only with the laws. However, it follows the same general schema that Lucretius follows, as the discussion of *epilogismos* that is taken to be characteristic of law-giving at *On Abstinence* I.8.2 and I.10.4. shows. The comments in Diogenes of Oenoanda (fr. 12 Smith) are compatible with such a reading as well.

of diseases.[18] They must have lived the life of hunters and gatherers.[19] And they must not have had fixed homes, but slept under the open sky and worn no clothes.[20] In short, human beings must have been very hardy creatures that lived a rather primitive life. At this point in time, humankind as a whole cannot yet have possessed the arts that are an important part of human culture today. Lucretius explicitly names plowing, which is a requisite for farming and characteristic of a sedentary lifestyle.[21] Furthermore, human beings also must have lacked the ethical and political knowledge that is the prerequisite for human communities to come into being. As Lucretius writes, "Nor could they [primitive human beings] look to the common good, nor did they know to make mutual use of any moral norms or laws [*nec commune bonum poterant spectare neque ulllis | moribus inter se scibant nec legibus uti*]."[22]

Let us look more closely at these important lines. At 958–9, Lucretius makes an epistemological claim (they "could not look [*nec ... poterant spectare*]") about the extent of moral knowledge in the original state. This claim distinguishes between moral norms (*mores*) and laws (*leges*), a distinction that will be mirrored in the separate descriptions of how moral norms and laws come to be later in the account. The most interesting part of the claim is the emphasis on the common good (*commune bonum*). Precisely what this is is not immediately clear. Lucretius does not define the term and does not repeat the expression elsewhere in his work. It could be understood in at least two ways. First, "common good" could merely refer to the good that is common to all. It would then be equivalent to the "natural good" that Epicurus mentions, for instance, at *KD* 7 and *Letter to Menoeceus* 128–9. This "natural good" is the Epicurean highest good or end that all agents pursue: pleasure (*hedonē*), understood as freedom from bodily pain (*aponia*) and mental distress (*ataraxia*), which according to the Epicureans in the cradle argument, all beings pursue from birth.[23] Yet such a reading is unsatisfactory. If the common good is the natural good, that is,

---

[18] Lucretius, *On the Nature of Things* V.925–30. [19] Ibid., V.937–42 and 966–9.
[20] Ibid., V.953–7.
[21] Ibid., V.933–6. An anonymous referee points to a possible connection between this passage and *Republic* II where Socrates realizes the need to enlarge his originally small community because the farmer depends on someone to manufacture the tools to plow the fields.
[22] Ibid., V.958–9. Trans. mine.
[23] See Cicero, *On Ends* I.30. For different readings of the cradle argument, see Brunschwig 1986 (who argues that the first good is kinetic pleasure) and Held 2007, 58–73 (who argues that the first good is katastematic pleasure). For a reading of the cradle argument that does not assign an important role to it for the understanding of Epicurean ethics, see Mitsis and Piergiacomi 2018. On the distinction between kinetic and katastematic pleasure, see Wolfsdorf 2009.

1.2 The Original State

Epicurean pleasure, it seems that human beings in the original state should also pursue it. But Lucretius claims as well that human beings in the original state cannot look to this good, which would result in a contradiction.

Let us therefore suggest a second, alternative reading. On this reading, the common good refers to the good of the group as a whole as opposed to the good of each individual. In other words, "*commune bonum*" at V.958 means that human beings in the original state have not yet grasped that there is an aspect to the good that pertains to life in community and that this good is a good that is beneficial to everyone. This is true regardless of which particular philosophy an agent ascribes to, although for the Epicureans, it will turn out to mean that for any given agent, being in a state of pleasure is compatible with the pleasure of the larger group as a whole.[24]

In making the epistemological claim that human beings could not look to the common good and could not make use of moral norms and laws, Lucretius leaves open whether the common good, moral norms, and laws already exist at this point in the account. On a first reading, being able to use moral norms and laws seems to presuppose that moral norms and laws must already exist so that they can in fact be used. Alternatively, however, one might take "use moral norms and laws" not to mean "apply moral norms and laws," but rather to set up moral norms in the first place. The latter reading seems to be the correct reading of Lucretius' comment insofar as human beings will only later in the account agree on what is just and decide on laws by which to abide (see Sections 1.3 and 1.4). Justice and law are, as we will see in more detail below, historical achievements on the Epicurean view. In regard to the common good, it seems, by contrast, that there is no reason to think that human beings cannot make out the common good because there exists no common good to make out.[25]

The main reason why Lucretius claims that human beings lack an understanding of the common good at this point in the development is that the first human beings, from a psychological perspective, have rather simple needs; what the earth produces is already enough to satisfy whatever human beings desire: "What the sun and rains had given them, what the earth had spontaneously produced, were gifts rich enough to content their hearts [*quod sol atque imbres dederant, quod terra crearat | sponte sua, stais id placabat pectora donum*]."[26] Accordingly, their individual, self-sufficient natures are completely enough to procure these individual needs; other

---

[24] See Chapter 2 for a more detailed discussion of this point.
[25] This point will become clearer in Chapter 2 when the beneficial will be discussed.
[26] Lucretius, *On the Nature of Things* V.937–8. Trans. Smith.

people are not needed. As Lucretius puts it, in the original state, "Individuals seized whatever prize fortune had offered them, trained as they were to live and use their strength for themselves alone [*quod cuique obtulerat praedae fortuna, ferebat | sponte sua sibi quisque valere et vivere doctus*]."[27]

The family, which is typically taken to be the basic unit of human community,[28] does not yet exist at this point in time. During this stage, men and women meet to have intercourse, but their encounters are fleeting and they do not form more lasting ties.[29] The power dynamic between the sexes seems generally to favor men insofar as Lucretius mentions not only the trade of food for sex and mutual love, but also rape, as the reasons why human beings unite. However, Lucretius does not claim that men establish a patriarchic dominance at this point in the account; this dominance was probably established only once the family comes to be during the next phase of societal development.

The most astonishing fact about this early stage, however, is that one wonders how children are raised and, in fact, *if* there are any children.[30] Lucretius only tells us *at a later stage* that men and women watched their children be born.[31] Do the early encounters between men and women also produce children? If they do, then they cannot be raised in a traditional family setting because, again, the family has not yet come into being. In this context we should recall that the very first human beings are literally children of the earth on the Epicurean view insofar as they, like all other animals, have emerged straight out of the earth.[32] Furthermore, the very first generation of human beings seems to come into existence in a relatively complete way, that is, as adults or – since we do not know anything about their exact age – at least as self-sufficient young beings; there is no description of them growing up. Given this account, one wonders whether human beings existed only in such a state for one generation or whether they were in this state for a longer period of time. This is again unclear since we do not have an indication of how long the original state actually lasted.

---

[27] Lucretius, *On the Nature of Things* V.960–1. Trans. Smith, modified.
[28] The Epicureans never explicitly call the "family" a community, as Aristotle, for instance, does. However, on the Epicurean view, the emergence of the family precedes the emergence of larger groups in time, and the family is a smaller unit of human group organization than the organization of neighbors that is the next larger unit of group organization (as we will see in more detail in the next section).
[29] Lucretius, *On the Nature of Things* V.962–5.
[30] On the connection between love and political development, see Morel 2019b.
[31] Lucretius, *On the Nature of Things* V.1013.   [32] Ibid., V.783–836.

1.2 The Original State 23

Democritus offers a similar account to the one we find in Lucretius.³³ The spontaneous generation of human beings directly from the earth in Lucretius echoes Democritus' claim that human beings are created out of earth and moisture.³⁴ Furthermore, Democritus also comments that the first human beings lived an uncivilized and savage life,³⁵ which mirrors Lucretius' observation that the first human beings "lived their lives in the roving manner of wild animals [*vulgivago vitam tractabant more ferarum*]."³⁶ Most importantly, however, Democritus also remarks that human beings at this point in time live "*sporadēn*,"³⁷ that is, "scattered," and there is some debate on what the term means, which incidentally is also used by Protagoras' account of how communities come to be in his Great Speech in Plato's eponymous dialogue.³⁸ According to one reading, "scattered" means that human beings live completely isolated lives without anyone else. According to an alternative reading, "scattered" must mean that there exist at least some smaller family-sized units. However, if the Democritean and Epicurean accounts are alike, then the testimony in Lucretius supports the former reading: human beings during the first stage of their existence really do live lives that are independent of the lives of other human beings because they really were not in need of others to live their respective lives as they are not able to conceive of the benefit that a cooperative life would provide.

While the Epicurean anthropological observation that human beings live isolated lives without children may seem implausible from a modern perspective, we should remind ourselves that similar claims were likely defended by Democritus and Protagoras.³⁹ More importantly, we should note that this observation will not refute the Epicurean account as a whole, since one could, from a modern perspective, begin the account once the family has come about and still have a coherent account. Within the context, the claim that human beings are completely self-sufficient beings

---

³³ On Democritus' account, see Robitzsch forthcoming a (including references to older literature).
³⁴ See DK 68 B 5.1 (= Diodorus of Sicily, *Library of History* I.7.3–5) and A 139 (= Censorinus, *The Natal Day* 4.9, and Lactantius, *The Divine Institutes* VII.7.9).
³⁵ DK 68 B 5.1 (= Diodorus of Sicily, *The Library of History* I.8.1).
³⁶ Lucretius, *On the Nature of Things* V.932. Trans. mine.
³⁷ DK 68 B 5.1 (= Diodorus of Sicily, *The Library of History* I.8.1).
³⁸ Plato, *Protagoras* 322b1. On Protagoras' account of how political communities come to be, see Robitzsch 2023. On the debate on what the term "*sporadēn*" could mean, see especially Nicholson and Kerferd 1982. See also Anonymous Iamblichus fr. 6 where human beings are said not to be able to live "*kath' hena*" (= DK 89 B 6 = Iamblichus, *Protrepticus* 100.10 Pistelli).
³⁹ An anonymous reader speculates that the lives of early human beings were similar to those of wild, predatory animals that led predominantly solitary lives, but come together for short periods of time to breed and care for offspring.

by nature also serves a very important argumentative function. It makes clear that the Epicureans do not endorse the Stoic and Aristotelian claim that human beings are social and political animals by nature.[40] This means that the Epicureans deny that human beings are by nature part of some community and that the life together with others is, under all circumstances, a prerequisite to achieve human fulfillment, as Aristotle and the Stoics claim. Such a reading is also supported by the overwhelming majority of other sources insofar as these sources clearly and unambiguously ascribe to the Epicureans the thesis that human beings are *not* social and political beings. In this vein, we read in fourth-century CE philosopher Themistius that Epicurus thinks that "human beings are not by nature sociable and cultivated [μὴ φύσει εἶναι τὸν ἄνθρωπον κοινωνικόν τε καὶ ἥμερον],"[41] and the Stoic Epictetus (first to second century CE) reports that

> ὅταν ἀναιρεῖν θέλῃ τὴν φυσικὴν κοινωνίαν ἀνθρώποις πρὸς ἀλλήλους, αὐτῷ τῷ ἀναιρουμένῳ συγχρῆται. τί γὰρ λέγει; μὴ ἐξαπατᾶσθε, ἄνθρωποι, μηδὲ παράγεσθε μηδὲ διαπίπτετε· οὐκ ἔστι φυσικὴ κοινωνία τοῖς λογικοῖς πρὸς ἀλλήλους, πιστεύσατέ μοι· οἱ δὲ τὰ ἕτερα λέγοντες ἐξαπατῶσιν ὑμᾶς καὶ παραλογίζονται.

> when [Epicurus] wishes to get rid of the natural communion of human beings with each other, he makes use of the same thing that is gotten rid of. For what does he say? "Do not be deceived, men, nor led astray or cheated. There is no natural communion among rational beings with each other, believe me. Those who say other things deceive and delude you."[42]

The only prima facie piece of evidence that communal life is natural for the Epicureans is another passage in Epictetus: "Epicurus understands as well that we are by nature sociable [ἐπινοεῖ καὶ Ἐπίκουρος ὅτι φύσει ἐσμὲν κοινωνικοί]."[43] Reimar Müller convincingly argues, however, that this passage does not mean that Epicurus actually endorses the position that

---

[40] For Aristotle, see *Politics* I.2.1253a2–3 and, for the Stoics, Cicero, *On Ends* III.62–3; Stobaeus, *Anthology* IV.671.7–673.11 (= Long and Sedley 1987, 57G); and Hierocles, *Elements of Ethics*, col. XI. For discussion of the Aristotelian claim, see Horn 2021 and Rapp 2021 (including references to older literature). This is true even if the Epicureans themselves will ultimately concede that families, a type of sociality, precede the existence of the society via social contracts and also that at least in terms of the creation of communities of neighbors, a certain sociality comes before the existence of society. See also the discussion in the next section of this chapter.

[41] Fr. 551 Usener (= Themistius, *Orations* XXVI, 390,21 Dindorf). Trans. mine.

[42] Fr. 523 Usener (= Epictetus, *Dissertations* II.20.6). Trans. mine. See also ibid. (= Lactantius, *Divine Institutes* III.17.42): "Epicurus says that there is no human society: everyone takes care of himself [*dicit Epicurus ... nullam esse humanam societatem: sibi quemque consulere*]." Trans. mine.

[43] Fr. 525 Usener (= Epictetus, *Dissertations* I.23.1). Trans. mine.

life in human communities is natural, but that he *should* do so (from Epictetus' Stoic perspective), if he were more reasonable.⁴⁴ After all, Epictetus continues, "but once having placed our good in the body he cannot say anything different [ἀλλ' ἅπαξ ἐν τῷ κελύφει θεὶς τὸ ἀγαθὸν ἡμῶν οὐκέτι δύναται ἄλλο οὐδὲν εἰπεῖν]."⁴⁵ As we will see in more detail below, the Epicureans do not deny that communal life becomes necessary at some point in the cultural development, namely, when human nature changes, but they do deny that it has always been so, and they would insist that the necessity is the result of a calculation of what is most beneficial, not part of an inherent drive to live with others.⁴⁶

In summary, then, communal life does not and cannot develop in the original state because human beings do not have any understanding of the common good and because such an understanding is necessary to form societies. Human beings are completely self-sufficient beings on the Epicurean view. Communities are not required at this point of development. First, they are not required because living in communion is not essential to human nature. And second, they are not required because communities do not provide goods that our primitive ancestors could not provide on their own. Accordingly, should communities come to be at some point, they – just as justice and the laws that accompany their emergence – will be a contingent historical achievement and as such not have been part of a greater design that in some way has always already been part of the human nature (as, for instance, on the Aristotelian and Stoic views).

1.3 The *Phusis* Phase

At V.1011, a new stage of development is described, one in which moral norms (*mores*) come to be and feature prominently as the social glue that makes life with other people possible. After all, *mores* are nothing other than the rules and principles that regulate human behavior in the interaction with other human beings, which is characteristic of life in groups. In particular, Lucretius now turns to describe the emergence of two forms

---

⁴⁴ Müller 1972, 36–7.   ⁴⁵ Fr. 525 Usener (= Epictetus, *Dissertations* I.23.1). Trans. mine.
⁴⁶ On the question of whether communities are natural or the product of convention, see also Philippson 1910, 294–5; Garbo 1936, 243–6; and Grilli 1953, 77–89. Note also in this context that the paradigm case of communal life for the Epicureans is the community of friends, which ideally will be self-sufficient and independent from mainstream society (at least insofar as it will try to avoid any political turmoil that may seize mainstream society), not the city-state or the cosmopolis, as on the Stoic and Aristotelian views.

of life with others: the life of men and women together in what might be called a family and the relationship of neighbors, that is, the relationship of families to each other in what might be called a community.[47] The moral norms that govern the first type of relationship are not explicitly named by Lucretius; the moral norms that pertain to the second relationship are called "justice." At this point in the account, we thus see clearly how the Epicurean account of justice involves conventions and that justice is a contingent, historical product on their view. Furthermore, we also see that the emergence of the family precedes the emergence of the social contract, which indicates that even on the Epicurean view certain levels of sociality will precede the sociality that comes about as a result of the social contract. Thus, once the actual social contract comes to be, the Epicurean view does not assume *pace* other contractarian theories that *completely* isolated individuals make agreements with each other. Instead, on their view, individuals who already live in families make agreements with each other. Finally, at this stage of the account, we also get an initial characterization of the scope and contracting agents involved in the Epicurean social contract (which will also be discussed in greater detail in Chapter 2).

Because the circumstances in the original state did not require that human beings live together with other people, let us begin to work out the Epicurean account by looking more closely at what changes compared with the previous phase of development so that human beings now decide to live with others. After the relatively stable original condition has become unstable, human beings will decide to change their ways of life. (Here, it is important to emphasize that every new phase of development will in a sense be an improvement vis-à-vis the previous phase, but will also have shortcomings of its own. For instance, while the change to life in community will take care of certain needs human beings develop, it will also itself be accompanied by the deficiency, which in turn will lead to an unstable state that the *logismos* phase of development will address.)

Recall that the main hindrance to life together with other people in the original state is that human beings, as self-sufficient beings, are able to satisfy their needs by themselves. Consequently, human beings must have new needs and/or no longer be self-sufficient in regard to all their needs, and, likewise, the life with other human beings needs to be able to make up for the new needs and the loss of self-sufficiency in some way.

---

[47] Neither term (that is, "family" or "community") is explicitly used in this text. For "*koinonia*" in Epicurus, see, for instance, *KD* 36–8.

1.3 The Phusis Phase

In line with these considerations, Lucretius opens the section that deals with the development of communal life with a comment related to human self-sufficiency. As we saw above, human beings in the original state are described as tough and enduring and they live the life of hunters and gatherers. Now, by contrast, human beings settle down and consequently their nature changes:

> Inde casas postquam ac pellis ignemque pararunt
> et mulier coniuncta viro concessit in unum
> [lacuna?]
> cognita sunt, prolemque ex se videre creatam,
> tum genus humanum primum mollescere coepit.
> ignis enim curavit, ut alsia corpora frigus
> non ita iam possent caeli sub tegmine ferre,
> et Venus inminuit viris puerique parentum
> blanditiis facile ingenium fregere superbum
>
> Next they provided themselves with huts and skins and fire, and woman, united to man, went to live in one <place with him. The advantages of cohabitation> were learned, and they saw the birth of their offspring. It was then that human beings first began to become gentle: The use of fire rendered their shivering bodies less able to endure the cold beneath the pavilion of the sky; Venus tamed their strength; and children with their charming ways easily broke down the stern disposition of their parents.[48]

The change from isolated hunters and gatherers to a sedentary family mode of life is surprising because Lucretius does not explain precisely what caused the change from one mode of life to the other. What suddenly made human beings build huts, wear clothing, establish more lasting unions between the sexes, and have children that led to the formation of families? It seems that the transition is missing here; nothing in the description of the state of nature gives us readers the answer to this question.

However, it is possible to fill in Lucretius' account. We merely need to assume that small changes ultimately can aggregate and so lead to a bigger and more significant change: the formation of a habit. Take an everyday case first. One might imagine that Scott the couch potato decides to become more active by taking a daily stroll through the park. After a while, he then expands the routine further by power walking. Furthermore, we might imagine him after another while to start running and to be out longer and, in the process, to change his dietary habits in order to accommodate his body's increased need for calories. Ultimately, Scott might even compete

---

[48] Lucretius, *On the Nature of Things* V.1011–18. Trans. Smith, modified.

in a 5k race. At that point at the latest, we would probably no longer refer to him as a couch potato.

Now, Lucretius may imagine a similar process happened to humankind as a whole, albeit in reverse. Human beings, chancing upon fire and skins and inventing huts, quickly see the advantages such innovations – and others similar to them – afford. Gradually, they begin to adopt these innovations and make them part of their daily lives. These innovations and changes may initially be independent of one another and not necessitated by each other. They may emerge one after the other and be small and insignificant at first. The pace of the development can thus appear to be rather slow. Eventually, a tipping point is reached; taken together, certain innovations, which individually altered the state of human beings only insignificantly, lead to bigger changes and ultimately result in a significant transformation of human nature. Human beings thus lose the nature they had in the original state and become gentle, having become accustomed to innovations that make their lives easier.[49] Constant dripping wears away a stone; this is the meaning of *"tum ... primum ... coepit."*

Human nature, then, changes and human beings become gentle and softer according to Lucretius' account. As a consequence, human beings are also no longer as self-sufficient as they originally were. This means that there are new needs that arise as a result of their changed nature, and the presence of children probably contributes to these needs as well insofar as it occasions the need to create a safe environment, in which these children can grow up.[50] The family comes to be and with it the requisite knowledge required to live with one's family members. Note that "advantages of cohabitation" in the passage quoted above is Martin Smith's addition, as the angle brackets make clear; the corresponding line in Lucretius' text is missing. However, there are good reasons in favor of Smith's suggestion or one similar in kind. Once relationships between the sexes are no longer casual, human beings need to acquire some understanding of how to live with a partner and, as a result, relationships become sustainable. As *"cognita sunt"* at V.1013 indicates, some intellectual act, some act of

---

[49] *"Mollescere"* at V.1014 does not mean "to become weak," but rather "to become soft/gentle," as Manuwald convincingly argues (1980, 56, fn. 212). We should note, however, that there is a rhetoric contrast between *"mollescere"* at V.1014 and the *"durius"* humankind of V.926.

[50] On the Epicurean view, the love for one's children is not natural. See frr. 525, 527–9 Usener (= Epictetus, *Dissertations* I.23.1, 5, and 7; III.7.19; IV.11.1.; Plutarch, *On Affection for Offspring 495a*, *Against Colotes* 1123a; and Lacantius, *Divine Institutes* III.17.6) as well as *PHerc.* 1012, cols. LXVI–LXVIII Puglia) along with McConnell 2017a (including references to older literature).

learning, takes place at this point of the development.[51] It seems very likely that this act pertains to some aspect of human interaction. Given the context of the passage that describes the first longer lasting relationships that are being formed, which probably amounts to the creation of the family, the lacuna probably contained the poem's first instance of human beings developing moral norms in regard to these relationships.

The family on its own, however, either is not enough to take care of all newly arisen needs or also creates new needs that need to be addressed. This is especially true for the need for protection. As a result, Lucretius turns to a second new kind of relationship that emerges at this stage: that between neighbors or family units, whose purpose it will be to make everyone safer. These new relationships are accompanied by the historical emergence of moral norms, which brings us to the most important passage in Lucretius' account of cultural development when it comes to justice:

> tunc et amicitiem coeperunt iungere aventes
> finitimi inter se nec laedere nec violari,
> et pueros commendarunt muliebreque saeclum,
> vocibus et gestu cum balbe significarent
> imbecillorum esse aequum misererier omnis.
> nec tamen omnimodis poterat concordia gigni,
> sed bona magnaque pars servabat foedera caste;
> aut genus humanum iam tum foret omne peremptum
> nec potuisset adhuc perducere saecla propago.

> It was then, too, that neighbors eagerly began to make *amicitia*[52] one with another, not to hurt or to be harmed, and claimed protection for their children and womenfolk, indicating by means of inarticulate cries and gestures that it is fair [*aequum*] that the weak [*imbecillorum*] are pitied [*misererier*] by everyone. Although it was not possible for concord [*concordia*] to be achieved universally, the great majority kept their agreements [*foedera*] loyally. Otherwise, the human race would have been entirely extinguished at that early stage and could not have propagated and preserved itself to the present day.[53]

---

[51] *Pace* Lachmann's and Bernays' suggestions to emend "*cognita sunt*" to "*conubium*" and "*coniugium*," respectively. Bailey fills the lacuna with "laws of marriage." This proposal seems less convincing than Smith's, however, insofar as laws (*leges*) come to be only at a much later stage of development, as we will see in more detail below. There is no need to introduce an anachronistic notion at this point.

[52] This key term is left untranslated for now so as not to bias the reader, but its meaning will be discussed in detail shortly.

[53] Lucretius, *On the Nature of Things* V.1019–27. Trans. Smith, modified.

It is possible that the "*et ... et ...*" at V.1019–27 indicates that the formation of ties between neighbors happens at the same time as the family comes into being; that is, men and women form more lasting ties with each other. This would indicate that the developmental process for Lucretius includes parallel developments. However, such a reading is not necessary insofar as the "*et ... et ...*" is still compatible with the idea that one relationship comes into being before the other; the sociality of the family precedes the sociality of the wider community and so in contrast to other contractarian theories, the Epicurean social contract is not the product of completely isolated individuals, but recognizes a preexisting form of sociality (the family).

The rich passage just quoted is the first to describe the *historical emergence* of justice (*aequum*) (1) in the full sense as (2) a kind of agreement. Both of these points can be or, in fact, have been challenged, though, and so it is worth defending both of them in more detail, starting with the second point.

Some commentators have objected that the contingently and historically arising ties between neighbors are forms of *amicitia*, that is, friendships, and not agreements.[54] According to such a reading, friendship rather than social agreements would thus stand at the beginning of the communal life for the Epicureans. This would be especially interesting because social contract theorists typically do not accord much significance to the notion of friendship, which, by contrast, is a feature of virtue-based approaches to the political, such as the one by Aristotle that even features a specific kind of political friendship. The reading just proposed would thus highlight the political importance of Epicurean friendship. The suggestion also gains additional plausibility insofar as Protagoras, in his account of how political communities come to be in Plato, claims that the move from an original condition to a state of society is characterized by the emergence of "bonds of friendship [*desmoi philias*]"[55] rather than more straightforwardly agreements of any kind. As is well known, Protagoras is from Abdera and his account of how political community comes to be shares some features with the account of his fellow Abderite Democritus, from whom, in turn, Epicurus is typically taken to have borrowed many ideas. In stressing the idea of friendship at this point, Lucretius could emphasize

---

[54] See, for instance, Long 1985, 310; as well as Aoiz and Boeri 2023, 25–32. Note that Smith translates *amicitia* twice as pacts and friendship: "Neighbors ... began to make *pacts of friendship*." Emphasis added. And Aoiz and Boeri, based on Smith's translation, even interpolate "*foedera*" into the translation, although the word is not found in line 1019.

[55] Plato, *Protagoras* 322c3.

features of the Epicurean account that have an Abderite origin, but that are elsewhere not highlighted in extant Epicurean texts. Furthermore, there is evidence in Cicero's *On Ends* that there were different accounts of friendship advanced by different Epicurean authors. Supposedly, "[t]here are also those [Epicureans]," of whom we do not know the identity, "who say that, among the wise, there is a kind of pact that they do not love friends less than themselves [*sunt autem, qui dicant foedus esse quoddam sapientium ut ne minus amicos quam se ipsos diligant*]."[56] This testimony does not allow us to infer that all types of friendship are indeed agreements, and it is an open question whether the friendship between sages that the Epicurean spokesperson Torquatus mentions in the passage is identical to the friendship we find in Lucretius. Nevertheless, Torquatus' comment would support the idea that at least in some circumstances some Epicurean philosophers understood friendship as a kind of agreement.

Despite these considerations, there is no need for an "Abderite" reading of lines 1019–27. As some commentators point out, "*amicitia*" need not be translated or in fact be understood as "friendship."[57] "*Amicitia*" can also mean "alliance" and so be a synonym for "*foedus*," which is used in the same passage quoted above and is a Latin equivalent of the Greek term "*sunthēkē*," which, as we shall see in more detail in Chapter 2, plays a prominent role in Epicurus' writings on justice and law. In addition, as we have seen already, what complicates matters is the fact that some Epicureans themselves seem to have understood friendship as kinds of agreement, and it may also be possible that the Epicureans understand friendship as "fellowship" rather than intimate bonds between people, that is, take them to come with only very minimal obligations.[58] As a result, the passage may not be asserting anything grandiose about friendship that would be unusual in any way. Lucretius' claim, by contrast, that the first alliance between neighbors concerns not harming and not being harmed (*nec laedere nec violari*) strongly echoes Epicurus' claim in the *Principal Doctrines* that agreements that are the basis for justice are over "not harming and not being harmed" (*mē blaptein mēde blaptesthai*).[59]

This brings us to the other point, the one regarding the use of the term "*aequum*." At line 1023, Lucretius for the very first time in the account of development claims that human beings make use of moral vocabulary or,

---

[56] Cicero, *On Ends* I.70. Trans. mine.
[57] See, for instance, Mitsis 1988, 106, fn. 14; Müller 1991, 118–19; and Konstan 2008, 89–93.
[58] See O'Connor 1989, 168.
[59] *KD* 35. See also *KD* 31–3. Chapter 2 will discuss this idea in more detail.

more specifically, communicate that something is "*aequum.*" In doing so, human beings communicate that one given course of behavior is preferable to another – in this case, pitying the weak is preferable to not doing so – or to other courses of behavior. However, it is unclear what Greek word the Latin term "*aequum*" translates. It could translate either "*dikaion*" (just) or "*ison*" (equal or fair). In the latter case, justice might have its beginnings in the idea of weighing and determining equal shares. The development of the notion of justice would thus begin with the equal, that is, with situations in which human beings apportion shares. According to this reading, the act of apportioning would be conveyed by simple language, perhaps even exclusively by pointing. In support of this suggestion, Lucretius claims that human beings at this point in the process of cultural development only communicate "by means of inarticulate cries and gestures."[60] One could then argue that the understanding of justice that the first human beings have (and that is captured in their preconception)[61] gradually evolves over time, and that it is not simple insofar as it presupposes the concept of equality.

While such a reading has some appeal prima facie, it ultimately fails to convince. First, in Epicurus and other Epicureans writing in Greek, we do not find the term "*ison*" in connection with justice. Of course, it is possible that we merely lack the relevant texts. However, it seems unlikely that such a key distinction is extant only in Lucretius. Second, Lucretius uses "*iustum*" once in its technical sense as "just" at III.950.[62] And so it is all the more surprising that book V, which contains a discussion of justice and the law, does not again use "*iustum*," but "*aequum*" instead. It thus seems more likely that Lucretius is using "just" and "equal," "*iustum*" and "*aequum*," as synonyms. This is also confirmed by looking at V.1149 where "*aequum*" is used to describe the laws ("*legibus aequis*"). The context is the final stage of communal development: here, it does not make sense to say that the laws are merely "fair" in the sense of a precursor to the full-fledged notion of justice (that is, the *iustum* or *dikaion*). At this point, the

---

[60] For Campbell (2003, 279), "*balbe* here indicates that the setting is that of the origins of language, with the formation of justice made possible by the development of the first efficient communication system which, although primitive and still relying heavily on gesture, is advanced enough to transmit ethical concepts." Lucretius is thus very optimistic about what can be achieved with only rudimentary language skills. It seems especially daunting that arrangements in regard to the weaker members of the community can be made without advanced, that is, fully developed, linguistic capabilities. Surely, human beings can apportion shares without language, but it is rather difficult, if not impossible, to convey the concept of equal shares without language.
[61] For a more detailed discussion of preconceptions, see Chapter 6.
[62] The other occurrence is at IV.1241.

1.3 The Phusis Phase

laws are just in the full sense precisely because they are in accordance with the preconception of justice, that is, the practical understanding of justice available to agents at the time. In short, then, "*aequum*" must translate "*dikaion*" at V.1023; for the Epicureans, human beings first make agreements about what is just during the first phase of development, and not merely think about apportioning shares.[63] Indeed, that justice, on their view, is more robust can also be seen by the fact that it includes provisions for the weak, who although not equal to contracting agents, are equally protected by the agreements. It is to these provisions that we turn to next, since they are quite revealing of the nature of the agreement that comes to be at this point in the account.

The historical agreements over harming and not being harmed are made by the heads of the families, according to Lucretius at line 1021; they include an additional provision to care for women and children, that is, household dependents, which is at odds with the idea that women generally are contracting partners.[64] Although this is not explicitly stated, this setup seems to imply that the political head of the household, the one who can negotiate with the neighbors, is likely male and, as a result, that a patriarchic hierarchy is established at this point in the account. That there is no mention of women making agreements here (or in fact in any other Epicurean text that is extant) might be considered a bit surprising insofar as the Garden had women as members and, thus, in contrast to other philosophical schools in antiquity, is often seen as having relatively progressive views on women.[65] For example, Leontion is supposed to have written a treatise against Theophrastus, which is unfortunately not extant.[66] Even if the treatise did not actually exist, the very mention of the treatise is predicated on the plausibility that on the Epicurean view, a woman could have been the author of such a treatise; otherwise, the polemic would not hit its mark. Accordingly, it seems possible that at least some women had the requisite mental capacities to make agreements on the Epicurean view. Yet we should also note in this context that the second- to first- century BCE Epicurean Zeno of Sidon is supposed to

---

[63] On the potentially problematic preexisting standard of *aequitas* at this point in the account, see Mitsis 1988, 106, fn. 15.

[64] *Pace* Aoiz and Boeri 2023, 24, who claim that parents more generally are the contracting parties.

[65] For discussions of women in Epicureanism, see, for instance, Erler 1994, 287–8; Gordon 2012, 72–108; and Arenson 2023. On the role of women and other members of the Greek and Roman household as well as their legal relationship to men more generally, see, for instance, Pomeroy 1975; Reinsberg 1989; and Dixon 1992.

[66] Fr. 28 Usener (= Cicero, *On the Nature of the Gods* I.93; and Pliny, *Natural History* Preface 29).

have categorically asserted the imperfection of the female sex.[67] As a result, there is no indication of (1) whether the Epicureans thought that the capability to make agreements extended to all women (if they in fact believed that women are able to make agreements) or (2) whether the Epicureans also thought that given the reality of gender dynamics in the ancient world and the dominance of men in general, women (or at least most women) would ever be in social situations – outside perhaps the communities of friends – that would enable them to make agreements

At 1023, Lucretius furthermore observes in regard to the dependents to whom protection is extended that it is part of the agreement that "it is just [*aequum*] that the weak [*imbecillorum*] are pitied [*misererier*] by everyone." This comment pertains to the question of what is agreed upon. Who the weak are who are mentioned in this passage is not clearly defined, and "*imbecillus*" is a word used only here in Lucretius. On a first reading, Lucretius could also make the more sophisticated point that the weaker members of the community more generally, perhaps first and foremost the elderly but also those with bodily and mental disabilities, ought to be the object of pity. On this reading, the social contract would be very quickly extended to needy relatives and perhaps even all members of society rather than being limited only to the core family members. However, "*imbecillus*" on a more restricted and perhaps safer reading could also merely refer to the women and children who were mentioned previously, not the infirm more generally. Put differently, although it seems theoretically possible that the Epicurean social contract can very quickly be extended to all, whether it actually will be extended in such a way will depend on whether the weak are (1) a threat to members of the community in terms of harm and (2) associated with a family in some way. If they are not (which is likely given their designation as "weak") and no one has an interest in them qua dependent, it seems that there is no requirement to include them in the agreements of justice on the Epicurean view.

Whoever the weak may exactly be, it is especially striking that Lucretius comments at 1023 that the weak are to be *pitied*. At this point, some commentators argue that this *emotional reaction* is wholly distinct from the *benefit* of not harming and not being harmed that is also mentioned as the

---

[67] Zeno of Sidon, fr. 28 Angeli and Colaizzo (= Soranus, *Gynecology* III.3 Ilberg): "By nature the female sex differs from the male to the point that both Aristotle and Zeno the Epicurean say that the female sex is imperfect, but the male sex is perfect [φύσει τε τὸ θῆλυ τοῦ ἄρρενος διαφέρει μέχρι τοῦ καὶ Ἀριστοτέλην καὶ Ζήνωνα τὸν Ἐπικούρειον εἰπεῖν ἀτελὲς μὲν εἶναι τὸ θῆλυ, τέλειον δὲ εἶναι τὸ ἄρρεν]." Trans. mine.

content of the agreements that are being formed at this point.[68] Accordingly, the Epicurean account of how communities come to be would not only be a result of a calculation of what is beneficial, but also be driven by an independent feeling of compassion. However, this reading seems dubious. After all, line 1023 does not have to be taken as giving the *reason why* human beings act in a certain way in regard to the weak, but rather can be taken as an alternate description of the *course of action that is decreed by the agreement*. In other words, it is not the case that everyone is compassionate with the weak *because* they feel pity for them, but rather the agreement recognizes that compassionate behavior toward the weaker members of the community is the right or just (*aequum*) course of action. On this alternative reading, the *reason why* human beings behave benevolently toward the weak would still be wholly dictated by what is beneficial: it may be significantly better for human beings to live in a community in which the weak in general are not harmed, since such a community might be more stable overall and therefore safer than a community that antagonizes its weaker members, and human beings might prefer to live in a community in which they know that should they become injured or infirm, they will also not be harmed in any way.[69] In short, any kind of pity would still be grounded on what is beneficial, which, as we will see in more detail in the next chapter, functions as the natural ground of the Epicurean account.[70]

Finally, *On the Nature of Things* V.1019–27 makes clear that the situation that is created as a result of the agreements is not stable. Agreements are kept most of the time, but – as we will see in light of Lucretius' later account of the development of civilization[71] – there is no way to sanction infringements at this stage. Here, we see once again Lucretius' nuanced appreciation of the cultural achievements of this stage: although it is a deficit of this stage that concord (*concordia*) is not universal, it must – as Lucretius points out – at least be widespread, for otherwise, humankind as a whole would have died out. Put again differently, the

---

[68] Westphalen 1957, 34 and 78; and Boyancé 1963, 243 (*pace* Müller 1972, 42 and fn. 71). See also Diogenes of Oenoanda fr. 3 Smith, in which Diogenes appeals to his love of humanity (*philanthrōpon*) to aid (*epikourein*) foreigners (*zenoi*).

[69] Such a process of thinking would of course speak in favor of the second, more expansive reading of who is included among the weak that was distinguished above. Again, though, whether the social contract will be actually extended to all will likely depend on the particular circumstances.

[70] There is also some discussion of whether the Epicureans are engaging with the Stoic doctrine of *oikeiōsis* at this point. See Appendix A.

[71] See Lucretius, *On the Nature of Things* V.1151–60.

historical process of the establishment of justice must therefore move into a last, final phase.

In his commentary on *The Nature of Things* V, Gordon Campbell points out that the observation that human beings almost died out at this point in the account is surprising because the description of the original state was not at all violent.[72] It therefore seems odd that suddenly violence is so widespread (even if not ubiquitous). Campbell explains this by referring to rational choice theory and changing evolutionary strategies among human beings:[73] what worked for primitive human beings no longer works for human beings in the first phase of cultural development. Human beings undergo a change in their nature, and as a result, there is more violence among them. And this violence needs to be kept at bay, which is the purpose of the newly made agreements.[74] However, these agreements are – as we saw – not always kept, and remedying or at least attenuating these injustices will thus be a major task for the next phase of development.

In reply to Campbell, one may remark that his criticism presupposes that agreements are made only to keep human beings from harming *each other*. But as we will see in more detail in the next chapter, this would mean to unduly restrict the content of the agreements. After all, there is much evidence for violence committed by animals and that wild animals are a huge threat to human beings during the early phase of cultural development.[75] A better reading of lines 1025–7 is thus that mankind would die out because some human beings do not always wholeheartedly participate in communal measures designed to ward off any kind of attack, which indeed would pose a great danger to human beings who are now weakened in their natures and thus even more vulnerable to such threats.

In summary, in this section, we have seen that both the family and the first human communities as aggregations of families arise at some point in history, and that the first human communities arise via agreements, which in turn decree which behaviors are just and which are not. It is thus clear

---

[72] Campbell 2003, 254.   [73] Ibid., 258–61; see also the alternative solutions discussed at 282–3.
[74] This passage might also be seen as evidence for the fact that Lucretius tries to cover up the violence of the original state (see also Blickman 1989, 166, who makes the same claim in regard to a different passage). Lucretius needs to reintroduce violent elements in order to justify the necessity of introducing laws and sanction mechanisms, which are a key feature not only of the Epicurean account but also of the phenomenal reality. Alternatively, one could also understand Lucretius' comment as a rhetorical overstatement. The comment that concord was not pervasive during the first phase of cultural development would then merely stress that this state was not complete and that this state of development was not a Golden Age either.
[75] See also V.988–98.

that some sociality precedes the social contract, on the Epicurean view, and that the origin of Epicurean justice is conventional, even if we also already saw in the previous section that the *commune bonum*, which itself is not conventional, will also be important in making Epicurean agreements of justice. In the next section, we will see how the account is extended to the laws.[76]

1.4 The *Logismos* Phase

During the third stage of development, justice is set on a more solid footing. It becomes codified into laws, which for the Epicureans are an extension of justice, bringing the developmental process that started in the original state to completion. Just like justice, the laws, on the Epicurean view, are thus a *historical* achievement. As a result, the Epicureans will also defend a kind of conventionalism in regard to the law, even if, just as in the case of justice, the conventional nature of the laws will ultimately be grounded in what is beneficial. By institutionalizing what is just and ultimately beneficial and putting in place enforcement mechanisms and punishments, the original agreements become binding in legal communities. While the deficit of the last phase (that agreements are often violated) is somewhat remedied, the resulting situation will not be perfect.

The development that leads to the establishment of the rule of law is not linear. In fact, it begins with the failure of the first attempts to set up government in the form of kingships:

> Inque dies magis hi victum vitamque priorem
> commutare novis monstrabant rebus et igni,
> ingenio qui praestabant et corde vigebant.
> condere coeperunt urbis arcemque locare

---

[76] One may note that it is quite striking how similar the Epicurean account of this stage of development is to what H. L. A. Hart observes in regard to "primitive" societies in *The Concept of Law* (2012 [1961], 91–2). Hart contends that for there to be a society without courts and legislature, one that lives only according to "primary rules of obligation," certain conditions need to be fulfilled. First, the rules themselves must contain provisions according to which members of society do not harm each other. Second, if there is a tension in society between those who obey the rules and those who free ride, the free riders cannot be in the majority. And third, such a model is only applicable to small groups of people, not large-scale societies. The first two points are explicitly addressed by the Epicureans, as should be clear from the above discussion. The third point is not addressed by them, which perhaps is unsurprising, since exponential population growth is a modern, not an ancient phenomenon. An anonymous referee, however, points out that Lucretius' account in *On the Nature of Things*, like the account of *Republic* II, does "associate the growth of the political community with the increase in the possibility of forms of deceit and a lack of direct interpersonal knowledge and affection."

praesidium reges ipsi sibi perfugiumque,
et pecudes et agros divisere atque dedere
pro facie cuiusque et viribus ingenioque.

> And more and more every day those who excelled in intellect and were strong in mind showed the others how to exchange their former way of life for new practices and, in particular, for the use of fire. Kings began to build cities and to choose sites for citadels to be strongholds and places of refuge for themselves; and they distributed gifts of flocks and fields to individuals according to their beauty, strength, and intellect.[77]

A problem in regard to this passage is whether "those who excelled in intellect and were strong in mind" of line 1107 are identical to the first kings of line 1109. This seems to be very likely, since a change in subject between the lines would be quite odd.[78] Understood in this way, then, the passage implies that the preeminent men/first kings use their superior capabilities to serve their own interest, not that of the public (see the pronouns *ipsi ... sibi*). The preeminent men thus try to use their preeminence to circumvent the terms of the original contract. They try to create special privileges for themselves: They order cities and citadels to be built so they can have a safe residence. And this place of refuge is then used as a power basis in order to amass other privileges.

The attempt of the first kings to usurp power does not succeed. According to Lucretius, the initial kingships fail because the interests of all are not sufficiently taken into account.[79] In the process of accruing power, the kings use their wealth to persuade and deceive the many. As Lucretius writes, "no matter how much physical strength and beauty people possess, they follow in the train of the rich [*divitioris enim sectam plerumque sequuntur | quamlibet et fortes et pulchro corpore creti*]."[80] However, such a deception of the many is not successful for long. Strife

---

[77] Lucretius, *On the Nature of Things* V.1105–10. Trans. Smith, modified.
[78] See also Hermarchus, fr. 34 Longo Auricchio (= Porphyry, *On Abstinence* I.10 [quoted below]).
[79] A parallel passage in Epicurus is *KD* 7: "Some wanted to become reputed and admired, thinking that they acquire security from other human beings in this way. And so, if the life of those [human beings] is secure, then they have received Nature's good. However, if it is not secure, they do not possess that which they desired from the beginning according to what is naturally appropriate [Ἔνδοξοι καὶ περίβλεπτοί τινες ἐβουλήθησαν γενέσθαι, τὴν ἐξ ἀνθρώπων ἀσφάλειαν οὕτω νομίζοντες περιποιήσεσθαι ὥστε, εἰ μὲν ἀσφαλὴς ὁ τῶν τοιούτων βίος, ἀπέλαβον τὸ τῆς φύσεως ἀγαθόν· εἰ δὲ μὴ ἀσφαλής, οὐκ ἔχουσιν οὗ ἕνεκα ἐξ ἀρχῆς κατὰ τὸ τῆς φύσεως οἰκεῖον ὠρέχθησαν]." Trans. mine. See also *KD* 6: "In order not to fear <other> human beings, there is the natural good of rule and kingship, with which one is possibly able to procure this <fearlessness> [Ἕνεκα τοῦ θαρρεῖν ἐξ ἀνθρώπων ἦν κατὰ φύσιν ἀρχῆς καὶ βασιλείας ἀγαθόν, ἐξ ὧν ἄν ποτε τοῦτο οἷός τ' ᾖ παρασκευάζεσθαι]." Trans. mine.
[80] Lucretius, *On the Nature of Things* V.1115–16. Trans. Smith.

1.4 The Logismos Phase

and power struggles very soon result. These lead to the dethronement of the first kings.[81] This experience makes people aware of the necessity of introducing the rule of law:

> inde magistratum partim docuere creare
> iuraque constituere, ut vellent legibus uti.
> nam genus humanum, defessum vi colere aevum,
> ex inimicitiis languebat; quo magis ipsum
> sponte sua cecidit sub leges artaque iura.
> acrius ex ira quod enim se quisque parabat
> ulcisci quam nunc concessumst legibus aequis,
> hanc ob rem est homines pertaesum vi colere aevum.

> At length some of them taught the others to create magistracies and established ordinances, so that [the others] might want to use laws.[82] The human race, utterly weary as it was of leading a life of violence and worn out with feuds, was the more ready to submit voluntarily to the restraint of laws and stringent ordinances. The reason why people were sick and tired of a life of violence was that each individual was prompted by anger to exact revenge more cruelly than is now allowed by just laws.[83]

The passage above mentions both "laws" (*leges*) and "ordinances" (*iura*). According to standard Latin legal vocabulary, "*ius*" is a broader term, encompassing all kinds of moral norms, written and unwritten, while "*lex*" is narrower and refers to written law. However, both terms can also be used as synonyms. If Lucretius used the terms as distinct in meaning, he would claim that the new sanction mechanisms helped codify both written laws as well as the (unwritten) moral norms in human communities, which would make the latter more pervasive. This would be difficult to make sense of. In the case of norms, societal reprimanding can be effective to enforce them. In this vein, it might be effective to reprimand agents in regard to certain behavior, for instance, to shout at them to enforce a social norm. But it seems surprising that such a way of reprimanding agents was not available in the previous stage of societal development. After all, the problem of the previous phase is that there are no sanction mechanisms in place to create pervasive adherence to norms and that such pervasiveness can only come

---

[81] Ibid., V.1136–42.
[82] The Latin text is not clear whether the preeminent men teach others to establish ordinances (as on Bailey's translation) or whether the preeminent men establish the ordinances themselves (as on Smith's translation quoted here). However, the parallel passage in Hermarchus, fr. 34 Longo Auricchio (= Porphyry, *On Abstinence* I.7–12) notes that not everyone will become a law-giver, which makes the latter reading of the Lucretius passage more likely than the former.
[83] Lucretius, *On the Nature of Things* V.1143–50. Trans. Smith, modified.

about by the punishments that are set down in conjunction with the law. It seems more likely, then, that Lucretius is using "*lex*" and "*ius*" as a hendiadys to express the same idea: codified law. This would also fit better with the Greek heritage of Epicurean thought. Epicurus, writing in Greek, had no way of distinguishing "*lex*" and "*ius*." In Greek, the word "*nomos*" covers the meaning of both moral convention and law, both written and unwritten.

The passage thus makes it clear that for Lucretius, the rule of law ("codified law") emerges as the result of a process that heavily involves trial and error and the recognition of what is best *faute de mieux*. Furthermore, as has been argued, Lucretius at this point draws on what seems like a theory of political change, according to which one form of government devolves into the next.[84] The original kingship deteriorates into a tyranny, the tyranny degrades into an oligarchy, and ultimately a form of government emerges that in virtue of its magistrate (*magistratus*) has some resemblance with the republican political order of Lucretius' day. Such a description is notably different from one that would capture the political realities of Athens in Epicurus' time, which lost at least some autonomy by becoming part of the empire of Alexander the Great. Therefore, Lucretius' account at this point is very unlikely a direct adoption of Epicurus' ideas, if indeed Epicurus himself dealt with this topic. (Unfortunately, no discussion is extant.) However, this is not to say that the idea of a change in forms of political order that is described in Lucretius is entirely novel, either. As is well known, other thinkers such as Plato, Aristotle, and – most systematically – the second-century BCE historian Polybius discuss the idea that certain forms of political order will decline into other forms, and it would be a desideratum of future scholarship to find out to what extent Lucretius may – either directly or indirectly – have found inspiration in these writers.

In this context, we should also note that it is even unclear which form of political order is truly the best on the Epicurean view and so which one Epicurus himself would have endorsed. While Abderite accounts of how political communities come to be, like those of Democritus and Protagoras, are often taken to be defenses of democratic ideology,[85] it is

---

[84] Schrijvers 1996 distinguishes six distinct phases in Lucretius. However, this distinction does not seem quite so clear, even if it is certain that Lucretius gives an account of how different forms of political order develop into others.

[85] Farrar 1988 discusses both authors as proponents of democratic thinking. For Democritus as a defender of democracy, see, for instance, Paneris 1977, 88–9 (including an overview of the literature up to 1977); Spinelli 1991; Mejer 2004; and Rechenauer 2019. The claim that Protagoras is in favor of democracy is defended in Moore 1988; Beresford 2013; and Manuwald 2014; among

not clear that this is also true of the Epicureans. There is, for instance, some evidence that the Epicureans endorsed monarchical kingships at least on some occasions, namely, on the condition that these kingships further Epicurean ends,[86] even if generally Epicureans were advised to avoid contact with kings.[87] The basic idea here is very simple: if a king is able to free Epicurean agents to live the good life without having to worry about political matters, then such an arrangement seems very favorable. In the same vein, Philodemus wrote a treatise *On the Good King According to Homer*, which in part is a work of literary criticism. More importantly, however, the work can be seen as an outline of the characteristics of a good ruler, with the intention of providing a model that real-life rulers can follow, a kind of mirror of princes like Xenophon's *Education of Cyrus*.[88] Moreover, Philodemus' work was dedicated to the Roman senator Piso, who was Philodemus' patron.[89] And, in the same vein, Plutarch also claims that the Epicurean Colotes (fourth to third century BCE) dedicated the treatise, in which he systematically refuted the doctrines of other philosophers, to Ptolemy II Philadelphus.[90] This again seems to indicate that the Epicureans at least in some instances had direct relationships with rulers and were favorable toward kingships. Nevertheless, as we will see in more detail in the course of this book, the Epicurean attitude toward the political is often dependent on particular circumstances. It therefore seems most prudent not to single out a given form of political organization as the preferred one, but rather to ascribe to the Epicureans a conditional attitude in regard to the question of which form of political order is best as well.

Having discussed the form of political order that is to be established, let us next turn to *how* the rule of law is established in Lucretius' account. For the Roman author, even those who have intellect are prone to errors and thus to "forgetfulness" when it comes to what is best for society as a whole. As a result, different preeminent men are needed, who give the laws after the first kingships fail. These men are more mindful of what is beneficial to all than the first kings were, and so we see clearly at this point – more clearly than when the agreements of justice emerged – that Epicurean legal agreements are not purely conventional but importantly need to take into consideration what is beneficial for everyone.

others. However, this claim is more controversial than the one about Democritus. For instance, see the critical discussion in Hoffmann 1997, 41 and 63–4.

[86] For a more detailed discussion, see McConnell 2010 as well as Fish 2011.
[87] Plutarch, *Against Colotes* 1127a.   [88] On Philodemus' work, see Asmis 1991 and Fish 2018.
[89] Philodemus, *On the Good King According to Homer*, col. XLIII.16–20.
[90] Plutarch, *Against Colotes* 1107e.

Furthermore, in stark contrast to the previous phase of societal development when all human beings directly agreed on what was to be just, this phase is no longer characterized by a joint effort of all. Instead, the hallmark of this phase of development is that distinct individuals are the driving force behind development, namely, those who have superior intellectual capacities. The majority of the population is left out. Although *all* human beings have some capabilities to grasp the basic moral vocabulary in the first cultural phase (after all, this capability is part of their nature and a prerequisite for society to function), not all have the ability to teach others and lead the way to introduce new ways of life.[91] In order to do this, different, superior intellectual capabilities are required. These, Lucretius seems to assume, are not distributed in the same way as the basic ability to get along with each other and form basic alliances. Therefore, during this phase of the development of civilization, some preeminent individuals are the principal agents of change.

Yet it would be wrong to think that the many play no role whatsoever in establishing the rule of law. The many concur with the laws that are given by their own will (*sponte sua*), likely because they have instrumental reasons to do so.[92] The process of law-giving nevertheless involves a form of consent, namely, insofar as the many decide that it is right to adhere to certain laws; the laws are not merely imposed on them.[93] This observation is confirmed by Hermarchus, who uses the verb "assent [*sugchōreō*]" to describe what the many do: "From the outset, no force was used to establish any of the laws, written or unwritten, which are still in use and are suited for handing on: the people who would use them also assented to them [Οὐδὲν γὰρ ἐξ ἀρχῆς βιαίως κατέστη νόμιμον οὔτε μετὰ γραφῆς οὔτε ἄνευ γραφῆς τῶν διαμενόντων νῦν καὶ διαδίδοσθαι πεφυκότων, ἀλλὰ συγχωρησάντων αὐτῷ καὶ τῶν χρησαμένων]."[94]

At this point, again, a comparison with Abderite theories of how the political communities come to be is interesting, even if these theories do not explicitly mention agreements as a means to move from the original state to a state of society.[95] Democritus very much stresses the idea of

---

[91] After all, not everyone in Epicureanism has the capability of becoming a sage. See fr. 226 Usener (= Clement of Alexandria, *Stromata* I.15, 130,37 Sylburg and Diogenes Laërtius, *Lives of Eminent Philosophers* X.117).
[92] Lucretius, *On the Nature of Things* V.1147. [93] *Pace* Farrington 1953, 334 and passim.
[94] Hermarchus, fr. 34 Longo Auricchio (= Porphyry, *On Abstinence* I.8.1.). Trans. Clark, modified.
[95] Note that the distinction between the formation of communities and the formation of the state is not clear in these theories.

concord (*homonoia*) as an important principle of political unity in his philosophy, even if this term is not used in the account of cultural development.[96] Accordingly, one might understand the willingness of the people to come together and express their support for the new rulers that is described in Lucretius and Hermarchus as comparable to the concord that Democritus takes to be instrumental for the coming to be and functioning of the political communities.[97]

It would be rash to conclude that the newly introduced laws are a hands-down triumph of justice for the Epicureans. During the *phusis* phase, human beings develop a notion of the *aequum*, but justice cannot triumph because it is not pervasive enough; there are many free-riders, which imperils the existence of human communities. During the *logismos* phase, the sanction mechanisms that accompany the law help establish the pervasiveness of justice. From now on, infringements against moral norms are prosecuted more effectively. This limits feuds and makes sure that there are clear ways of deescalating conflicts. But this positive aspect of the law is accompanied by the following downside according to Lucretius:

> inde metus maculat poenarum praemia vitae.
> circumretit enim vis atque iniuria quemque
> atque, unde exortast, ad eum plerumque revertit,
> nec facilest placidam ac pacatam degere vitam
> qui violat factis communia foedera pacis.
> etsi fallit enim divum genus humanumque,
> perpetuo tamen id fore clam diffidere debet;
> quippe ubi se multi per somnia saepe loquentes
> aut morbo delirantes protraxe ferantur
> et celata <diu> in medium et peccata dedisse.

> Ever since that time [when laws were introduced] fear of punishment has poisoned the blessings of life. Violence and hurt[98] enmesh all those who practice them: they generally recoil on the wrongdoers, and it is not easy for those who by their actions violate mutual pacts of peace to pass a placid and peaceful life; for even if their crime goes undetected in heaven and on earth, they are bound to fear that it will not remain hidden forever. And indeed many people, so it is said, by talking in their sleep or in the delirium of

---

[96] DK 68 B 250 and 255 (= Stobaeus, *Anthology* IV.1.40 and IV.1.46).
[97] Lucretius explicitly mentions *concordia* at V.1024. See also above.
[98] The word that is translated as hurt here is "*inuiria*," which could also mean "injustice." The point of the passage, however, is not that justice and its opposite came to be when the laws were introduced. We already saw that justice came to be at an earlier stage in the process of development of communal life.

disease, have betrayed their own guilt and disclosed long hidden matters and their misdeeds.[99]

In other words, a new kind of fear makes its appearance at this point of the process of societal development. It is true that the laws can first be said to offer advantages. For instance, those who abide by the law are surely better off than they would be in a society without laws, for it must be better for them to live in a society free from random violence. Likewise, those whose "blessings are poisoned by the laws" seem to be precisely those who do not abide by the law; those who abide, by contrast, can be thought to have nothing to fear. Yet laws introduce fear into the world, and if the goal of Epicurean philosophy is to remove fear overall, the laws, on the Epicurean view, cannot, as David Konstan rightly observes, be an unequivocally good thing, even if they yield certain advantages.[100] Most importantly, the introduction of the laws is linked with the coming to be of new irrational fears that were completely absent from the human life of the original condition. Recall here that the discussion of gods and religion immediately follows the discussion of the fear that results from punishments associated with the laws, and the fear connected with the laws is importantly linked with the fear of the gods.[101] Philodemus observes that there were different ways in which stories of the gods were introduced into the world.[102] One of these is that individuals tell stories about the gods to procure their own security. While this description is not explicitly linked to phases in human development and it is in fact unclear whether Philodemus is making a developmental claim at all, this description is reminiscent of the first kings in Lucretius who usurped power to be safe and of what the law-givers could have done in order to make sure that their laws are more widely obeyed.

In the same vein, Diogenes of Oenoanda discusses the connection between laws and divine punishments in what is today referred to as the "Theological Physics Sequence" of his inscription. He makes the related point that instilling the fear of the gods is not an effective means to prevent

---

[99] Lucretius, *On the Nature of Things* V.1151–60. Trans. Smith, modified.
[100] Konstan 2008, 119–20. See also Müller 1972, 72–3; and Blickman 1989, 175. *Pace* Manuwald 1980, 59, fn. 219, who denies that there is anything negative about the law. On the role of fear in regard to obeying the law, see also Chapter 5.
[101] See Lucretius, *On the Nature of Things* V.1161–240; Konstan 2008, 112–19; and Perelli 1967, 222.
[102] Philodemus, *On Piety* I.2150–81 Obbink. A similar account is also found in Hermarchus: The first law-givers first try to frighten those who do not obey with punishments (fr. 34 Longo Auricchio = Porphyry, *On Abstinence* I.8.2). Later, they also add a religious dimension to keep the many from breaking the law (ibid. I.9.4).

1.4 The Logismos Phase

people from doing wrong. And this comment seems to be aimed at individuals who have attempted to do this or think that it is necessary:

φασὶ γάρ τινες μὴ συμφέρειν τῷ βίῳ τὸ δόγμα τοῦτο. τοὺς γὰρ ἀνθρώπους καὶ ἐπὶ τοῦ παρόντος μὲν ἀδικοπραγεῖν ἐφ' ὅσον δή ποτε· ἂν μέντοι καὶ τῶν ἐκ θεῶν φόβων ἀπολυθῶσι, τελέως ἀδικοπραγήσειν, ἐγ δὲ τούτου συνχυθήσεσθαι τὸν ὅλον [βίον. τοιοῦτοι] μὲν καὶ ν[ῦν πε]φ[ύ]κασι[ν] οἱ μὴ [δ]ε[δ]οικότες τοὺς θεούς ([συ]νκεχωρημένον [εἴη τ]οῦτο· εἰ γὰρ ἐδεδοίκεσαν, οὐκ ἂν ἠδίκουν)· [τ]ῶν δ' ἄλλων ἀποφαίνομαι τοὺς μὲν φυσικῶν ἁπτομένου<ς> λόγων μὴ διὰ τοὺς θεοὺς εἶναι δικαίους, διὰ δὲ τὸ βλέπειν [ὀ]ρθῶς τάς τε ἐπιθυμίας τίν' ἔχουσιν φύσιν κα[ὶ] τὰς ἀλγηδόνας καὶ τὸν θάνατον (πάντη τε γὰρ πάντως ἢ διὰ φόβον ἢ διὰ ἡδονὰς ἀδικοῦσιν ἄνθρωποι), τοὺς δ' αὖ χυδαίους διὰ τοὺς νόμους εἶναι δικαίους, εφ' ὅσον γέ εἰσιν δίκαιοι, καὶ τὰς ἀπὸ τούτων ἐπικρεμαμένας αὐτοῖς ζημίας. ἀλλὰ κἂν ὦσιν τινες ἐν αὐτοῖς διὰ τοὺς θεοὺς εὐγνώμονες, οὐ διὰ τοὺς νόμους, ὀλίγοι δὲ οὗτοι· καὶ δυ' ἢ τρεῖς μόλις κατὰ μεγάλας πληθῶν ἀποτομὰς εὑρισκόμενοι, βεβαίως οὐδὲ οὗτοι διακαιοπραγοῦσιν.

For some say that this doctrine [that is, that the gods are not to be feared] does not benefit our life, for human beings even in the present situation act wrongly so far as they possibly can; that if, however, they are also released from their fears derived from the gods, they will act completely wrongly, and in consequence the whole [of life] will be confounded. However, [people of such behavior] are even now those who do not fear the gods ([let] this [be] agreed; for if they feared the gods, they would not do wrong). But, as for the others, I declare that those of them who grasp the arguments based on nature are not just on account of the gods, but on account of their having a correct view of the nature of desires and pains and death (for indeed invariably and without exception human beings do wrong either on account of fear or on account of pleasures), and that ordinary people on the other hand are just, insofar as they are just, on account of the laws and the penalties, imposed by the laws, hanging over them. But even if some of their number are conscientious on account of the gods, rather than on account of the laws, they are few; only just two or three individuals are to be found among great segments of multitudes, and not even these are steadfast in acting justly.[103]

---

[103] Diogenes of Oenoanda, frr. 167 II.4–III.14 + 126.I.1–III.4 Smith. Trans. Hammerstaedt and Smith, modified. In contrast to Diogenes' skepticism regarding the efficiency of the fear of the gods as an instrument to compel people to be just, Philodemus seems to be more optimistic in regard to what the fear of the gods may accomplish. See *PHerc.* 1251 (= Philodemus, *On Choices and Avoidances*?), col. XII.4–19 Indelli and Tsouna-McKirahan. As Hammerstaedt and Smith observe, the Epicureans' unnamed opponents (*tines*) may be the Stoics here (since the Stoics are also Diogenes' target a little later in the text).

Accordingly, one may say that, on the Epicurean view, the fear of the gods, which is one of the worst fears that Epicureanism combats (as the Fourfold Remedy makes clear),[104] is at least in part connected to the introduction of the law, since the latter seems to have precipitated the necessity of the former. Again, then, this should make clear that the introduction of the law on the Epicurean view cannot be all positive.

In summary, we have seen that the laws, just like the agreements of justice, come to be by conventional means during a second phase of communal development. Likewise, the laws are a historical product on the Epicurean view. However, they are also established in light of what is beneficial to all, hinting at the natural side of Epicurean justice (that will be more fully explored in the next chapter).

1.5 Epicurean Social Contract Theory

This chapter showed that the Epicurean theory of the social contract clearly distinguishes between (1) an original state; (2) a *phusis* phase of development, during which human beings unite for the first time; and (3) a *logismos* phase, during which human beings create legal and political states. Accordingly, these three different stages of development correspond to different degrees of historical establishment and human knowledge of justice and the law, which according to the Epicureans do not exist by nature. While neither justice nor laws exist in the original state, the *phusis* phase features justice without laws. Finally, the *logismos* phase features both justice and laws.

The chapter also showed that for the Epicureans, human beings at the beginning of the account are not "by nature" social beings (as they are, for instance, for Aristotle or the Stoics), but rather self-sufficient beings who do not need to live with others. The transition from the original state of human beings to the life with others (during the *phusis* phase) is caused by a change in human nature and needs; a sedentary lifestyle, family ties, and technological achievements affect their nature gradually, but importantly, and this change is accompanied by new desires, for instance, of protecting both the agents themselves as well as their loved ones. Moral norms such as the just (*aequum*) first come into being at this stage of development, as a historical achievement, by means of an agreement, once the family as a more basic form of sociality has already emerged. As was emphasized above, while agreements do play a key role in the account, the agreement

---

[104] Philodemus, *To the . . .*, col. V. 8–13 Angeli. See also *KD* 1.

are made with an eye toward what is beneficial, which itself is not a conventional feature (as will be argued in more detail in the next chapter).

After the coming to be of justice, life in community is still fraught with difficulties, on the Epicurean view: preeminent men usurp political power in order to use it for their own ends, leading to a state of strife. As a response, laws are introduced as a check to those in power, but they are a mixed blessing: they introduce a new kind of fear into the world.

While more needs to be said about the natural feature of Epicurean justice to see how exactly the Epicureans argue for a middle position in the *nomos-phusis* debate, the Epicurean multistage developmental account of how justice and law come to be certainly invites comparisons to early modern conceptions of the social contract. Accordingly, the chapter will close with a few remarks on some commentators' attempts to assimilate the Epicurean contractarianism to that of Thomas Hobbes, primarily on the strength of the idea that the original state in Epicurus is a violent or potentially violent state: a war of all against all.[105]

On the basis of the close investigation of the textual evidence, one can easily show that such an assimilation to Hobbes' theory of the social contract is unwarranted. First, Lucretius recognizes advantages and disadvantages of the original state, which is a wholly negative condition in Hobbes. In addition, the reference to Hobbes is misleading insofar as the latter does not discuss the creation of the society at all in his theory, but rather exclusively focuses on the creation of the state. Put differently, there is no separate discussion of a *pactum unionis* and a *pactum subjectionis* in Hobbes as there is in Epicurean authors, since the former does not at all discuss the emergence of the sociality prior to the social contract (as the Epicureans do). Furthermore, according to Hobbes, human nature is constant throughout his account: dominated by fear, man is a wolf to man. Yet this is not true according to the Epicureans: they stress that human beings undergo a change in human nature (prior to entering society) and only this change makes it necessary that societies come to be. Likewise, Epicurean agents are not motivated principally by fear. In fact, it is only the creation of the state and the connected emergence of religion that really instills human beings' anxieties (especially in regard to the gods).

If one had to relate the Epicurean account of the social contract to a schema of an early modern account of the social contract, Jean-Jacques

---

[105] For references and discussion, see Robitzsch 2017 (*pace* Spinelli 2019, 389–90; and Perelli 1967, 166–71). See now also Aoiz and Boeri 2023, 6, 16, 33, and 160.

Rousseau's version would be a much better fit than Hobbes'.[106] Rousseau endorses the key Epicurean idea that human beings undergo a change prior to entering society. And in addition to this, he not only assumes that the original state is an overall peaceful state of existence but he also distinguishes between the bad process of the formation of society (described in the *Second Discourse*) and the more positive and later project of creating a better society in *On the Social Contract*, which in some ways might be said to correspond to the Epicurean *logismos* phase that features the emergence of the rule of law.

---

[106] For a detailed discussion of the similarities between the Epicurean and the Rousseauean account, see Müller 1997.

CHAPTER 2

Contractual Justice

Whereas Lucretius' *On the Nature of Things* was the focus of the previous chapter, this chapter will draw primarily on writing by Epicurus himself as well as by some later Epicureans. The goal is to elaborate on three claims in regard to Epicurean justice and social contract theory. The first claim concerns the fact that the etiological account of how justice and law come to be in Lucretius left some room for justice to be grounded in something natural. This chapter completes the argument by showing more clearly what exactly this is and why the Epicureans can be said to occupy a middle position in the *nomos-phusis* debate. Furthermore, the chapter will describe in more depth what agents agree to exactly when they make agreements (claim 2) as well as how noncontracting parties are also covered by the agreements, on the Epicurean view (claim 3).

The first section of this chapter will discuss the connection between justice and benefit and the extent to which there is something naturally just on the Epicurean view (Section 2.1). The second section will then turn to the functional role of agreements within Epicurean philosophy as well as their content (Section 2.2). The third and last section will deal with agreements with animals and non-Greeks (Section 2.3).

2.1 The Naturally Just: *Nomos* Grounded in *Phusis*

Given that justice is a historical achievement, it is surprising to read at the outset of the discussion of justice in *KD* 31 that there is something naturally just (*to tēs phuseōs dikaion*) on the Epicurean view:

> Τὸ τῆς φύσεως δίκαιόν ἐστι σύμβολον τοῦ συμφέροντος εἰς τὸ μὴ βλάπτειν ἀλλήλους μηδὲ βλάπτεσθαι.
>
> The naturally just is a *sumbolon* of benefit in regard to not harming each other and not being harmed.[1]

[1] Trans. mine.

What is the "naturally just"? The maxim tells us that it is the *sumbolon* of benefit, but unfortunately, there is also some disagreement on the precise meaning of the word "*sumbolon*."[2] According to the traditional reading, "*sumbolon*" is taken to be a synonym for "agreement [*sunthēkē*]." On this reading, then, *KD* 31 makes the same point as *KD* 32, 33, and 35. All four maxims, on this reading, claim that justice is a kind of agreement, albeit in somewhat different language. However, according to an alternative reading, "*sumbolon*" in *KD* 31 is taken to mean "token" or "expression."[3] On this reading, Epicurus makes a more general point, namely, that what is naturally just is an expression of benefit. Regardless of what one takes "*sumbolon*" to mean in this maxim, however, this chapter will show that Epicurus and his followers accept both claims: that there is a close relationship between justice and agreements (as the traditional reading of *KD* 31 highlights) *and* that there is a close relationship between justice and benefit (which the alternative reading of *KD* 31 emphasizes).[4] Accordingly, not much hinges on the precise meaning of the word "*sumbolon*" in this maxim.

What "*to tēs phuseōs dikaion*" exactly is has regularly puzzled scholars, especially because of the strange genitive.[5] In the context of the *nomos-phusis* debate, one would rather expect the dative "*phusei*." Given the habitual usage of the dative "*phusei*," the claim that there is something "just by nature" would then mean that justice is natural in the world in the sense of a nonartificial thing, which has a permanent essence that does not vary according to circumstances or observer. Accordingly, if *KD* 31 means that there is something "just by nature [*to phusei dikaion*]," the maxim would express the idea that Epicurean agreements of justice do not vary according to circumstances or observers. Yet such a conclusion would be strange. As we saw in Lucretius' *Kulturentstehungslehre*, justice really is an agreement, and for the Epicureans, it arises anew from place to place, as shown by *KD* 37 and 38 (which will be quoted in detail below). Consequently, it would be strange if *KD* 31 asserted that justice exists naturally (*phusei*) in the sense just described.

---

[2] On the meanings of the word in general, see Müri 1976 and Struck 2004.
[3] See, for instance, Schofield 2010 [2000], 440, fn. 11; and Brown 2010 [2009], 192, fn. 44. While indeed the meaning of "*sumbolon*" is first and above all "agreement," Aristotle (*On Interpretation* 16a4 and 24b2) already uses "*sumbolon*" in a philosophical context to mean "token" or "expression." Epicurean usage of "*sumbolon*" as "token" or "expression" could thus be said to merely follow the precedent set by earlier thinkers such as Aristotle.
[4] Besides *KD* 31, *KD* 36–8 also discuss the close relationship between justice and benefit.
[5] See Bollack 1975, 353–4, for an overview of the different ways of translating the maxim.

2.1 The Naturally Just: Nomos Grounded in Phusis

Instead, "*to tēs phuseōs dikaion*" is better understood as a way of referring to what really characterizes justice in terms of its "nature," although one should quickly add that the "nature" of justice cannot be a fixed permanent essence.[6] To explain this further, it will be helpful to consider a parallel case. In *KD* 7, Epicurus writes about "what is naturally good [*to tēs phuseōs agathon*]."[7] This is usually not taken to mean that there are things that are naturally good in the sense of being once and for all good (as on the above reading of the dative "*phusei*," which implies such a permanent essence). Rather, it is taken to mean that given how the world is set up, a certain thing is good at this very moment. The world could be structured differently and the things that are good now would not be good then, but at least now they are good. In other words, following Anthony Long and David Sedley, we can translate the genitive "*phuseōs*" literally as "nature's," and keep in mind that nature for the Epicureans here does not refer to a permanent essence, but rather to a *natural process* that reflects the changing structure of the world.[8] Put differently, "nature's justice" is the nature of justice as it is found in the world at a given moment, not a *permanent* essence of justice.

Against such a nonessentialist reading of "*to tēs phuseōs dikaion*," one might be tempted to adduce a passage in the later Epicurean Philodemus, which mentions something naturally just (*phusei dikaion*): "... τοῖς δυν[αμένοις τὴν] φύσει δικαίου κ[αὶ ἀδίκου χ]ώ[ρ]αν ἔχειν, [ὥστ' ἐν τού]τωι κατὰ μη[θὲν ἀλλάτ]τειν, τὰ δ' ἐναντία τὴν τῶν ἐναντίων, ἔνια δὲ κατὰ τόπους καὶ περιστράσεις."[9] Harry Hubbell translates: "Some things are just or unjust by nature [*phusei*] and never change, others vary according to locality and condition." At first sight, this translation thus suggests that there are things that are just by nature in the sense that was flagged as problematic, namely, in the sense of a kind of justice that exists as an essential nature, independently of agents or circumstances. In response to such a reading, one first has to note that the text is part of those Epicurean texts preserved on Herculaneum papyri. As a result,

---

[6] See also *KD* 37 (quoted in detail below) for an alternate way of referring to the nature of justice.
[7] For further parallel cases, see *Letter to Menoeceus* 133: *KD* 15; and *SV* 25. *KD* 7 mentions "what is naturally appropriate [*to tēs phuseōs oikeion*]."
[8] Francesco Verde rightly observes: "the Epicurean concept of 'nature,' in a certain sense, is not a stable and immobile notion, but vigorously and actively dynamic, and for this reason, in my opinion, one could speak of a 'natural process' rather than nature [*il concetto epicureo di 'natura,' in un certo senso, non è una nozione stabile, immobile ma energicamente e attivamente dinamica, per questo, a mio parere, occorrerebbe parlare di 'processo naturale' più che di natura*]" (2010, 215). See also the discussion in Robitzsch 2017.
[9] Philodemus, *Rhetoric* I.259, col. XXIV.26–33 Sudhaus.

there are several lacunae in the text, and the reading of the sentence strongly depends on additions by a modern editor, Siegfried Sudhaus. However, even if one accepts the reading offered by Sudhaus, a more literal translation than the one by Harry Hubbell quoted above is the following: "... to/by those things[10] able to have the status of the just and unjust by nature [*phusei*],[11] so as to never change in this [regard], but the opposites that of the opposites,[12] while some change according to locality and condition." In short, the sentence does not at all present the clear-cut contrast between just things by nature and just things that are not by nature, which is falsely suggested by Hubbell's translation, which leaves out a part of the Greek. Admittedly, the passage clearly claims that there is something just by nature (*phusei*), but without more context, it is impossible to say what – if anything – this implies about something being just by nature in Epicureanism.[13] Consequently, the reading of nature proposed above, namely that there is no justice by nature, understood as a permanent essence, is not threatened by this passage in Philodemus.

Even if our analysis up to this point is correct, this still leaves the naturalness of the Epicurean conception of justice in *KD* 31 quite indeterminate. After all, so far we have only noted that natural justice is the justice that is found at a given point in time. Accordingly, let us take a closer look at the second half of the maxim to determine of what the nature of justice exactly consists. Here, the nature of justice is connected with benefit, which means that on the Epicurean view, what is just is dependent on what is beneficial. What is beneficial, in turn, on the Epicurean view, can change with time and circumstances, as *KD* 37 and 38 make clear:

> Τὸ μὲν ἐπιμαρτυρούμενον ὅτι συμφέρει ἐν ταῖς χρείαις τῆς πρὸς ἀλλήλους κοινωνίας τῶν νομισθέντων εἶναι δικαίων ἔχειν τοῦ δικαίου χώραν <δ>εῖ, ἐάν τε τὸ αὐτὸ πᾶσι γένηται ἐάν τε μὴ τὸ αὐτό. ἐὰν δὲ νόμον θῆταί τις,[14] μὴ ἀποβαίνῃ δὲ κατὰ τὸ συμφέρον τῆς πρὸς ἀλλήλους κοινωνίας, οὐκέτι τοῦτο τὴν τοῦ δικαίου φύσιν ἔχει. κἂν μεταπίπτῃ τὸ κατὰ τὸ δίκαιον

---

[10] The quotation begins with a definitive article and a participle in the dative. Since the beginning of the sentence is lost, it is unclear how the text that has come down to us connected to the lost part of the sentence.

[11] For a similar expression, see *KD* 37 according to one manuscript reading: "ἔχει τὸ τοῦ δικαίου χώραν."

[12] A verb needs to be supplied here from the part of the sentence that is not preserved in the papyrus.

[13] In this context, note that Demetrius Lacon spends some time clarifying the expression "by nature," distinguishing three different senses in which it can be used. *PHerc.*, 1012 col. LXVII Puglia. This seems to be a later development in the school, though, in response to criticism from rival philosophers, which could suggest that Demetrius employs a different conception of "by nature" than Epicurus did. On the meaning of the term "nature" in Epicureanism, see also O'Keefe 2021.

[14] The manuscript readings "μόμον θῆταί τις" and "νόμοτεθῆται τι" cannot be correct here.

2.1 *The Naturally Just:* Nomos *Grounded in* Phusis

συμφέρον, χρόνον δέ τινα εἰς τὴν πρόληψιν ἐναρμόττῃ, οὐδὲν ἧττον ἐκεῖνον τὸν χρόνον ἦν δίκαιον τοῖς μὴ φωναῖς κεναῖς ἑαυτοὺς συνταράττουσιν ἀλλ' ἁπλῶς εἰς τὰ πράγματα βλέπουσιν.

Among the things that are acknowledged to be just, whatever is attested to be beneficial in the requirements of mutual intercourse necessarily has a place in the domain of justice, whether or not it turns out to be the same for all. But if someone makes a law and it does not happen to accord to the beneficial of mutual intercourse, it no longer has the nature of justice. And even if what is beneficial in the sphere of justice changes but fits the preconception for some time, it was no less just throughout that time for those who do not confuse themselves with empty utterances but simply look at the facts.[15]

Ἔνθα μὴ καινῶν γενομένων τῶν περιεστώτων πραγμάτων ἀνεφάνη μὴ ἁρμόττοντα εἰς τὴν πρόληψιν τὰ νομισθέντα δίκαια ἐπ' αὐτῶν τῶν ἔργων, οὐκ ἦν ταῦτα δίκαια· ἔνθα δὲ καινῶν γενομένων τῶν πραγμάτων οὐκέτι συνέφερε τὰ αὐτὰ δίκαια κείμενα, ἐνταῦθα δὴ τότε μὲν ἦν δίκαια ὅτε συνέφερεν εἰς τὴν πρὸς ἀλλήλους κοινωνίαν τῶν συμπολιτευομένων. ὕστερον δ' οὐκ ἦν ἔτι δίκαια ὅτε μὴ συνέφερεν.

Where, provided the facts have not been altered, things that were acknowledged to be just have been shown not to accord with the preconception in actual practice, then they are not just. But where, when the circumstances have changed, the things acknowledged to be just no longer lead to benefit, there they were just at the same time when they were of benefit for the dealings of fellow-citizens with one another; but subsequently they are no longer just, when no longer of benefit.[16]

Note that neither these maxims nor in fact any other passage in the Epicurean corpus makes what is beneficial the product of an agreement in the way that justice is. On the contrary, as especially *KD* 37 makes clear, those who look at the facts (*ta pragmata*) see directly that the beneficial in the realm of justice aligns with the preconception of justice.[17] Accordingly, at any given time, what is beneficial is thus best understood as a natural fact, where this means that what is beneficial is based on the determinate, objective condition of the world. Accordingly, the entirety of facts about the world at a certain point in time determines what will be beneficial at that time. This means that anthropological, sociological, psychological, and political facts about human beings; zoological facts about possible

---

[15] *KD* 37 (= Long and Sedley 1987, 22B). Trans. Long and Sedley, modified.
[16] *KD* 38. Trans. Bailey, modified.
[17] Aoiz and Boeri 2023, 60. Note that *KD* 38 also acknowledges that the facts are the basis for assessing whether the agreements of justice align with the preconception of justice.

predators and prey; geographical facts about the terrain; and physical facts about the laws of nature, among many other facts, all help determine at any given moment in time what things are beneficial. Put differently, the view that *benefit itself* is the result of an agreement would have rather strange consequences. Imagine, for instance, that human beings agreed that it would be beneficial to their health to eat thirty chocolate bars every day or that they would agree that brushing one's teeth is a waste of time and that dental health can be obtained without it. Surely, such agreements would not *make* eating chocolate or not brushing one's teeth beneficial toward achieving the end of health. They would merely ignore what we know about dieting and what is conducive to obtaining health, an objective fact about what is beneficial. Of course, our state of knowledge may progress and we may find out that a certain thing or action does not have the desired benefit after all. For instance, blood-letting has largely been abandoned in modern medicine, because it is now believed to cause more disadvantages than benefit in patients. Again, however, this was not a matter of agreement among human beings (agreements would not make blood-letting beneficial), but rather a finding, a fact about what is beneficial for human beings like us in certain circumstances and what is not.

In short, then, on the Epicurean view, facts about the world – or more precisely about what is beneficial – provide the foundation for justice as an important constraint: At any given time, what is beneficial is based on an objective, determinable state of affairs, namely, what is beneficial at time t, and it can receive the *additional* status of being just, when (1) what is beneficial pertains to the dealings with other people (that is, is specific to a certain domain) and (2) human beings have agreed on it, giving the theory a constructivist element. Put again differently, while the Epicureans emphasize the importance of agreements in their theory of justice, as we also saw in the previous chapter, they also place agreements on a firm basis, namely, nature itself (understood as what is beneficial), which mitigates the fear that Epicurean theory is *only* artificial and as such arbitrary; the state of the world, including human nature, thus constrains which agreements will indeed, in particular circumstances, promote good human lives and which will not. However, this constraint is not deterministic and it is only the agreement itself that, in the end, *makes* a certain behavior just or unjust (compared with other courses of behavior, which may be beneficial but not just).

In summary, then, in terms of the ancient *nomos-phusis* debate, we can thus conclude that Epicurean justice occupies a sophisticated middle position. On the one hand, justice is the result of an agreement and only the agreement makes something just. On the other hand, however, it is not possible that merely anything becomes the subject of the agreement, but merely what is beneficial. As a result, Epicurean justice certainly distinguishes itself from the Platonic conception of justice. There is also no indication that Plato held a view according to which the Form of justice itself changes over time (rather than always staying the same), even if Plato, like Epicurus, accepted the claim that what is actually just may depend on the particular circumstances at hand, although he did not recognize agreements.

2.2 Benefit, Harm, and Security: Agreements and Their Role in Epicurean Philosophy

In discussing the naturally just, *KD* 31 connects justice and benefit. In particular, the maxim also claims that justice is not any kind of benefit, but the benefit of not harming and not being harmed. This section will spell out this claim further by making clear (1) what harm is for the Epicureans and (2) what functional role the prevention of harm and thus the agreements have more broadly within Epicurean philosophy.

Since there is no extant account of what counts as harm in the extant writings of Epicurean authors, it must be supplied. A good starting place for this is that on the Epicurean view, the highest goal in life, the normative structuring principle, that all agents should adopt in their actions is that human beings should live a life that is free from bodily pain (*aponia*) and mental distress (*ataraxia*). Harm would thus turn out to a bad that hinders agents to be able to live a life of *aponia* and *ataraxia*, and in agreeing not to harm and not to be harmed, agents would pledge both to not impose a bad on others and, in exchange, to not have a bad imposed on them. Since we find a variety of different forms of harm in Epicurean authors, it will be argued in what follows that "harm" entails (1) direct and (2) indirect harm, (3) against other contracting and (4) against third parties, and (5) physical and (6) nonphysical harm. Furthermore, it will be argued that beyond refraining from harm and contributing to the communal project of self-defense, Epicurean agreements do not entail any further positive duties to help others (for instance, to share resources with those who are needy or assist them in another way), which may figure prominently in modern conceptions of justice that emphasize distributive justice.

On a first reading (and perhaps intuitive understanding), harm can refer to the *direct harm* any individual may commit and suffer. Refraining from harm then means that agents pledge in agreements, for instance, not to rob each other and not to kill each other. Epicurean contractarianism thus might be seen as the answer to a problem of collective action: agents are better off not being harmed, but because harming others is in some scenarios supposedly beneficial to agents, agents do not abstain from harming because the cost of abstaining is higher than the confidence that they will actually receive the greater good of not being harmed. This results in a stalemate that is only resolved by the agreements, recalling the mixed motive or assurance games of rational choice theory (prisoners' dilemma, stag hunt, or hawk-dove) that commentators have drawn on in order to model the difficult choice that Epicurean agents face prior to contracting.[18]

In contradistinction to these rational choice models and agents, however, Epicurean theory and enlightened Epicurean agents do not seem to struggle to deal with scenarios in which it may be beneficial for an agent to make an agreement that will guarantee that the agent will be free from harm, while harming others or the group as a whole. For example, the usurpation of political power may be beneficial to the tyrant, but only at the expense of the tyrant's subjects. And in contrast to the question of whether the concern for the self can be reconciled with the concern for others in discussions of Epicurean friendship,[19] the conflict in regard to the benefit of not harming and being harmed may be less serious and thus easier to explain. For the Epicureans, what is beneficial for the community or for the group may simply align with what is beneficial for the individual,[20] that is, at least insofar as several agents can simultaneously achieve the state of *aponia* and *ataraxia*. This assumption becomes more plausible when one recalls that Epicurean hedonism is not a maximizing theory, even if some contemporary scholars falsely interpret the theory in this way.[21] Once agents have reached the state of *aponia* and *ataraxia*, on the Epicurean view, their happiness can no longer be increased.[22] Furthermore, the resources needed to reach this state are, in fact, for the Epicureans so abundant that there will be no conflicts for resources among agents. Likewise, agents above all are called on to focus on their natural

---

[18] See Denyer 1983, 144–9; Campbell 2002a; Campbell 2003, 256–8; Thrasher 2013, 431–2; and Vanderschraaf 2022.

[19] See especially O'Connor 1989; Annas 1993a, 236–44; O'Keefe 2001b; Brown 2002; Evans 2004; Rossi 2017; Mitsis 2020; and Carnes 2021.

[20] See also Müller 1983, 161.

[21] See, for instance, Thrasher 2013, 425; and Erler 2020, 12–13. Porter (1938, 14) argues that the misrepresentation of the Epicurean position can already be seen in Cicero's *On Ends* I.30 where "*appetere*" translates the Epicurean technical term "*euaresteisthai*." Whereas "*appetere*" "implies a restless seeking," "*euaresteisthai*" does not; it merely implies that something is pleasing and hence accords with the idea that the state of *ataraxia* is not one that can be maximized.

[22] See, for instance, *KD* 18.

2.2 Benefit, Harm, and Security

and necessary desires, and these desires are characterized by the fact that they can be easily satisfied.[23] As a result, it is difficult to see how a great deal of conflict can arise in regard to them. A king usurping the power in his community might thus be said to not pursue what is beneficial after all, but is likely reaching beyond what is beneficial in the mutual interactions with others, creating mental turmoil for himself through the threat of being disposed, by following empty desires. The enlightened ruler, by contrast, is unlikely to overstep his mandate, and also unlikely to pursue his own good by sacrificing the good of his subjects. In short, then, if the Epicurean view is properly understood, there may not be much of a conflict between the goal of an individual and the goal of the community as a whole, between what is beneficial in regard to harming and being harmed for an individual and what is beneficial in regard to harming and being harmed for the community as a whole. The reason is, again, that the conception of what is beneficial in the dealings with others may well be quite thin, and so what is required of agents to fulfill the pledge of the agreement is quite minimal. As a result, the Epicurean approach contrasts with modern contractarian and, especially, contractualist approaches that try to justify the existence of a more expansive state, that is, one that goes beyond the basic function of providing protection from harm to its inhabitants.

In addition to direct harm, harm may also include the *indirect harm* agents could do to each other on the Epicurean view.[24] For instance, it may include the provision that agents do not poison the local well or stream, which other members of the community use to fulfill one of their natural and necessary desires, that is, the desire for drink. In this vein, Hermarchus explicitly mentions provisions that were put in place to refrain from killing certain animals like sheep and cattle, because they are useful to human beings to procure their daily livelihood.[25] Accordingly, when agents pledge not to harm each other in a mutual agreement, they – at times – oblige themselves to cause neither direct nor indirect harm to those with whom they make an agreement.[26]

---

[23] On the Epicurean classification of desires, see Chapter 4 as well as Robitzsch 2022a.
[24] O'Keefe 2001a, 143 and passim. O'Keefe distinguishes between a narrow reading and an expansive reading of the claim that justice is an agreement not to harm each other. According to the narrow reading, justice as an agreement not to harm each other excludes indirect harm, and according to the expansive reading, justice as an agreement not to harm each other includes indirect harm.
[25] Hermarchus, fr. 34 Longo Auricchio (= Porphyry, *On Abstinence* I.11.2–5). The idea here is that not being able to use these animals would constitute a harm to the agent.
[26] A potential problem for including indirect harm under harm is that the passage in Hermarchus – in fact the only passage that backs up such a reading – deals with law and not justice, that is, with agreements of law, which are later, instead of agreements of justice, which are prior. However, it

In addition to direct and indirect harm, "harm" also leaves open whether "not to be harmed" means "not to be harmed by other people" or more broadly "not to be harmed by other people *as well as* by animals *and* any other potential sources of harm." Put differently, are agreements made only among contracting parties or are they made among contracting parties *and simultaneously* against third parties?

While *KD* 38 suggests that justice pertains to the "benefit for the dealings of fellow-citizens with one another [συνέφερεν εἰς τὴν πρὸς ἀλλήλους κοινωνίαν τῶν συμπολιτευομένων],"[27] emphasizing that justice concerns the protections against fellow *human beings*, other extant textual evidence suggests that harm from third parties is also to be included in the agreements. Hermarchus, for instance, argues that our early ancestors came together and made agreements in order to fend off wild animals.[28] And while Lucretius does not explicitly claim that agreements are directed against third parties, he mentions that the only threat that human beings face prior to making agreements are wild animals.[29] Consequently, like Hermarchus, Lucretius could be said to endorse the idea that the harm human beings preempt in agreements is any kind of physical harm, not just the harm that could be committed by the parties making the agreement. It follows, then, that although potential harm from third parties is not mentioned in the *Principal Doctrines* or elsewhere in Epicurus' own writings, it is best not to restrict unduly the harm to the harm caused by other human beings. In summary, then, Epicurean agents make agreements about things that cause direct harm and things that would cause harm indirectly both by the contracting parties themselves and by third parties.

So far, the discussion has centered on *physical harm*. Yet there is no reason to restrict harm to physical harm when it comes to the Epicurean

---

seems to be a fair assumption that there are also agreements of justice whose content resembles the content of the laws and so that the Hermarchus passage can provide support for the view that harm also includes indirect harm when it comes to the agreements of justice.

[27] On the traditional reading, *KD* 33 also makes clear that justice pertains to the dealings with other people: "Justice is not anything in itself, but a kind of agreement over not harming and not being harmed in the dealings with each other in any place whatever [Οὐκ ἦν τι καθ' ἑαυτὸ δικαιοσύνη, ἀλλ' ἐν ταῖς μετ' ἀλλήλων συστροφαῖς καθ' ὁπηλίκους δή ποτε ἀεὶ τόπους συνθήκη τις ὑπὲρ τοῦ μὴ βλάπτειν ἢ βλάπτεσθαι]." As Morel 2000, 403–4 points out *pace* the *Little, Scott, Jones Ancient Greek Lexicon* (LSJ) that lists "*sustrophē*" at *KD* 33 (and only this passage) with the meaning "dealings," the term is in other Epicurean texts used in a technical sense of an agglomeration of bodies in a cosmological context. See *Letter to Herodotus* 73 and 77 as well as Diogenes of Oenoanda, fr. 14.4 Smith. See also Hermarchus, fr. 34 Longo Auricchio (= Porphyry, *On Abstinence* I.10.2).

[28] Hermarchus, fr. 34 Longo Auricchio (= Porphyry, *On Abstinence* I.10.1).

[29] Lucretius, *On the Nature of Things* V.988–98.

view, either. After all, the actual physical harm that agents experience is only one aspect that the Epicurean theory as a whole addresses: a key component of Epicurean philosophy is to alleviate the mental distress that agents experience in regard to *potentially* being physically harmed. According to the Epicureans, the highest goal in life is the pursuit of pleasure (*hēdonē*).[30] However, by pleasure, the Epicureans do not mean the sensual pleasures of food, wine, and sex (although the pursuit of some such pleasures is not precluded by their theory), but rather a state that is characterized negatively by the absence of bodily pain and mental distress, *aponia* and *ataraxia*, as was already pointed out above.[31] Consequently, the removal of fear is a pillar of Epicurean philosophy, which – in certain ways – can be understood as a predecessor to modern psychotherapy.[32] This understanding of pleasure is quite unorthodox and even in antiquity was already the subject of much criticism – as the long complaint about Epicurus' unorthodox usage of the notion of pleasure in Cicero indicates.[33]

Finally, it is important to emphasize that Epicurean agreements center on the prevention of harm and nothing beyond this goal. For instance, the promotion of some other good, like actively helping others by providing them assistance in procuring food, is *not* part of the Epicurean agreements. Here, the Epicurean conception significantly differs from views of justice that, for instance, emphasize distributive justice. This finding is confirmed in the *Principal Doctrines* insofar as these maxims do not mention such a good, and the three texts that might be taken to refer to the promotion of a good that might not pertain to security, one passage in Hermarchus and two in Lucretius, do not have to be taken to mean that anything besides the prevention of harming and being harmed, that is, self-defense, is the focus of Epicurean agreements.

In Hermarchus, one reads that the first law-givers "tried to restrain firmly those who readily destroyed each other and who weakened the [mutual] aid because of forgetfulness of past events [ἐπειράθησαν βεβαιοτέρως ἀνεῖρξαι τοὺς προχείρως φθείροντας ἀλλήλους καὶ τὴν βοήθειαν ἀσθενεστέραν κατασκευάζοντας διὰ τὴν τοῦ παρεληλυθότος λήθην]."[34] Even if Hermarchus is speaking about the law in the passage and so not of agreements of justice, one might think that the passage

---

[30] See, for instance, *Letter to Menoeceus* 128. [31] Ibid., 131–2.
[32] For Epicurean philosophy as a kind of therapy, see especially Nussbaum 1994.
[33] See Cicero, *On Ends* II.6–15.
[34] Hermarchus, fr. 34 Longo Auricchio (= Porphyry, *On Abstinence* I.11.1). Trans. mine.

indicates that agreements of justice also confer positive obligations not related to self-defense, namely, of aiding others in other contexts as well. However, it is not clear what precisely aid entails in the passage just quoted. It may mean that the aid that agents render to each other consists in promoting goods, for instance, by sharing resources with others who do not at the moment or cannot in general have access to them. Yet it may also mean that the mutual aid pertains exclusively to the mutual aid in the case of self-defense against third parties that was already discussed above.[35] On this reading, then, the passage in Hermarchus is compatible with the idea that Epicurean agreements do not entail positive obligations to help others in regard to goods not related to security, for instance, by providing them with food.

The second passage that could be taken to argue for positive obligations in regard to goods not related to self-defense is *On the Nature of Things* V.1019–23, a passage that was already commented on in detail in the previous chapter. Here, neighbors "claimed protection [*commendarunt*] for their children and womenfolk, indicating by means of inarticulate cries and gestures that it is just that the weak are pitied by everyone." Yet note that while pitying probably refers to the right attitude that agents ought to take vis-à-vis the weak, as was argued in the previous chapter,[36] it is unclear how far-reaching the attitude of pity really has to be. It might involve the obligation to help someone by giving them resources of some kind that do not pertain to self-defense, but it may also – more realistically and more in line with what the Epicureans say elsewhere – be restricted to not harming someone who is already weak. However, even if pitying in Lucretius were to be taken to include duties to help others in regard to issues not related to self-defense, one might wonder whether such a view is the orthodox Epicurean position. Lucretius in regard to other points of detail diverges from the view of other Epicurean authors.[37] Accordingly, one might think that here, too, Lucretius advances a position that is not identical with Epicurus' position, either, and therefore, that a safer reading

---

[35] According to such a reading, then, Hermarchus' account is compatible with Lucretius' in regard to its treatment of the free-rider problem. See *On the Nature of Things* V.1025–7 as well as the more detailed discussion in the previous chapter.

[36] We unfortunately do not get a definition of pitying in Lucretius. At III.881, it is clear that pitying implies an emotional response of some kind, but it is unclear what kind of practical response is also part of having pity for someone.

[37] For instance, in regard to the cognitive capacities of animals and the role of *oikeiōsis*. See below and Appendix A.

will assume that Epicurean agreements are limited to refraining harm and helping with self-dense only.

The third and last passage that might provide evidence for obligations that are not merely limited to refraining from harm is found in a section of Lucretius' poem that contrasts the deficits of the original condition with the disadvantages of modern life. In this context, Lucretius identifies the lack of food as a harm that early human beings suffered: "Moreover, whereas in those times it was lack of food that consigned people's languid limbs to death, nowadays it is surfeit of food to which they succumb [*tum penuria deinde cibi languentia leto | membra dabat, contra nunc rerum copia mersat*]."[38] Since lack of food is a harm, one might think that this potential harm is also addressed by the agreements that human beings made with each other.[39] However, this is not at all clear. After all, immediately after the lines just quoted, Lucretius says that human beings inadvertently poisoned themselves in the original condition: "and whereas in those times they often served poison to themselves unwittingly, nowadays they make away with themselves more expertly [*illi imprudentes ipsi sibi saepe venenum | vergebant, nunc dant <allis> sollertius ipsi*]."[40] Certainly, randomly eating a poisonous food is a harm that human beings encountered during the original condition. Yet it is implausible to assume that this potential harm was solved by the agreements of justice. Accordingly, not all harms of the original state are addressed by agreements of justice, which, on a more conservative reading, aim only at preventing harm from other people and third parties. The agreements of justice are therefore not understandings to help others in a positive sense in times of need; rather, this seems to be the role of friendships. Agreements of justice thus would only pertain to a food shortage deliberately caused by human beings, but it does not seem that Lucretius has those in mind at line 1007.

Finally, let us end this section by supplementing the point that Epicurean agreements are restricted to preventing harm in regard to self-defense with the observation that the functional role of agreements within Epicurean philosophy is to promote security (*asphaleia*), a technical concept that figures prominently in Epicurean writings. Within Epicurean philosophy, security complements the program of scientific investigation that serves the purpose of mitigating the threat that natural phenomena pose (including the divine) – as *KD* 13, for instance, clearly sets out:

---
[38] Lucretius, *On the Nature of Things* V.1007–8. Trans. Smith.
[39] O'Keefe 2001a, 140, seems to understand this passage in this way.
[40] Lucretius, *On the Nature of Things* V.1009–10. Trans. Smith.

"There is no profit in procuring security in relation to human beings if things above and beneath the earth and indeed all in the boundless universe remain matters of suspicion [Οὐθὲν ὄφελος ἦν τὴν κατὰ ἀνθρώπους ἀσφάλειαν παρασκευάζεσθαι τῶν ἄνωθεν ὑπόπτων καθεστώτων καὶ τῶν ὑπὸ γῆς καὶ ἁπλῶς τῶν ἐν τῷ ἀπείρῳ]."[41]

Security can be achieved in different ways in Epicurean theory. The best means to achieve security, on the Epicurean view, is friendship, as *KD* 28 makes clear:

Ἡ αὐτὴ γνώμη θαρρεῖν τε ἐποίησεν ὑπὲρ τοῦ μηθὲν αἰώνιον εἶναι δεινὸν μηδὲ πολυχρόνιον καὶ τὴν ἐν αὐτοῖς τοῖς ὡρισμένοις ἀσφάλειαν φιλίας μάλιστα κατεῖδε συντελουμένην.

The same understanding produces confidence about there being nothing terrible which is eternal or [even] long-lasting and has also realized that security amid even these limited [bad things] is most easily achieved through friendship.[42]

By this, Epicurus means a life in a community of friends, withdrawn from the many of mainstream society:[43]

Τῆς ἀσφαλείας τῆς ἐξ ἀνθρώπων γενομένης μέχρι τινὸς δυνάμει τε ἐξερειστικῇ καὶ εὐπορίᾳ, εἰλικρινεστάτη γίγνεται ἡ ἐκ τῆς ἡσυχίας καὶ ἐκχωρήσεως τῶν πολλῶν ἀσφάλεια.

The purest security is that which comes from a quiet life and withdrawal from the many, although a certain degree of security from other men does come by means of the power to repel [attacks] and by means of prosperity.[44]

In the same vein, Epicurus famously advises his disciples to "live unnoticed [λάθε βιώσας]"[45] and explicitly claims that the sage "will not

---

[41] Trans. Bailey, modified. Even if it were inauthentic, the *Letter to Pythocles* in this context is a great example of how Epicurean research into natural phenomena contributes to freedom from mental distress by educating agents about the true nature of things.
[42] Trans. Inwood and Gerson. On the supreme importance of friendship in Epicureanism, see also *KD* 27 as well as *SV* 52 and 78.
[43] The distinction between the Epicurean community and the rest of humanity is very important in Epicureanism. For "*hoi polloi*" in Epicurean writings, see, for instance, *KD* 14; *Letter to Menoeceus* 123 (three times), 124, 125, and 134; as well as fr. 187 Usener (= *Gnomologium Parisinum* 1168 f. 115 r.).
[44] *KD* 14, trans. Inwood and Gerson. See also *KD* 6 and 7. In *KD* 7, *asphaleia* is even referred to as "the natural good [τὸ τῆς φύσεως ἀγαθόν]."
[45] Fr. 551 Usener (= Plutarch, *Is "Live Unnoticed" a Wise Precept?* as well as Philostratus, *Life of Apollonius* VIII.28).

be politically active [οὐδὲ πολιτεύσεται]."⁴⁶ However, Epicureans acknowledge that it is not always possible to obtain security by withdrawing from the life of the many.⁴⁷ First, not everyone is a sage and it would be wrong to reduce the Epicurean theory to one directed only at sages. In contradistinction to the Stoics, who argue either that the figure of the sage is only a regulatory ideal or that there are only very few people who have achieved the status of being a sage, the Epicureans argue that there is a large number of sages in the world. Accordingly, Philodemus (probably directly responding to the Stoic claim that all sages are friends with each other) writes that "one must not suppose that all [sages] are friends of all – at least according to what 'friends' are usually called. For it is not possible that many of them will come to know each other [οὐ μὴν ἀπάντα[ς] ἀ[πάν]των οἰητέον εἶναι [φίλ]ους, ἢ κατὰ τὸ σύν[η]θές γε φίλοι καλοῦνται· τοὺς γὰ[ρ] ἀπείρους [ο]ὐ δυνατὸν ἀλλήλ[οις εἴ]ς γνῶσιν ἀφικνεῖσθαι]."⁴⁸ However, not everyone has the disposition necessary to live the life of a sage. Some people lack the bodily constitution (*sōmatos hexis*) or ethnic background (*ethnos*) to become a sage,⁴⁹ which is a prerequisite for leading such a life. Likewise, Epicurus explicitly mentions people whose disposition is to lead a political life.⁵⁰ People who have such a disposition are not to be stopped from following their nature, but rather encouraged to pursue the life that best fits them. Given the vagaries of the political sphere, security from others will be a special concern for such people.

Second, the circumstances might make it impossible for an agent to live a secure life by withdrawing from the many. In such a case, an Epicurean has no choice but to live with other human beings; reciprocal agreements thus become a path to produce the sought-after security that contributes to

---

⁴⁶ Fr. 8 Usener (= Diogenes Laërtius, *Lives of Eminent Philosophers* X.119). Note that "πολιτεύσεται" is the manuscript reading in manuscripts B, P, and F; Dorandi prints "πολιτεύσεσθαι." This attitude already brought the Epicureans much ridicule in antiquity, culminating in Cicero's remark at *On the Orator* III.63–4. that if all eminent men who had reached the state of *ataraxia* withdrew from public life, they would not be able to remain in this blissful state for a long time. See also Plutarch, *Against Colotes* 1126e–27c.

⁴⁷ See, for instance, Müller 1972, 78–80; Long 1985; Fish 2011; and especially Roskam 2007 and Roskam 2020. There is even some evidence that Epicurus himself had some interest in political matters. See Roskam 2007, 50.

⁴⁸ Philodemus, *On the Gods* III, col. 1.3–7 Diels. Trans. mine. Given that not everyone is capable of being a sage (see below), "*apeiron*" here has to mean "many" (that is, so many that not everyone can befriend everyone), not literally an infinite number. See also Delattre 2003.

⁴⁹ See fr. 226 Usener (= Diogenes Laërtius, *Lives of Eminent Philosophers* X.117). See also Diogenes of Oenoanda's inscription, which is addressed only to those who are already well constituted (*hoi eusunkritoi*). See frr. 2 and 3.

⁵⁰ See fr. 555 Usener (= Plutarch, *On the Tranquility of the Soul* 2, 465f.). See also Grilli 1996 and the typology of Epicurean forms of life in Liebich 1960, 104–18.

a life of *aponia* and *ataraxia*.⁵¹ In the same vein, Epicurus emphasizes in *KD* 39 that agents should do the best they can in order to prevent external threats, but where this is not possible, to at least acquaint themselves with them. Finally, even trying to be secure by withdrawing from the life of the many, this does not mean that Epicurean agents capable of withdrawing will live the life of hermits, completely isolated from others. As Elizabeth Asmis emphasizes, the imperative "live unnoticed" does not mean that one ought to live in a physically concealed way, that is, in hiding, but rather that one ought to blend in with mainstream society, to adopt a certain inner attitude, a kind of inner detachment from the affairs of the larger sociopolitical community.⁵² So this means that even Epicureans living in communities of friends might still need political knowledge and, as we will see in Chapter 3, agreements in order to live the good life.

In other words, while there is a considerable amount of evidence that, all things being equal, Epicureans advise agents not to be implicated in political matters,⁵³ there is also some evidence that there were politically active Epicureans⁵⁴ and that one cannot be politically inactive all the time.⁵⁵ Political theorizing and making agreements about harming and not being harmed thus fulfill an important function in Epicureanism. They help agents attain security in situations, in which this is necessary, but not otherwise possible. This in turn helps agents achieve the Epicurean goal of living a life of *aponia* and *ataraxia*.⁵⁶ In summary, then, we may say that agreements and so the theorizing about the life with others plays an important role in Epicureanism. While the Epicureans do not claim that such a life is the best life, they understand well that the conditions for living the best life may not always be met.⁵⁷

---

⁵¹ See Müller 1972, 117–18. ⁵² Asmis 2001, 214.
⁵³ See especially the examples in Fowler 1989.
⁵⁴ See, for instance, Castner 1991; Griffin 1997; Sedley 1997; Benferhat 2005; Sedley 2010 [2009]; Valchova 2018; and Tutrone 2022, 207. The historical evidence is particularly rich for later Epicureans living in modern-day Syria and in Rome.
⁵⁵ See Sedley 1997.
⁵⁶ To show that political theorizing played some role in Epicureanism, finally, one may also add a quantitative argument: eight of the forty *Principal Doctrines* deal explicitly with justice and the law. If thinking about justice and law, that is, the political realm, were completely unimportant to the Epicureans, it would be very surprising that one in five, or 20 percent, of the most important maxims were devoted to it.
⁵⁷ In a recent paper, Jeffrey Green argues for the view that the Epicureans should be understood as extrapolitical thinkers, rather than merely apolitical or antipolitical ones. He characterizes such a view as follows: "[A]n extrapolitical perspective does not necessarily reject politics once and for all but continually looks to achieve a temporary or episodic transcendence of political commitments and concerns, often with the expectation of a future reentry into political life" (2015, 493). While it is true that the Epicureans do not reject politics unconditionally, there is no textual evidence for the

2.3 The Parties of Epicurean Agreements

On the interest-based contractarian view of justice that the Epicureans defend, the ability to make agreements is the prerequisite for articulating one's own point of view. Without this ability, agents simply have to accept the determinations that other agents make on their behalf. While men of a certain age are certainly able to make agreements according to the Epicurean view, as we saw in Chapter 1, this likely excludes women, children, and weaker members of society. Nevertheless, these groups profit from the agreements indirectly, insofar as they are associated with contracting parties. This section aims to say more about how third parties are covered by agreements and what conditions need to be fulfilled to make an agreement on the Epicurean view by examining the possibility of agreements with animals and foreigners.[58]

On the Epicurean view, animals are never explicitly acknowledged to be able to make agreements, and, in fact, not being a contracting party is what makes them marginalized insofar as they cannot be said to have their own place at the bargaining table. Yet this does not mean that their interests are not taken into account at all. They can become part of agreements of justice insofar as these are considered beneficial for the contracting parties themselves. The Epicureans thus offer an indirect duty view when it comes to animals, just as they did in regard to women, children, and weaker members of society more generally, and in this regard, their view resembles that of other contractarians such as Hobbes and Gauthier.[59] A common objection against an indirect duty view is that it exposes those indirectly protected by the agreement to harm should the agreement be terminated prematurely for some reason: for instance, should an animal's patron pass away, the animal would no longer be protected from harm and could be killed without consequence. In regard to such an objection, the Epicurean view offers at least some consolation. Epicurean agents ideally have no reason to harm others who are not a threat to them, whether or not they have made an agreement with them, as we will see in more detail in Chapter 4.

A discussion of the question of who the contracting parties are must begin with *KD* 32 where the question of who is able and willing to form an agreement is explicitly addressed:

---

claim that the Epicureans hope merely for a temporary or episodic transcendence of the political life and that they expect to return to it when living in their Epicurean communities.

[58] In what follows as well as elsewhere, "animals" will be used to refer to nonhuman animals.

[59] See Tanner 2013 for a discussion of marginal humans and animals in modern neo-Hobbesian views.

Ὅσα τῶν ζῴων μὴ ἐδύνατο συνθήκας ποιεῖσθαι τὰς ὑπὲρ τοῦ μὴ βλάπτειν ἄλληλα μηδὲ βλάπτεσθαι, πρὸς ταῦτα οὐθὲν ἦν δίκαιον οὐδὲ ἄδικον· ὡσαύτως δὲ καὶ τῶν ἐθνῶν ὅσα μὴ ἐδύνατο ἢ μὴ ἐβούλετο τὰς συνθήκας ποιεῖσθαι τὰς ὑπὲρ τοῦ μὴ βλάπτειν μηδὲ βλάπτεσθαι.

Nothing is just or unjust in relation to however many of those animals not able [*mē edunato*] to make agreements over not harming each other and not being harmed; so too with however many of the peoples [*ethnōn*] unable or unwilling [*mē edunato ē mē ebouleto*] to make agreements over not harming and not being harmed.[60]

Before getting into the details of the passage, we need to address a linguistic point. There is some disagreement on how to understand and hence translate "*pros*" in *KD* 32.[61] On a first reading, it could mean that there is no justice *in regard to* those animals that cannot make agreements, as in the translation quoted above. On an alternative reading, which is to be rejected in what follows, it can also mean that there is no justice *among* certain animals, namely, those that cannot make agreements. On this reading, the text merely says that there is no justice within a given species, but it leaves open whether human beings can make agreements of justice with the species in question. For instance, on the condition that wolves cannot make agreements with each other, one might say the following: while there is no justice *among* wolves, human beings might still be able to make agreements with them or be required to be just *in regard to* them. This alternative reading (that there is no justice *among* wolves), however, seems less convincing than the first (that there is no justice *in regard to* wolves). The context of the maxim, that is, observations on justice, makes it unlikely that Epicurus is merely making the ethnological observation that there are some species (and peoples) that lack justice in interacting with others from the same species. The more interesting observation is about how *human beings* should act in regard to these species (and in the second part of the maxim: in regard to foreign peoples). Furthermore, it also seems strange (even if not impossible) that if there is no justice *among* members of a certain species, there is at the same time justice between the members of this species and the members of another species. It seems more natural to suppose that intraspecies agreements in a certain sense are a prerequisite for interspecies agreements.

---

[60] = Long and Sedley 1987, 22A. Trans. Long and Sedley, modified. On the dialectic context of the maxim, see especially Moraux 1957, 100–8.
[61] Perelli 1967, 180, fn. 1; and Goldschmidt 1977, 44–57 (with references to older literature).

2.3 The Parties of Epicurean Agreements

In *KD* 32, Epicurus distinguishes between agreements with animals and agreements with other peoples. What is striking about the passage is that he does not directly rule out either type of agreement. "However many of" could stand in for some, all, or perhaps even an empty set. In regard to animals, we will therefore need to investigate whether the "however many of" set is empty or whether there are at least some animals that are capable of making agreements. In regard to other peoples, it is noteworthy that "*ethnos*" is a broad term and may thus include not only non-Greeks but also Greeks who are disposed in such a way that they cannot make agreements. The key question in regard to these peoples is therefore whether the Epicureans think that some people are in general incapable or unable to make agreements, and in the case of animals, if they are not able to make agreements, how they can still become privy to protections of justice. In what follows, let us therefore investigate in more detail the possibility of agreements with animals (Section 2.3.1) and agreements with other peoples (Section 2.3.2).

2.3.1 Agreements with Animals

If the Epicureans allowed agreements with animals, this would have some interesting consequences from a modern perspective. It would imply that the Epicureans truly extend justice to animals. On this reading, human beings would have contractual obligations toward them, which could be seen as an important step on the way to arguing for the interests of animals and so perhaps even their rights.[62] As we will see in more detail in this section, though, the textual evidence suggests that animals cannot make agreements on the Epicurean view. This is true even if some passages in Lucretius suggest that there are certain arrangements between human beings and animals, which in certain respects resemble agreements of justice (although they ultimately fall short of them), and if the discussion of interspecies agreements makes clear that the broader Epicurean theory of agreements is tiered (that is, consists of arrangements that are different in type, but still bear some resemblance with each other).

Since *KD* 32 leaves open whether there are some animals that are able to make agreements, we need to examine whether animals on the Epicurean view have the cognitive capacities to make agreements. After all, only if they are *capable* of making agreements, that is, if they have the requisite

---

[62] For the ancient debate, see especially the discussion in Sorabji 1993, 153–7. On the usage of the term "rights" in an ancient context, see Miller 1995, 87–140.

capacities to make agreements, is it possible that they are also *able* to make agreements, that is, they are in circumstances that enable them to make agreements. We thus need to examine the Epicureans' remarks about cognitive capacities of animals.[63] In particular, we will see that early Epicurean authors and Philodemus are pessimistic about the cognitive capacities of animals, while Lucretius is more optimistic. Nevertheless, even Lucretius does not endorse the idea that human beings can make agreements of justice with animals.

Let us begin with the founder of the school, Epicurus, himself. In *On Nature* XXV,[64] a notoriously cryptic text that is not only lacunose but also contains much difficult and unexplained technical vocabulary, we read:

> ἔτι μᾶλλον ἐνίοτ[ε κ]ακίζομεν, ἐν νουθετητ[ικ]ῶι μέντοι μᾶλλον τρόπω[ι], καὶ οὐκ ὥσπερ [τ]ὰ ἄγρια τῶν ζώιων [καθ]αίρομεν μὲν ὁμοίως αὐτὰ τὰ ἀπογεγε[νν]ημένα [κ]αὶ τὴ[ν] σύστασιν εἰς ἕν τι συμπ[λέ]κοντες, οὐ μὴν ο[ὔ]τε τῶι νουθε[τ]ητ[ι]κῶι τρόπωι καὶ ἐπανορθωτικῶι οὔτε τῶι ἁπλῶς ἀ[ντι]ποι[η]τικῶι χρώμεθα.

> We sometimes reproach it [that is, an animal capable of having "developments"][65] all the more, but in an admonitory mode – and not in the way in which we exonerate those animals which are wild by combining their developments and their make-up alike into a single thing, and indeed do not use either the admonitory and reformatory mode or the simply retaliatory mode.[66]

While many details of this passage are unclear and a detailed discussion would exceed the scope of this chapter, Epicurus seems to claim here that wild animals are in some way significantly different from nonwild animals

---

[63] In doing so, we will see that the Epicureans have quite a nuanced appreciation of animals, especially compared with other schools of the time. See also Dierauer 1977; Annas 1992, 134–7; Annas 1993b, 65–70; and Sorabji 1993, 161–6.

[64] The following passage is still listed under "*Deperditorum librorum reliquae*" in the second edition of Arrighetti's works of Epicurus, but Laursen identified the text as belonging to *On Nature* XXV. The translation follows Long and Sedley's. However, the critical edition of the text that has been provided by Laursen is invaluable, since it also includes a detailed commentary on the text. For a more recent commentary on this difficult text, see Masi 2006 (including references to older literature).

[65] What exactly Epicurus means by the technical term "developments" is not clear.

[66] Long and Sedley 1987, 20j (= fr. 34.25 Arrighetti). Trans. Long and Sedley, modified. On this passage, see especially Huby 1967; Laursen 1988; and Verlinsky 1996. Laursen translates: "We occasionally criticize even more – that is, not in the primary blaming way and not as wild animals do, we rinse, in that we plait together the products themselves and the composition – and we do not at all use the blaming or correcting or the simply opponing way" (1988, 17). Note that the gamma in "*agria*" is no longer legible in the original papyri and a nineteenth-century drawing of the papyrus has "*aeria tōn zōiōn*" (air animals).

2.3 The Parties of Epicurean Agreements

in that the latter, but not the former, may be blamed for their actions. It could follow from this that the distinction between wild animals and tame or domestic ones overlaps with the distinction between those animals that are able to make agreements and those that are not. However, deducing any firm conclusion from this passage seems problematic, given the state of the text and a lack of context. Let us therefore turn to a different and perhaps more conclusive piece of evidence to address the cognitive capabilities of animals in Epicureanism.

In *On Irrational Contempt for Common Conceptions*, Polystratus, the third head of the Garden, who is perhaps one of the last Epicureans to have studied with the school founder himself (which would make doctrinal continuity between his views and Epicurus' own views more likely), explicitly discusses the cognitive capacities of animals. Unfortunately, much of Polystratus' argument is lost due to the poor condition of the papyrus scroll it was preserved on, and the passages that are relevant in this context are too long and too dispersed to quote in full. Nevertheless, in his treatise, Polystratus is concerned with demonstrating that human beings and animals crucially differ in regard to their reasoning capacity (*logismos*). Animals, Polystratus claims, "do not share in reason *or not in one like ours* [τὸ μὴ κοινωνεῖν λογισμοῦ ἢ μὴ οἵου ἡμεῖς]."[67] Polystratus does not outright deny reason to animals, but he insists that there are certain cognitive operations that animals cannot perform and that these distinguish animals from human beings. More explicitly, Polystratus names the following related differences:[68] he points out that animals are not able to remember past events.[69] Furthermore, Polystratus explicitly claims that animals do not have the ability to grasp the beautiful and shameful and other such things or to understand signs (*sēmeia*), omens (*oiōnoi*), and tidings (*klēdones*).[70] On this view, animals take in sensory information, but they are not able to process this information as human beings do. To make this point, Polystratus uses several verbs that stress understanding and comprehension,[71] claiming in each case that this "understanding" is unique to human beings – and so distinguishes them from animals.

The ability to make agreements is not explicitly discussed in Polystratus' treatise. However, it seems that it could be added to the list. After all, the description of the cognitive capacities of animals in Polystratus is enough

---

[67] Polystratus, *On Irrational Contempt for Common Conceptions*, col. VII.5–7 Indelli. Trans. mine, emphasis added.
[68] See also Haussleiter 1935, 286–8.
[69] "[οὔτε τὰ παρελθ]όντα μνη[μ]ονε[ύειν]." Polystratus, *On Irrational Contempt for Common Conceptions*, col. IV.1–3 Indelli. Admittedly, the text is here very uncertain.
[70] Ibid., col. VII.1–2.   [71] See *sunoraō* at ibid., cols. I.2 and VII.4–5 and *eulabeomai* at col. III.4–5.

to dismiss the possibility. Without memory, the ability to learn, and a grasp of things that are beneficial, it is difficult to see how animals could be capable of making agreements. Given how animals are described, any other conclusion would be very odd.

This overall impression is confirmed in Hermarchus, Epicurus' immediate follower as the head of the Epicurean school. In the following passage, his view of animals on the whole is less nuanced than that of Polystratus:

> Εἰ μὲν οὖν ἠδύναντο ποιήσασθαί τινα συνθήκην ὥσπερ πρὸς ἀνθρώπους οὕτω καὶ πρὸς τὰ λοιπὰ τῶν ζῴων ὑπὲρ τοῦ μὴ κτείνειν μηδὲ πρὸς ἡμῶν ἀκρίτως αὐτὰ κτείνεσθαι, καλῶς εἶχε μέχρι τούτου τὸ δίκαιον ἐξάγειν· ἐπιτεταμένον γὰρ ἐγίγνετο πρὸς τὴν ἀσφάλειαν. Ἐπειδὴ δὲ τῶν ἀμηχάνων ἦν κοινωνῆσαι νόμου τὰ μὴ δεχόμενα τῶν ζῴων λόγον, διὰ μὲν τοῦ τοιούτου τρόπου τὸ συμφέρον οὐχ οἷόν τε κατασκευάσασθαι πρὸς τὴν ἀπὸ τῶν ἄλλων ἐμψύχων ἀσφάλειαν μᾶλλόν περ ἢ τῶν ἀψύχων, ἐκ δὲ τοῦ τὴν ἐξουσίαν λαμβάνειν, ἣν νῦν ἔχομεν, εἰς τὸ κτείνειν αὐτὰ μόνως ἔστι τὴν ἐνδεχομένην ἔχειν ἀσφάλειαν.

> Now if people had been able [*edunato*] to make a kind of agreement with the remaining animals [*ta loipa tōn zōōn*], as with human beings, over not killing and not being killed indiscriminately by us, it would have been fine to push justice up to this point; for it would tend to security. But since it was impossible [*tōn amēchanōn ēn*] to associate with law animals that lack reason, it was not possible [*ouk hoion te*] to use such an instrument as the means of providing for utility in our security from other living beings any more than from lifeless things. That is why the only way to achieve such security as is possible is to take the license which we now have to kill them.[72]

According to Hermarchus, agreements with animals would be desirable because they extend security for human beings: threats from animals would greatly diminish. This argument is wholly anthropocentric: animals are not to be protected and included in the sphere of justice because of themselves, but because this would mean that human beings would be exposed to fewer threats. Yet Hermarchus also claims that such agreements are impossible to make because nonhuman beings do not possess reason (*ta mē dechomena tōn zōōn logon*), varying Polystratus' claim that animals do not have reason like ours. Accordingly, Hermarchus insists that animals do not partake in justice – at least not in the way being discussed here,

---

[72] Hermarchus, fr. 34 Longo Auricchio (= Porphyry, *On Abstinence* I.12.5–6). Trans. Clark, modified.

namely, by making agreements with human beings. However, Hermarchus also speaks about "the remaining animals" (*ta loipa tōn zōōn*), which – on an alternative reading – could again imply that only certain animals are unable to make agreements, while others indeed are able to do so, even if such a reading is unlikely given the evidence about the cognitive capacities of animals according to Epicurean psychology.

Overall, then, the case against agreements with animals in early Epicureanism is quite compelling. While the passages in Epicurus and Hermarchus leave open the possibility that there may be some animals with whom human beings can make agreements, Polystratus' condemnation of animals is categorical and makes this possibility seem rather remote.

Roughly the same view on the capabilities of animals is found in Philodemus.[73] He maintains that in contradistinction to human beings, animals are not able to be happy, that is, be free from bodily pain and mental distress. This is because animals lack reasoning (*logismos*), which human beings possess. In addition, Philodemus also claims that animals do not have an understanding of the gods (which on the Epicurean view is acquired through a kind of mental perception) and that they do not have beliefs (*doxai*). Finally, according to Philodemus, animals do not experience distress in regard to political matters, which could mean that they do not participate in political actions – such as making agreements – either.[74]

Lucretius is the sole exception to this more or less uniform characterization of animals in Epicureanism; of all Epicurean authors whose work on the subject is extant, Lucretius grants animals the most extensive cognitive capacities.[75] Most significantly, Lucretius claims that animals have an *animus*, which is the Epicurean technical term for a rational soul.[76] And as we already saw above, it is above all having certain cognitive capacities that will ultimately decide whether animals are capable of making agreements. It seems, then, that this claim makes Lucretius' account suspicious, and he does not seem to be the Epicurean "fundamentalist"[77] some readers take him to be.

Be this as it may, we find the following passage in Lucretius' account of cultural development in book V of *On the Nature of Things*:

---

[73] Philodemus, *On the Gods* I, cols. XIII–XV Diels.   [74] Ibid., col. XIV.31 Diels.
[75] See Sorabji 1993, 28–9. See also the brief remarks in Shelton 1995 as well as the longer discussion in Zinn 2015.
[76] Lucretius, *On the Nature of Things* II.270. On the distinction between *animus* and *anima*, see Wald 1968; Lathière 1972; and Mehl 1999.
[77] Sedley 1998b, 71.

> Multaque tum interiisse animantum saecla necessest
> nec potuisse propagando procudere prolem.
> nam quae cumque vides vesci vitalibus auris,
> aut dolus aut virtus aut denique mobilitas est
> ex ineunte aevo genus id tutata reservans.
> multaque sunt, nobis ex utilitate sua quae
> commendata manent, tutelae tradita nostrae.
> principio genus acre leonum saevaque saecla
> tutatast virtus, vulpis dolus et fuga cervos.
> at levisomna canum fido cum pectore corda
> et genus omne quod est veterino semine partum
> lanigeraeque simul pecudes et bucera saecla
> omnia sunt hominum tutelae tradita, Memmi.
> nam cupide fugere feras pacemque secuta
> sunt et larga suo sine pabula parta labore,
> quae damus utilitatis eorum praemia causa.
> at quis nil horum tribuit natura, nec ipsa
> sponte sua possent ut vivere nec dare nobis
> utilitatem aliquam quare pateremur eorum
> praesidio nostro pasci genus esseque tutum,
> scilicet haec aliis praedae lucroque iacebant
> indupedita suis fatalibus omnia vinclis,
> donec ad interitum genus id natura redegit.

At that time, too, many species of animals must have perished and failed to propagate and perpetuate their race. For every species that you see breathing the breath of life has been protected and preserved from the beginning of its existence either by cunning or by courage or by speed. There are also many that survive because their utility has commended them to our care and committed them to our guardianship. In the first place, the fierce breed of savage lions owes its preservation to its courage, the fox to its cunning, and the deer to its speed in flight. On the other hand, the light-slumbering and loyal-hearted dog and every kind of beast of burden, as well as the fleecy flocks and horned herds, are all committed, Memmius, to the guardianship of human beings. They were glad to escape from the wild beasts and seek peace and the plentiful provisions, procured by no exertion of theirs, which we give them as a reward for their utility. But those animals that nature endowed with none of these qualities, so that they were unable either to be self-supporting or to render us any useful service, in return for which we might allow their kind to have sustenance and security under our protection, were of course an easy prey and prize for others, shackled as they all were by the bonds of their own destiny, until nature brought their species to extinction.[78]

---

[78] Lucretius, *On the Nature of Things* V.855–72. Trans. Smith.

2.3 The Parties of Epicurean Agreements

The text distinguishes two kinds of animals, which gives additional grounds for singling out wild animals in *On Nature* XXV, as suggested above. On the one hand, the text claims, there are wild animals such as lions, foxes, and deer that cannot be domesticated. On the other hand, it continues, there are those animals that can be domesticated: working animals that one would typically encounter on a farm and that are common in any agrarian society such as those of antiquity. Whereas wild animals according to Lucretius possess certain natural capacities that enable them to procure protection and survival on their own, domestic animals do not. However, animals such as dogs, cattle, and sheep provide valuable services to human beings. Despite their inability to protect themselves and procure security and survival on their own, they can compensate for this lack by the benefit (*utilitas*) they provide for human beings. Human beings, in turn, provide protection and survival for them. Accordingly, it is beneficial for a farmer to take care of his watchdog or sheepdog or the survival of his flock that yields milk and wool (in the case of sheep) or milk (in the case of cows).

To sum up, then, there are three clues that suggest that agreements between human beings and animals might be possible on Lucretius' view. First, there is the frequent use of the word "*utilitas*," which is a nominalized Latin translation of the Greek adjective "*sumpheron*" and thus recalls the Epicurean description of justice as the expression of benefit in *KD* 31. Second, there is the idea that there is an exchange of goods and services between domestic animals and human beings ("*damus utilitatis eorum praemia causa*"), which recalls the idea of a barter and hence a type of agreement. And then, finally, some content of the barter between humans and animals involves security and protection, which also play a key role in human-human agreements.

Are agreements with animals then in fact possible on the Epicurean view? We have already seen above that Lucretius is an unlikely representative of Epicurean orthodoxy, given that he also thinks animals have an *animus*, which other Epicurean authors explicitly deny.[79] Furthermore, note that the passage quoted above does not explicitly talk about agreements; the word "*foedus*," which is the Latin translation of the Greek "*sunthēkē*," does not appear in the text. Lucretius explicitly calls the relationship between animals and human beings "guardianship [*tutela*]."[80]

---

[79] See Sorabji 1993, 28–9 (*pace* Annas 1992, 134–7; and Campbell 2003, 126–7). See also Campbell 2008.
[80] Lucretius, *On the Nature of Things* V.861 and 867.

Guardianship, however, is a technical term from Roman law that implies an asymmetrical relationship: the patron ensures that the patronized is secure and the patronized provides some other benefit to the patron, but this benefit need not be related to harming and being harmed. The Roman jurist Gaius (second century CE), for instance, writes the following:

> Permissum est itaque parentibus liberis, quos in potestate sua habent, testamen<to tu>tores dare: masculini quidem sexus inpuberibus, <feminini vero inpuberibus puberibus>que, <vel> cum nuptae sint. veteres enim voluerunt feminas, etiamsi perfectae aetatis sint, propter animi levitatem in tutela esse.
>
> Where the head of a family has children in his power he is allowed to appoint guardians for them by will. That is, for males while under puberty but <for females however old they are, even> when they are married. For it was the wish of the old lawyers that women, even those of full age, should be in guardianship as being scatter-brained.[81]

In the case of cows and other "beasts of burden," the fact that the guardianship relationship cannot exclusively relate to security is especially clear, since cows are not used in any way to fend off enemies. Furthermore, a dog can be said to keep human beings secure, but it seems that even here human beings would not be said to enter the agreement to be safe from dogs, but rather so that dogs can help them to be safe from third parties. Consequently, tending to animals is not the same as making an agreement of justice with them.[82] However, interactions with animals have certain features that are similar to the interactions that are characteristic of Epicurean agreements insofar as they are a kind of exchange that involves benefit in some way, and, at least in some cases, security also seems to play a role. It seems, then, that at least in Lucretius, agreement-like arrangements with animals are possible, even if these are not agreements in the sense of those that lead to the existence of justice.

This finding can be furthermore confirmed by another observation. Lucretius often describes earlier stages of cultural evolution in a way that prefigures elements that are characteristic of later stages of development. For instance, describing the relationships among our early ancestors even

---

[81] Gaius, *Institutes* I.144. Trans. Gordon and Robinson modified. See also the texts on guardianship in Lefkowitz and Fant 2016, 124–6. While there is no direct equivalent to guardianship in Greece, one may assume, however, that women are de facto understood to be in a similar dependency relationship. See Pomeroy 1975 and Reinsberg 1989.
[82] Konstan 2008, 91, fn. 15 *pace* Goldschmidt 1977, 53.

2.3 The Parties of Epicurean Agreements

at a time when human beings had not yet come together and made agreements, Lucretius writes:

> et Venus in silvis iungebat corpora amantum;
> conciliabat enim vel mutua quamque cupido
> vel violenta viri vis atque inpensa libido
> vel pretium, glandes atque arbita vel pira lecta.
>
> And Venus joined the bodies of the lovers in the woods; for either mutual desire united them or the violent force of the man and his excessive lust or presents, acorns and gathered strawberries or pears.[83]

The context of this passage is to explain how lovers unite to procreate. Besides rape, Lucretius mentions mutual attraction and desire of the partners as well as what could be called prostitution: the exchange of sexual favors for delicacies. In both these cases, mutual consent to have sexual intercourse plays a role. Consequently, one may even say that a mutual benefit is recognized by both parties. However, again, while Lucretius does not call the exchange of strawberries for sexual favors or the decision of men and women to have sex "agreements," these interactions may be said to be similar to agreements of justice insofar as they also involve mutual benefit.

On the basis of the above comments, it is thus tempting to assume a multitiered view of what counts as an agreement in Epicureanism.[84] Besides the agreements that lead to justice, on the one hand, and those that lead to the existence of the laws, on the other hand, there would also be agreements with animals and the agreements of the original state between men and women that were just discussed. One could even add to this the "agreements of nature [*foedera naturae*]" that play a prominent role in Lucretius' account and that also metaphorically take up the notion of an agreement and apply this to the domain of physics.[85]

Unfortunately, the textual evidence for such a reading of Epicurean agreements is rather slim. Lucretius is the only source for such a view. Accordingly, one might also think that Lucretius, who, as we saw above, in other contexts values the cognitive abilities of animals very highly (*pace* other Epicurean authors), not only is keen on finding a firmer place for them in his ethical, social, and political philosophy, but also has the theoretical means at his disposal to do so by drawing on the guardianship relationship, for instance, which has no equivalent in Greek and Greece.

---

[83] Lucretius, *On the Nature of Things* V.962–5. Trans. mine.   [84] See also Campbell 2008.
[85] On agreements of nature, see the discussion in Asmis 2008.

More importantly, however, even if the arrangements with animals were part of the orthodox Epicurean view, it would still imply that there are no agreements with animals in the full sense of the term. This is equivalent to saying that there is no justice in regard to animals because again justice with animals presupposes the existence of agreements that lead to justice in the full sense, that is, those that have to do with preventing harm in some way or other. The "agreements" with animals described in Lucretius thus seem to be of a completely different type than the ones that human beings make with each other. An "agreement" with an animal would never be on par with an agreement with a human being.

Put differently, then, just as children and women are covered by the agreements of justice insofar as they are related to a (male) contracting party in some way, so too domestic and farm animals are covered by the agreements of justice insofar as they belong to some (male) contracting party. In this case, the animals are under their patron's guardianship, which presumably will protect them not only from harm from the patron but also from other people's aggressions insofar as the animals' patrons have made agreements of justice with other people as well as from the aggressions from other animals insofar as it will be beneficial to the patron that the animals in question are healthy. It thus seems that animals will be protected by the agreements in the same way that women and children are protected, with the notable difference that there is no extant discussion on the precise nature of the arrangement between the (male) patrons and their dependents (woman and children), which prima facie might also be described as a kind of tutelage relationship.[86]

Again, we should emphasize at this point that even if an agent does not have an arrangement with certain animals, there is no reason why an Epicurean agent would deliberately harm them. First, the animal may be *someone*'s animal, in which case they would be protected through agreements human beings make with each other. Second, it is unclear what would motivate an Epicurean agent to harm animals. Prudential reasons for the most part speak against harming animals on the grounds of entertainment, diet, or religious rituals. Let us spell this out in more detail in what follows.

---

[86] The fact that Lucretius claims that women and children are to be pitied in the contract, whereas we do not have a comparable statement about animals, may be insignificant. After all, as it was argued in Chapter 1, pitying may amount to merely not harming and it is possible that (male) contracting parties can also agree on the fact that it is just not to kill each other's domestic and farm animals.

It is difficult to see why Epicurean agents would harm an animal for entertainment. As we will see in more detail in Chapter 4, when we will look at the desires that agents ought to cultivate, it is quite certain that desires relating to cock fighting, horse racing, or other enjoyments at the expense of animals are desires for unnecessary luxuries that are to be avoided on the Epicurean view.

In regard to diet, by contrast, an Epicurean agent could rather easily be vegetarian, given that plant food can typically be obtained more easily and in a more worry-free way than meat (which may require a perilous hunt). In fact, the Epicureans argue in numerous passages that agents should be content with simple foods such as water and barley cakes, which are typically vegetarian foods.[87] This observation is in line with the fact that for the majority of the population in antiquity, a vegetarian diet was more common than a meat-based one.[88] Of course, domestic animals might be a special case, since they might be more easily slaughtered than wild animals, but even goats and chickens are, for instance, sustainable producers of milk and eggs, and it seems prima facie hardly beneficial to destroy a sustainable food source prematurely (although they of course could be slaughtered once keeping them alive no longer provides a net benefit).

Finally, religious rituals often involved animal sacrifice in antiquity. But one might here first point to the fact that such sacrifice will only affect a very small number of animals. Second, because the Epicureans also argue that the gods have no direct influence on human affairs, it seems difficult to assess what value the Epicureans bestow on religious rituals involving animal sacrifice. Certainly, they hold that piety is a virtue and so that participating in religious rituals contributes to their *aponia* and *ataraxia* by helping agents meet the expectations bestowed on them by the community around these rituals. But one may wonder whether there is, for instance, really any value for religious rituals that involve the sacrifice of animals in an ideal Epicurean community.

In summary, these considerations do not rule out that any animals will ever be harmed on the Epicurean indirect duty view. Again, if a chicken is old and no longer lays eggs, that is, no longer provides a benefit, it can be slaughtered and eaten; there are no categorical reasons that would prevent animals from being harmed on the Epicurean view. However, again, on

---

[87] For instance, *Letter to Menoeceus* 130–2. Note that eating fish is here characterized as an unnecessary luxury.
[88] See Hardach 2007. Campbell 2008, 13–15, discusses a passage in Porphyry's *On Abstinence* that makes a case for the view that the Epicureans were proponents of vegetarianism, but it is not clear that the passage Campbell quotes can really be reliably ascribed to the Epicureans.

prudential grounds, it seems that the cases in which animals be harmed can at least be reduced somewhat, since in many cases it will not be more beneficial to harm an animal than not to harm it.

2.3.2 Agreements with Other Peoples

Having discussed agreements with animals, let us next comment on the second part of *KD* 32, which deals with agreements with other peoples: "so too with however many of the peoples [*ethnōn*] unable or unwilling [*mē edunato ē mē ebouleto*] to make agreements over not harming and not being harmed."

As was already pointed out above, "*ethnē*" here can refer to Greeks and non-Greeks alike, which means that there might also be Greeks who are unable to make agreements on the Epicurean view. In contrast to the case of animals, which were said not to be able to make agreements, Epicurus adds in regard to other peoples that there may be some who are not *willing* to make agreements. As a consequence, one may distinguish three criteria that an agent needs to fulfill in order to make agreements: First, as we saw in the discussion of animals, an agent needs to be capable of making agreements, that is, possess the prerequisite capacities. Second, agents need to be able to make agreements, that is, circumstances must be such that it is possible for agents to make agreements. And third, finally, agents also have to want to make agreements.

In regard to other peoples, it seems likely that at least some peoples seem to be capable and able to make agreements, since asking whether a people is willing to make an agreement is only an intelligible question if the other two criteria are already fulfilled in some people. However, an interesting issue is whether the Epicureans think that some people are completely incapable of making agreements. Here, the textual evidence is slim. Epicurus notes that not everyone has the capacity of being a sage and that sages do not arise in every people.[89] Furthermore, he maintains that only Greeks are able to practice philosophy.[90] It is unclear whether these pronouncements entail that all non-Greeks are unable to make agreements as well. Diogenes of Oenoanda explicitly addresses non-Greeks with his inscription, which shows that at least some non-Greeks might able to become sages and live the Epicurean good life on his view.[91] A fortiori

---

[89] Fr. 226 Usener (= Diogenes Laërtius, *Lives of Eminent Philosophers* X.117).
[90] Ibid. (= Clement of Alexandria, *Stromata* I.15, 130,37 Sylburg).
[91] Diogenes of Oenoanda, fr. 3 Smith.

such a view entails that at least some foreigners are able to make agreements. However, Diogenes' claim is in tension with Epicurus' pronouncements and so might reflect a later change in Epicurean doctrine.

In summary, then, let us briefly restate the main conclusions of this chapter, which was dedicated to specific features of Epicurean contractarianism. First, we saw that on the Epicurean view, agreements are about what is beneficial and that what is beneficial is not simply a conventional feature of the world, but a natural one. Accordingly, we specified in what way the Epicureans adopt a middle position in the *nomos-phusis* debate. Second, the chapter showed that the content of Epicurean agreements is the prevention of harm, which was glossed as a deprivation of *aponia* and *ataraxia*, the highest good in Epicureanism. It was argued that harm on the Epicurean view includes direct and indirect, physical and nonphysical harm, against other contracting as well as third parties. Finally, the last section of the chapter showed that the Epicureans defend an indirect duty view when it comes to making agreements. While agreements of justice with animals are not possible, human beings and animals can make other kinds of arrangements. In regard to other peoples, by contrast, we saw that the Epicureans do not in principle rule out the idea that it is possible to make agreements with them, even if the textual evidence is very slim.

CHAPTER 3

Aretaic Justice

In early modern social contract theories, such as those of Thomas Hobbes and John Locke, virtue does not play a significant role. Likewise, however, defenders of virtue ethics like Aristotle, for instance, reject the claim that agreements alone are sufficient to bring about morality. On their view, morality would be downgraded to merely a matter of coordination and neglect its essential function to make citizens just and good in an absolute sense, if agreements brought about and determined what is moral. Discussing a legislative theory that claims that laws come to be as a matter of agreement, which is ascribed to the sophist Lycophron, about whom otherwise not much is known, Aristotle writes in the *Politics*:[1]

> περὶ δ' ἀρετῆς καὶ κακίας πολιτικῆς διασκοποῦσιν ὅσοι φροντίζουσιν εὐνομίας. ᾗ καὶ φανερὸν ὅτι δεῖ περὶ ἀρετῆς ἐπιμελὲς εἶναι τῇ γ' ὡς ἀληθῶς ὀνομαζομένῃ πόλει, μὴ λόγου χάριν. γίγνεται γὰρ ἡ κοινωνία συμμαχία τῶν ἄλλων τόπῳ διαφέρουσα μόνον, τῶν ἄπωθεν συμμαχιῶν, καὶ ὁ νόμος συνθήκη καί, καθάπερ ἔφη Λυκόφρων ὁ σοφιστής, ἐγγυητὴς ἀλλήλοις τῶν δικαίων, ἀλλ' οὐχ οἷος ποιεῖν ἀγαθοὺς καὶ δικαίους τοὺς πολίτας.

> By contrast, political virtue and vice are closely investigated by those concerned with good legislative order. Thus it is quite evident that the city-state must be concerned about virtue – at any rate, the city-state that is truly, and not just for the sake of argument, so called. For otherwise the community becomes an alliance, differing only in location from others in which the allies live far apart, and law becomes an agreement, and as Lycophron the sophist said, "a guarantor of just behavior towards each other," but not such as to make citizens good and just.[2]

This chapter will argue that Epicurus and his followers split the difference between these two opposing views: they claim that agreements are

---
[1] For a brief discussion of Lycophron's view, see Mulgan 1979.
[2] Aristotle, *Politics* III.9.1280b5–12. Trans. Reeve, modified.

central to justice, while nevertheless maintaining that there is a robust virtue of justice. In particular, on their view, contractual justice specifies the content of aretaic justice and provides the developmental basis for aretaic justice to emerge. This means that the content of contractual justice will be slightly more expansive than the content of aretaic justice. Furthermore, the chapter will suggest that since in an ideal society, some form of contractual justice is needed for society to function, contractual and aretaic justice can be said to work in tandem to fulfill the crucial function of providing security.

To set the stage for a discussion of the Epicurean virtue of justice, the first section of this chapter will examine the Epicurean theory of the virtues (Section 3.1). The second section will then turn to the examine the textual evidence on the virtue of justice (Section 3.2). Finally, the third section of the chapter will examine the relationship between contractual and aretaic justice on the Epicurean view (Section 3.3).

3.1 The Epicurean Virtues

The main sources for the Epicurean account of the virtues are the *Letter to Menoeceus* and Torquatus' summary of Epicurean ethics in Cicero's *On Ends*.[3] Both of these sources have to be taken with a grain of salt, however. The *Letter to Menoeceus* is not a systematic discussion of Epicurean ethics, but rather a protreptic treatise[4] that outlines Epicurean moral ideas. As a result, more technical ideas are not found or elaborated on in the text, for instance, the important distinction between kinetic and katastematic pleasures. This means that the letter cannot be taken as the last word on the Epicurean virtues. The account in *On Ends*, by contrast, is written by Cicero, an author who is generally hostile to Epicureanism and addresses a Roman, not a Greek, audience. This makes it unlikely that this account can be fully trusted, either, although it is unclear to what extent exactly the account is unorthodox. Fortunately, however, there is additional textual evidence, preserved in Diogenes Laërtius and Philodemus as well as other authors, that can complement the discussion of the *Letter to Menoeceus* as well as *On Ends*.

The goal of this section is to identify some key characteristics of the Epicurean virtues in the *Letter to Menoeceus*, the only complete ethical

---

[3] This section is substantially modified and developed from material originally published in Robitzsch 2020b.
[4] Hessler 2014, 40–71.

treatise by Epicurus himself that has come down to us, as well as other Epicurean sources. The next section will then focus on the account in *On Ends*, which discusses the virtue of justice in more detail and supplements the account outlined in this section.

The structure of the *Letter to Menoeceus* follows the order of the so-called Fourfold Remedy, a set of four statements expressing the most important Epicurean ethical doctrines that both open the *Principal Doctrines* and the (ethically oriented) *Vatican Sayings* and do not deal with virtue.[5] However, Epicurus eventually uses the word "virtue [*aretē*]" in a passage at 132. For easier reference, the sentences of the subsequent passage are numbered:

> (1) Τούτων δὲ πάντων ἀρχὴ καὶ τὸ μέγιστον ἀγαθὸν φρόνησις. (2) διὸ καὶ φιλοσοφίας τιμιώτερον ὑπάρχει φρόνησις, ἐξ ἧς αἱ λοιπαὶ πᾶσαι πεφύκασιν ἀρεταί, διδάσκουσα ὡς οὐκ ἔστιν ἡδέως ζῆν ἄνευ τοῦ φρονίμως καὶ καλῶς καὶ δικαίως, <οὐδὲ φρονίμως καὶ καλῶς καὶ δικαίως> ἄνευ τοῦ ἡδέως. (3) συμπεφύκασι γὰρ αἱ ἀρεταὶ τῷ ζῆν ἡδέως καὶ τὸ ζῆν ἡδέως τούτων ἐστὶν ἀχώριστον.

> (1) Practical wisdom is the source of all of these and it is the greatest good. (2) Therefore, practical wisdom, from which all the remaining virtues naturally have arisen, is more valuable than philosophy, teaching that it is not possible to live pleasurably without living prudently and honorably and justly <nor to live prudently and honorably and justly> without living pleasurably. (3) For the virtues have naturally arisen together with living pleasurably and living pleasurably is inseparable from them.[6]

The passage makes several claims, but for the purposes of this chapter, the most important one is that "it is not possible to live pleasurably without living prudently and honorably and justly <nor to live prudently and honorably and justly> without living pleasurably" in sentence (2), which is also rephrased in sentence (3) as "living pleasurably is inseparable from [the virtues]." In other words, the passage makes important points concerning (i) the relationship of virtue and pleasure and (ii) the virtues to each other, and (iii) it gives examples of Epicurean virtues. Let us spell out these points in greater detail, beginning with (i).

---

[5] The four statements are the following (somewhat simplified): (1) Do not fear the gods. (2) Do not fear death. (3) Pain is easy to endure. (4) Pleasure is easy to obtain. Note that while *KD* 1, 2, and 4 are identical with *SV* 1, 2, and 4, *KD* 3 and *SV* 3 are slightly different. The term "Fourfold Remedy" derives from Philodemus, who uses it to refer to the first four *Principal Doctrines* at *To the ...*, col. V.8–13 Angeli. See also Giovacchini 2019.

[6] Trans. mine.

3.1 The Epicurean Virtues

Since the claim that it is not possible to live pleasurably without living prudently and honorably and justly and vice versa is also found in *KD* 5 and *SV* 5 and so immediately follows the Fourfold Remedy in three different presentations of Epicurean ethics, the prominent location of the claim in several Epicurean texts signals that it expresses a key precept; in fact, it expresses a teaching that comes right after the Fourfold Remedy in importance, which highlights the role of virtue in general and of justice in particular in Epicureanism.[7]

Sentence (2) claims that for Epicurus the pleasurable life and the virtuous life are inter-entailing.[8] This claim is also emphasized in various passages, in which Epicurus stresses that the virtues only have instrumental value: they are the (only) means to obtain (true) pleasure, understood as the absence of bodily pain and mental distress. Diogenes Laërtius, for instance, observes that on the Epicurean view, "the virtues are also chosen because of pleasure, not because of themselves, just as medicine is chosen for the sake of health [διὰ δὲ ἡδονὴν καὶ τὰς ἀρετὰς αἱρεῖσθαι, οὐ δι' αὐτάς, ὥσπερ τὴν ἰατρικὴν διὰ τὴν ὑγίειαν]."[9] Such a view starkly contrasts with those of Plato and Aristotle, who maintain in their respective theories that virtue is an end in itself and that the virtuous person will feel pleasure as a result of virtuous activity, not be virtuous for the sake of pleasure.

Furthermore, the three terms "practical wisdom," the "honorable," and "justice" in sentence (2), in addition to their specific meanings, can also be understood to be a stand-in for "virtue in general," giving further support to the thesis that the pleasurable life and the virtuous life are inter-entailing. Let us explain this in greater detail by looking at the meaning of the three terms.

---

[7] As the angle brackets indicate, sentence (2) as well as *KD* 5 and *SV* 5 contain a textual emendation that was first proposed by Henri Estienne (Henricus Stephanus) and is today generally accepted. Without emendation the text merely claims that it is not possible to live pleasurably without practical wisdom and, likewise, that it is not possible to live justly and honorably (*kalōs*) without living pleasurably. In other words, without the emendation, the passage merely asserts a connection between pleasure and practical wisdom, on the one hand, and pleasure and justice and the honorable, on the other hand, but leaves the connection between the four terms open. However, the emendation can be easily justified in reference to Cicero's and Diogenes of Oenoanda's writings where the four terms are explicitly connected with each other. Cicero, *On Ends* I.57; and Diogenes of Oenoanda, fr. 37 Smith. For further discussion, see especially Warren 2014, 225–31.

[8] See, for instance, Mitsis 1988, 61.

[9] Fr. 504 Usener (= Diogenes Laërtius, *Lives of Eminent Philosophers* X.138). Trans. mine. See also the other texts that make up fragment fr. 504 Usener as well as fr. 509 Usener (= Clement, *Stromata* II.21). The link between the virtue of courage and benefit is established at Diogenes Laërtius, *Lives of Eminent Philosophers* X.120: "courage does not come to be by nature, but rather by a calculation of benefit [τὴν δὲ ἀνδρείαν φύσει μὴ γίνεσθαι, λογισμῷ δὲ τοῦ συμφέροντος]." Trans. mine.

First, "practical wisdom [*phronesis*]." Any mention of this term of course reminds the seasoned reader of ancient Greek philosophy of Aristotle's discussion of this intellectual virtue in the *Nicomachean Ethics*.[10] Accordingly, commentators of Epicurus frequently think of Aristotle as well when discussing Epicurean practical wisdom,[11] even if the Epicurean version of "practical wisdom" is also identified with "sober calculation [*nēphōn logismos*]," which is used at *Letter to Menoeceus* 132. Given the scarcity of textual evidence, it is difficult to say what practical wisdom exactly amounts to in Epicureanism. Perhaps an appropriately cautious gloss is that in saying that Epicurean agents should live "prudently," the Epicureans mean to say that agents should live in accordance with good practical decisions, which pertain to the selection of pleasures and pains. However, as sentence (1) in the passage quoted above makes clear, practical wisdom is also conceived of as a kind of super-virtue on the Epicurean view: it is the source of all the other virtues, and so can serve as a *pars pro toto* synecdoche for virtue. If this is right, then the claim that the Epicureans should live "prudently" also amounts to saying that the Epicureans should live virtuously in general.

The second term mentioned in the above statement is "*to kalon.*" The translation of the term is difficult, but by it, Epicurus probably means a form of morally good conduct.[12] More precisely, the term "*kalōs*" is used as a generic adverb for all kinds of moral conduct, whether of a legal or an extra-legal nature. Although the "*kalon*" is not itself a virtue, the term can also be used to sum up all the other virtues in the same way as the term "practical wisdom."

Finally, justice. We already discussed contractual justice and the sociopolitical dimension of Epicurean justice in the previous chapters. However, it is more likely that justice in this statement refers to justice as a virtue, since "*dikaiōs*" modifies "living [*zēn*]" and does not refer explicitly to agreements. This idea is further supported in *KD* 17: "The just is freest from disturbance, the unjust is full of the greatest disturbance [Ὁ δίκαιος ἀταρακτότατος, ὁ δ' ἄδικος πλείστης ταραχῆς γέμων]."[13] The

---

[10] Aristotle, *Nicomachean Ethics* V.5.1140a24–31.
[11] See especially Morel 2010 and Morel 2019a for a comparison between practical wisdom in Aristotle and in Epicurus. See also De Sanctis 2010, who offers a very useful overview of the usage of the term "practical wisdom" in different Epicurean authors.
[12] For an overview of different usages of "*kalon*" and its derivates in Epicurean authors as well as a more detailed defense of the claim that in Epicurean authors, the "*kalon*" refers to good moral conduct in general, see Robitzsch 2020b, 424–5.
[13] Trans. mine. The same connection between freedom from mental distress and justice is also drawn in fr. 519 Usener (= Clement of Alexandria, *Stromata* VI.2): "Result of justice is greatest freedom from mental distress [δικαιοσύνης καρπὸς μέγιστος ἀταραξία]." Trans. mine.

maxim is somewhat tricky to understand because it is unclear whether the subject of the sentence is the just life (*bios*) or the just person (*anthropos*) or something else entirely. Nevertheless, the meaning of the maxim is clear insofar as it connects the most pleasurable way of living with justice and the least pleasurable with injustice. Furthermore, that justice is a virtue is attested elsewhere. Diogenes Laërtius, for instance, claims Epicurus wrote a treatise *On Justice and the Other Virtues* (Περὶ δικαιοσύνης καὶ τῶν ἄλλων ἀρετῶν), which unfortunately has not come down to us.[14] This work is especially important because its title not only explicitly identifies justice as a virtue, but also makes clear that justice has a special place among the virtues. The idea that justice is to be given a special place among the virtues is also found in Aristotle, for whom justice, in a certain sense, is a designation used to speak about all the virtues together.[15] When Epicurus therefore claims that agents should live justly, he could be claiming that agents should live virtuously. On such a reading, justice would be synonymous with practical wisdom and the *kalon*, which were discussed above, and the claim that agents should live prudently, justly, and honorably in the second sentence of the passage of *Letter to Menoeceus* 132 would amount to a hendiatris.

We will say more about justice as a virtue in the next section, but taking stock so far, we see that the Epicureans attribute a significant role to virtue in general and justice in particular and they claim that the pursuit of virtue and of pleasure inter-entail each other.

This brings us to (ii), the relationship between the virtues on the Epicurean view. According to the first sentence of *Letter to Menoeceus* 132, "practical wisdom is the source of all of these and it is the greatest good."[16] According to the third sentence of the same passage, by contrast, "the virtues naturally arise with living pleasurably." This prima facie suggests a view, according to which practical wisdom brings about certain virtuous choices and these choices in turn bring out practical wisdom. This model is usually closely associated with Aristotle and might be dubbed the reciprocal model of the connection of virtues.[17] But such a reading of the Epicurean theory might be a bit rash, given that Epicurus' claim about practical wisdom as the source can also be understood as meaning that all

---

[14] Diogenes Laërtius, *Lives of Eminent Philosophers* X.28.
[15] Aristotle, *Nicomachean Ethics* V.1.1229b25–1130a13.
[16] On different readings of "all of these," see Morel 2010, 21–2. The most plausible reading seems to be that "all of these" refers to the sober calculation of choices and avoidances mentioned immediately before the quoted passage.
[17] Aristotle, *Nicomachean Ethics* VI.12–13.

virtues can be reduced to practical wisdom, that they are really just forms of practical wisdom. On this alternative model, defended prominently by Socrates and the Stoics, the connection between the virtues is stronger than on the previous model: rather than reciprocally entailing each other, the virtues are *in fact* conceived as a unity. Plato's metaphors for this in the *Protagoras* are a piece of gold and a face: the virtues are not like parts of a piece of gold that are all gold and, as gold, indistinguishable from each other, but like the parts of a face, which are distinguishable and complementary to each other in making a face.[18]

Which view, then, did Epicurus hold in regard to the unity of the virtues? Given the importance of practical wisdom as the source, Epicurus may have been closer to the Socratic and Stoic position than to the Aristotelian one. It is noteworthy, however, that the Epicureans never explicitly discuss the thesis of the unity of the virtues.[19]

This brings us to (iii). So far we have spoken about *the virtues* in Epicureanism, but only justice and (practical) wisdom are explicitly mentioned in the *Letter to Menoeceus*. Piety and moderation make indirect appearances. At *Letter to Menoeceus* 123 the correct views on the gods are discussed: "Impious is not the one who does away with the gods of the many, but the one who ascribes to gods the opinions of the many [ἀσεβὴς δὲ οὐχ ὁ τοὺς τῶν πολλῶν θεοὺς ἀναιρῶν, ἀλλ' ὁ τὰς τῶν πολλῶν δόξας θεοῖς προσάπτων]."[20] While piety is not directly mentioned, the passage makes clear that something like piety is important for the Epicureans. This idea is independently supported not only by the fact that Epicurus and Philodemus wrote treatises titled *On Piety* (Περὶ ὁσιότητος and Περὶ εὐσεβείας)[21] but also by the fact that both authors wrote a treatise called *On the Gods* (Περὶ θεῶν). In addition, there is some evidence in

---

[18] Plato, *Protagoras* 329c–e. For the Stoics, see Stobaeus, *Anthology* II.63.6–64.12 Wachsmuth and Hense [= Long and Sedley 1987, 61D and 63G].

[19] If Dirk Obbink's reconstruction of the text of *On Piety* is correct, Philodemus claims that "piety and justice *almost* appear to be the same thing [[ὅ]τι σχεδὸν ταὐτ[ὸ φαίν]εται τὸ ὅσιο[ν καὶ δί]και[ον]]." Philodemus, *On Piety* I.2263–5 Obbink. Trans. mine, emphasis added. But since piety and justice are both interpersonal virtues and a pairing of these two virtues is also common elsewhere (see, for instance, Plato, *Euthyphro* 11e–12d or *Gorgias* 507a9–b4), the passage is less significant than one that would affirm, for instance, that courage and justice are the same thing. Note also that in the passage, Philodemus is concerned with the *dikaion* and *hosion*, not with *dikaiosunē* and *hosiotēs*. Yet while the passage thus deals with the extension of moral terms, not virtues, the underlying problem addressed in the passage remains the same as in the discussion on the unity of the virtues. In addition, immediately before this passage, an opponent raises an objection against Epicurean justice by referring to "*diakiosunē*."

[20] Trans. mine.

[21] Diogenes Laërtius, *Lives of Eminent Philosophers* X.27. *Eusebia* and *hosiotēs* are names for a virtue that seems to aim at the same object (the right attitude toward the gods), just as *enkrateia* and

3.1 The Epicurean Virtues

Philodemus, but also elsewhere, that the Epicureans engaged in prayer, not to please the gods but to contemplate the divine as an ideal to emulate.[22] Accordingly, one might think that piety – or at least the behaviors that are otherwise summed up by the umbrella term "piety" – is also important on the Epicurean view.

In the same vein, at *Letter to Menoeceus* 131, Epicurus recommends that agents ought to lead a moderate life in most circumstances:

> μᾶζα καὶ ὕδωρ τὴν ἀκροτάτην ἀποδίδωσιν ἡδονήν, ἐπειδὰν ἐνδέων τις αὐτὰ προσενέγκηται. τὸ συνεθίζειν οὖν ἐν ταῖς ἁπλαῖς καὶ οὐ πολυτελέσι διαίταις καὶ ὑγιείας ἐστὶ συμπληρωτικὸν καὶ πρὸς τὰς ἀναγκαίας τοῦ βίου χρήσεις ἄοκνον ποιεῖ τὸν ἄνθρωπον καὶ τοῖς πολυτελέσιν ἐκ διαλειμμάτων προσερχομένοις κρεῖττον ἡμᾶς διατίθησι καὶ πρὸς τὴν τύχην ἀφόβους παρασκευάζει.

> Barley cakes and water provide the highest pleasure when someone in want takes them. Therefore, becoming accustomed to simple, not extravagant ways of life makes one completely healthy, makes man unhesitant in the face of life's necessary practices, puts us in a better position for the times of extravagance which occasionally come along, and makes us fearless in the face of chance.[23]

From this, then, one might also infer that moderation (or again the behaviors that are typically summed up by this term) is important on the Epicurean view, even if the term "moderation [*sōphrosunē* or *enkrateia*]" is not explicitly used in the above passage.

To complete the list of cardinal virtues, one would have also expected courage to be mentioned in the *Letter to Menoeceus*, even if this virtue is discussed in other, independent sources that confirm that courage was indeed a virtue for the Epicureans.[24] One reason for the omission of courage may be that the Epicureans had overall a fluid list of the virtues, that is, one that could be expanded given the particular needs of the context. Take, for instance, the following passage from *PHerc.* 1251, which its latest editors Giovanni Indelli and Voula Tsouna identify with Philodemus' *On Choices and Avoidances*. It clearly echoes the passage from

---

sōphrosunē can, as we will see below, refer to the same virtue, namely, moderation, which aims at the right attitude toward pleasure.

[22] Piergiacomi 2013. See also Hahmann and Robitzsch 2022.
[23] Trans. Inwood and Gerson, modified.
[24] For additional textual evidence on the Epicurean virtues, see frr. 504–22 Usener. Courage is discussed in frr. 516 and 517 (= Origen, *Against Celsus* V.47; and Diogenes Laërtius, *Lives of Eminent Philosophers* X.120).

the *Letter to Menoeceus*, *KD* 5, and *SV* 5, but also makes clear that there are more virtues than those mentioned in these texts:

[... οὐκ ἔστιν ἡδέως ζῆν] ἄνευ [τοῦ φρονί]μως κ[αὶ καλ]ῶς [καὶ δικαί]ως, ἔτι δ' ἀνδ[ρ]είως [κ]α[ὶ ἐγ]κρατῶς καὶ μεγαλο[ψύ]χ[ω]ς καὶ φιλοποιητικῶς κα[ὶ φιλανθρ]ώπως καὶ καθόλ[ου πασῶν] τῶν ἄλλων ἀρετῶν ὑπα[ρ]χουσῶν.

... it is not possible to live pleasurably without living prudently and honorably and justly, and also courageously and temperately and magnanimously and by making friends and by caring about others and, in general, without having all the other virtues.[25]

PHerc. 1251 expands the list of Epicurean virtues at *Letter to Menoeceus* 132 by courage, temperance, magnanimity,[26] and what seem to be two virtues concerning friends,[27] both of which are difficult to translate into English. More importantly, however, *PHerc.* 1251 *explicitly* emphasizes that even the expanded list of the Epicurean virtues is still incomplete; there are other virtues that the author of *PHerc.* 1251 knows, but chooses not to name at this point, as "all the other virtues" makes clear. And piety is certainly one example of a virtue that is not included here, although it is elsewhere recognized by the Epicureans as a virtue, as we saw above.

We do not need to conclude that new virtues of *PHerc.* 1251 are all the product of later innovation within the Epicurean school. We know from Diogenes Laërtius that Metrodorus is also supposed to have written a treatise on magnanimity and so may have already had a fully developed account of this virtue, which has not come down to us.[28] However, innovation is more likely in the case of the two other virtues. *Philopoēsia* (translated as "making friends" above) is not mentioned in any other

---

[25] *PHerc.* 1251, col. XIV.1–8 Indelli and Tsouna-McKirahan. Trans. Indelli and Tsouna, modified.

[26] In Aristotle, magnanimity is a kind of crowning virtue: it designates a kind of generosity that aristocrats can exercise to elevate their already otherwise virtuous lives to a higher level. Magnanimity, so understood, would thus be a strange virtue for the Epicureans to advocate for. However, as Sean McConnell argues in more detail (2017b), the Epicureans can be said to have importantly redefined magnanimity into a virtue that is not in principle open only to an elite, but rather open to all. As such, it can be said to deal with the proper understanding of one's status in the world and the necessity of possessing certain external goods for achieving freedom from bodily pain and mental distress.

[27] First, *philopoēsia* seems to refer to a capacity to make friends, while the second, *philanthrōpia*, may refer to a certain general care for others. It is not clear how these relate to *phila* and the claim of *SV* 23 that friendship is a virtue: All friendship is a virtue in itself, but it takes its origin in benefit [πᾶσα φιλία δι' ἑαυτὴν ἀρετή· ἀρχὴν δὲ εἴληφεν ἀπὸ τῆς ὠφελείας]. Trans. mine. (Following Usener, note that many commentators emend "*aretē*" in *SV* 23 to "*hairetē*." For discussion, see Brown 2002.)

[28] Diogenes Laërtius, *Lives of Eminent Philosophers* X.24.

Epicurean text besides the one just quoted. By contrast, *philanthrōpia* (translated as "caring about others" above) is also mentioned in Diogenes of Oenoanda, who uses the term to refer to love of foreigners.[29] Since *philanthrōpia* is not mentioned in Epicurus, it is possible that the term may have been a later innovation, an additional virtue not found in Epicurus. This suggestion gains plausibility by the idea that over the course of time, later Epicureans may have felt some pressure to introduce cosmopolitan elements into their philosophy. Alternatively, we could also insist that absence of evidence is not evidence of absence; given the Garden's relative openness to women and slaves, *philanthrōpia*, as a virtue, may have been a virtue that from the beginning underscored the Garden's openness toward others.[30]

The take-home message of the examples in Philodemus, then, is that on the Epicurean view, the list of virtues may have become more expansive over time and that it is, at least to a certain degree, fluid and expandable. Nevertheless, it seems that justice and (practical) wisdom as well as moderation and piety were all discussed as virtues by early Epicurean authors and so in a sense among the most important virtues, even if there is no evidence of a formal ranking of the virtues in Epicureanism.[31] Finally, it is striking to observe how little the Epicureans say about the content of the particular virtues in the passages we have examined so far. This is true not only of *philopoesia* and *philanthrōpia*, which are mentioned, without being described more concretely, but also of the other virtues and in particular of justice, as we will see in more detail in the next section.

3.2 Justice as an Epicurean Virtue

With this general background on the Epicurean theory of virtue, let us turn to the Epicurean spokesperson Torquatus' presentation of Epicurean ethics and more specifically his account of justice in book I of Cicero's *On Ends*. In his exposition, Torquatus mentions four virtues: wisdom, temperance, courage, and justice. This list is noticeably different from the lists articulated in the *Letter to Menoeceus* and in *PHerc.* 1251, yet identical with

---

[29] Diogenes of Oenoanda, frr. 3.V.5 and 119.III.4–5 Smith.
[30] If there is a love for foreigners, this might give an independent reason for the Epicureans to adopt the *oikeiōsis* doctrine. For some discussion of the doctrine in Hermarchus and Lucretius, see Appendix A.
[31] With the exception of the Epicurean claim that practical wisdom is the source of the other virtues (discussed above).

the cardinal virtues that play a decisive role not only in Plato's *Republic* but also in the Stoic account of the virtues.[32] Torquatus' account of justice is the most detailed discussion of justice as a virtue and so, despite its length, ought to be quoted in a generous excerpt:

> Iustitia restat, ut de omni virtute sit dictum; sed similia fere dici possunt. ut enim sapientiam temperantiam fortitudinem copulatas esse docui cum voluptate ut ab ea nullo modo nec divelli nec distrahi possint, sic de iustitia iudicandum est, quae non modo numquam nocet cuiquam, sed contra semper <adfert> aliquid cum vi sua atque natura quod tranquillet animos, tum spe nihil earum rerum defuturum quas natura non depravata desiderat. <et> quem ad modum temeritas et libido et ignavia semper animum excruciant et semper sollicitant turbulentaeque sunt, sic <improbitas si> cuius in mente consedit, hoc ipso, quod adest, turbulenta est; si vero molita quippiam est, quamvis occulte fecerit, numquam tamen id confidet fore semper occultum ... invitat igitur vera ratio bene sanos ad iustitiam aequitatem fidem, neque homini infanti aut impotenti iniuste facta conducunt, qui nec facile efficere possit quod conetur nec optinere, si effecerit ... praesertim cum omnino nulla sit causa peccandi. quae enim cupiditates a natura proficiscuntur facile explentur sine ulla iniuria, quae autem inanes sunt, iis parendum non est; nihil enim desiderabile concupiscunt, plusque in ipsa iniuria detrimenti est quam in iis rebus emolumenti quae pariuntur iniuria. itaque ne iustitiam quidem recte quis dixerit per se ipsam optabilem, sed quia iucunditatis vel plurimum adferat. nam diligi et carum esse iucundum est propterea, quia tutiorem vitam et voluptatem pleniorem efficit. itaque non ob ea solum incommoda quae eveniunt inprobis fugiendam inprobitatem putamus, sed multo etiam magis quod, cuius in animo versatur, numquam sinit eum respirare, numquam adquiescere.

> Only justice remains, and then we will have discussed all the virtues. But here too there are pretty similar things to be said. I have demonstrated that wisdom, moderation and courage are so closely connected with pleasure that they cannot be severed or detached from it at all. The same judgement is to be made in the case of justice. Not only does justice never harm anyone, but on the contrary it brings some benefit. Through its own power and nature it calms the spirits; and it also offers hope that none of the resources which an uncorrupted nature requires will be lacking. Foolhardiness, lust and cowardice unfailingly agitate and disturb the spirits and cause trouble. In the same way, when dishonesty takes root in one's heart, its very presence is disturbing. And once it is activated, however secret the deed, there is never a guarantee that it will remain secret.... That is why true reason calls those of sound mind to justice, fairness and integrity. Wrongdoing is of no avail to one who lacks eloquence or

---

[32] See also Mitsis 1988, 69.

resources, since one cannot then easily get what one is after, or keep hold of it even if one does get it.... Above all there is never a reason to do wrong. Desires which arise from nature are easily satisfied without resort to wrongdoing, while the other, empty desires are not to be indulged since they aim at nothing which is truly desirable. The loss inherent in any act of wrongdoing is greater than any profit which wrongdoing brings. Thus the right view is that not even justice is worthy of choice in its own right, but only insofar as it affords the greatest abundance of pleasure. To be valued and esteemed is agreeable just because one's life is thereby more secure and full of pleasure. Hence we consider that dishonesty is to be avoided not simply because of the troublesome turn of events which it leads to, but much rather because its presence in one's heart prevents one ever breathing freely or finding peace.[33]

In what follows, let us emphasize four points in regard to Torquatus' account of Epicurean justice. First, Torquatus highlights in this passage that justice is not different from the other Epicurean virtues. Whatever we have said of the other virtues such as moderation, (practical) wisdom, and courage also applies to justice: justice is not valuable in and of itself, but only instrumentally valuable, namely, insofar as it produces or contributes to pleasure, described in terms of a freedom from mental disturbance. Furthermore, the passage connects the instrumental value of justice with the idea of benefit; namely, insofar as justice helps agents be secure, it provides a benefit. That justice involves a calculation of what is beneficial in certain circumstances is completely in line with these ideas as well.

Torquatus' observation on the instrumental value of justice directly relates to points (i) and (ii) of the previous section and is further confirmed by Philodemus. In *On Property Management*, Philodemus stresses that justice is instrumentally valuable for obtaining freedom from mental distress, connecting discussions of justice to questions of moral psychology:

> Καὶ ἀδικία δὲ νομίζεται μὲν ἑκάστερον ποιεῖν, στερίσκει δ' [ἔπ]ειτα τὸ πλεῖστον οὐ μόνον τῶν κ[ερ]δανθέντων ἀλλὰ καὶ τῶν προϋπαρχόντων, ὥστε ἂν καὶ δικαιοσύνην ἀσκῆι, τό γ' ἐπὶ ταύ[τ]ην [ἀ]κινδύνως καὶ ποριεῖ καὶ φ[υλ]άξει.

> Injustice too is thought to bring about each one of these things (sc. the acquisition and preservation of property), but, in fact, afterwards it takes away the greatest part not only of what one has gained but also of what one

---

[33] Cicero, *On Ends* I.50–3. Trans. Woolf.

has had beforehand. It follows that, if one actually practices justice, one will both obtain and safeguard the gain acquired in conformity with it.[34]

Second and relatedly, Torquatus mentions what motivates agents to act justly in the Epicurean view and so touches on the topic of moral psychology. Torquatus identifies the fear of one's wrongdoing being detected and subsequently in some way being punished as a major motivation for acting justly and cultivating the virtue of justice. This obviously relates to the Epicurean highest ethical goal of being free from mental distress and bodily pain. (We will have an opportunity to discuss Epicurean moral psychology in more detail in the next chapter, which will be dedicated to the question of whether a sage, an Epicurean ideal agent, would violate a law, if he knew that he would escape detection.)

Third, Torquatus unfortunately gives us only a limited indication of the scope of the virtue of justice. This is in line with observation (iii) of the previous section. Justice is described negatively as not committing wrongs and not being dishonest. This description is compatible with the description of Epicurean agreements of justice, which, as we saw, were described as being about not harming and not being harmed. (Note again here that an *inuiria* can be a harm as well as an injustice.) However, the description still leaves quite indeterminate what justice is and there is no text that claims explicitly that justice is a disposition (*hexis*) of the soul as Plato, Aristotle, and the Stoics would claim. However, it seems that we are entitled to this conclusion insofar as we know that the sage who is a virtuous agent has a certain disposition that distinguishes him from other agents.[35]

What then is this disposition of justice about? Given the content of Epicurean agreements, it seems that the disposition is not merely a disposition to follow the laws; otherwise, as we will see in more detail in Chapter 4, we would also expect that there is an unconditional requirement to be lawful on the Epicurean view. Yet justice also does not exist independently of agreements on the Epicurean view, as *KD* 33 makes clear: "[the virtue of] justice is not anything in itself [*ti kath' heauto*], but [only] a kind of agreement [*sunthēkē tis*] over not harming and being

---

[34] Philodemus, *On Property Management*, col. XXIV.11–19 Tsouna. Trans. Tsouna. In addition to this passage, justice is also mentioned in three other passages of Philodemus' extant writings: *On Piety* I.2149–50 and 2260–1 Obbink; and *On Anger*, col. XXIV.39 Armstrong and McOsker. And perhaps one also needs to add Philodemus, *Rhetoric* II.282, fr. IX Sudhaus as well as *On Poems* V, col. XXXIV.3 Mangoni to this list. However, these passages are rather lacunose so that they add little to the present discussion.

[35] Fr. 226 Usener (= Diogenes Laërtius, *Lives of Eminent Philosophers* X.117).

3.2 Justice as an Epicurean Virtue

harmed in the dealings with each other in any place whatever."[36] This maxim is rather difficult to understand, especially because of its implications for the ontological status of justice within Epicurean philosophy, which we will address in more detail in Chapter 6.[37] Yet, for now, we may limit ourselves to the observation that the maxim makes clear that the virtue of justice cannot be understood independently of any agreements that exist in different places. This seems, in turn, to imply that the virtue of justice cannot be a commitment to what is beneficial in regard to not harming and not being harmed *independently* of whether the beneficial thing in question has been agreed upon or not. This leaves us with the conclusion that on the Epicurean view, justice as a virtue must concern the agreements of justice that are formed in different places, not the benefit for the community in the abstract. Yet this statement needs to be quickly qualified: agents will be obligated to adhere to agreements of justice only *insofar as these agreements also are beneficial*. This qualification is important because it would be strange if agents were virtuous when they adhered to an agreement that yields no benefit, given everything we have said about Epicurean agreements so far. The qualification also makes clear that justice must involve an element of discernment adapted to the circumstances at hand (which may be related to the idea that all virtues stem from practical wisdom, which at *Letter to Menoeceus* 132 is said to be the source of all the virtues).

Fourth, and finally, the account of justice Torquatus offers introduces some elements that go beyond what we find in other Epicurean authors and that thus might be thought to be un-Epicurean.[38] To give two examples: First, terms like "lust [*libido*]" or "cowardice [*ignavia*]" or "dishonesty [*improbitas*]," for instance, are negatively connoted moral terms. To find such terms associated with Epicurean justice or the consequences of injustice is strange because generally justice, understood as an agreement, is usually not cast in such negative moral terms. Furthermore, when Torquatus uses the term "to do wrong [*peccare*]," this, for a Roman audience, has religious overtones that are otherwise absent from the Epicurean account of justice that focuses on self-interest. This suggests that Torquatus' Epicurean account of the virtue of justice may at least be partially unorthodox, although, again, the features of Epicurean justice that were discussed above, namely, that justice relates to benefit in an

---

[36] οὐκ ἦν τι καθ' ἑαυτὸ δικαιοσύνη, ἀλλ' ἐν ταῖς μετ' ἀλλήλων συστροφαῖς καθ' ὁπλίκους δήποτε ἀεὶ τόπους συνθήκη τις ὑπὲρ τοῦ μὴ βλάπτειν ἢ βλάπτεσθαι.
[37] For a detailed discussion of this maxim, see Robitzsch 2022b and Robitzsch forthcoming c.
[38] See especially the discussion in Mitsis 1988, 69–70 *pace* Sedley 1998a, 148–50.

instrumental way and that justice entails a commitment not to do wrong, are well attested in other Epicurean texts.

3.3 Two Kinds of Justice?

A desideratum of a convincing theory of justice is that it is internally consistent, and it was already suggested above that the existence of aretaic justice crucially depends on contractual justice. The goal of this section is to characterize the relationship between these two kinds of justice further.[39] After all, on the basis of the so-called Golden Age fragment by Diogenes of Oenoanda, one might think that there is no need for agreements in a perfectly just community, since there will also be no laws in such a community. On this view, contractual justice for the Epicureans would be like a ladder that can be kicked away, once it has been climbed:

> δυνατὴν δὲ αὐτὴν ἂν ὑποθώμεθα, τότε ὡς ἀληθῶς ὁ τῶν θεῶν βίος εἰς ἀνθρώπους μεταβήσεται. δικαιοσύνης γὰρ ἔσται μεστὰ πάντα καὶ φιλαλληλίας, καὶ οὐ γενήσεται τειχῶν ἢ νόμων χρεία καὶ πάντων ὅσα δι' ἀλλήλους σκευωρούμεθα. περὶ δὲ τῶν ἀπὸ γεωργίας ἀνανκαίων, ὡς οὐκ ἐσομένων ἡμεῖν τότε δούλων] καὶ γὰρ ἀ[ρόσομεν αὐτοὶ] καὶ σκάψο[μεν, καὶ τῶν φυ]τῶν ἐπιμελ[ησόμεθα], καὶ ποταμο[ὺς παρατρέ]ψομεν, καὶ τὰ[ς φορὰς] ἐπιτηρήσο[μεν] ... καὶ διακόψει [κατὰ τὸ δέον τὸ] συνε[χῶς συνφι]λοσοφεῖν τοια[ῦτα· τὰ] γὰρ γεωγρ[ήματα ὧν ἡ] φύσις χρῄζει [παρέξει].

> But if we assume it[40] to be possible then truly the life of the gods will pass onto men. For everything will be full of justice and mutual love, and there will come to be no need of fortifications or laws and all the things which we contrive on account of one another. As for the necessities derived from agriculture, since we shall have no [slaves at that time] (for indeed [we ourselves shall plough] and dig and tend [the plants] and divert rivers and watch [the crops ...]) and such activities, [in accordance with what is] needful, will interrupt the continuity of the [shared] study of philosophy, for [the] farming operations [will provide what our] nature wants.[41]

Yet as Timothy O'Keefe argues, the text does not say that there will be justice without the existence of any kind of agreements.[42] In particular,

---

[39] For discussion of this problem, see Mitsis 1988, 91–2; Annas 1993a, 293–301; Armstrong 1997; and O'Keefe 2001a.
[40] The referent of "αὐτὴν" is not clear in the text. Commentators generally assume "it" to be that all human beings are or can become wise.
[41] Diogenes of Oenoanda, fr. 56.I.2–II.7 Smith. Trans. Smith. For some discussion and further references on this important text, see Robitzsch forthcoming b, fn. 23.
[42] O'Keefe 2001a, but see already Müller 1983, 164, fn. 30.

3.3 Two Kinds of Justice? 95

while indeed the passage in Diogenes claims that there will not be any laws in a perfectly just community, it does not say that there will not be agreements of justice. Even a community of Epicurean sages will thus need at least some agreements to solve coordination problems that will inevitably arise; for instance, they need to make agreements with each other to make sure that no agent will deplete resources at the detriment of others or harm others through inefficiencies caused by a lack of coordination. An example of the former would be that a meadow is used for farming instead of some other purpose. An example of the latter would be traffic rules such as who has the right of way.

Likewise, however, on a more fundamental level, according to the etiological account of Epicurean justice examined in Chapter 1 as well as *KD* 33 discussed above, there cannot be aretaic justice antecedent to agreements on the Epicurean view. In order for there to be aretaic justice in the first place, there must have been agreements in existence at some prior point that specified the content of justice. Justice, on the Epicurean view, is *historically* the product of an agreement, and without this agreement there is simply no justice (contractual or aretaic). Contractual and aretaic justice are both socially beneficial. And so certainly these social benefits exist whether agents have agreed to them or not; after all, social benefit is a natural, not a conventional fact about the world. However, there may be something socially beneficial that, given the lack of agreements, is not just. Put differently, then, for it to be possible to speak intelligibly about an Epicurean community of sages, in which everything is full of justice, we have to admit the antecedent existence of agreements that create what is just at least somewhere in some circumstances. These agreements subsequently make it possible to call an Epicurean community of sages just. Recall in this context as well that society is not something natural for the Epicureans, and there is no evidence that (contractual and aretaic) justice is a natural kind that exists independently of human invention once and for all.

If this is correct, then the most natural way to think of the relationship between contractual and aretaic justice is that the latter is nested in the former.[43] (And both kinds of justice are thus, in turn, dependent on the natural category of benefit.) The idea here is that in the Epicurean view, aretaic justice could not exist without contractual justice, which specifies the content of the personal virtue of justice in different places and at

---

[43] Versions of this view are offered in Annas 1993a, 293–301; Armstrong 1997; O'Keefe 2001a; and Brown 2010 [2009].

different times. Both kinds of justice aim at the achievement of the Epicurean goal in life, freedom from pain and mental distress. Nevertheless, contractual justice also entails rules of coordination that may not be directly included in the content of aretaic justice proper; this is the reason why even sages need to make agreements with each other. Contractual justice for the Epicureans thus has a wider scope than aretaic justice, which, however, might additionally include an element of discernment that itself is not part of the agreements of justice. In short, then, contractual justice is the ground on which aretaic justice can arise, and although the overlap between the two kinds of justice will be considerable, they are not identical.

Having determined the relationship between contractual justice and aretaic justice in this way, we may still wonder why both kinds of justice are needed. The answer is not found explicitly in any text but can be easily supplied. We have already seen that (1) even fully (aretaically) just agents will rely on agreements to some extent in order to resolve coordination problems and (2) aretaic justice will only be able to develop if contractual justice is already in place. Furthermore, (3) laws, which are crucially dependent on the existence of contractual justice, are crucial to bring "slow learners" up to speed and protect sages against suffering injustices. While Diogenes' Golden Age fragment clearly shows that laws will not be needed in ideal circumstances, we also know that Epicurean philosophy is very much concerned with providing pragmatic help in nonideal circumstances. In this vein, Seneca reports that the Epicureans recognize natural differences in moral progress and ability among human beings and recommend that those who cannot reason out the most beneficial course of action need to be brought along and, if need be, forced to behave correctly:

> Quosdam ait Epicurus ad veritatem sine ullius adiutorio exisse, fecisse sibi ipsos viam. hos maxime laudat quibus ex se impetus fuit, qui se ipsi protulerunt. quosdam indigere ope aliena, non ituros si nemo praecesserit, sed bene secuturos.... praeter haec adhuc invenies genus aliud hominum ne ipsum quidem fastidiendum eorum qui cogi ad rectum conpellique possunt, quibus non duce tantum opus sit, sed adiutore et, ut ita dicam, coactore. hic tertius color est.

> Epicurus remarks that certain men have worked their way to the truth without anyone's assistance, carving their own passage. And he gives special praise to these, for their impulse has come from within, and they have forged to the front by themselves. Again, he says, there are others who need outside help, who will not proceed unless someone leads the way, but who will follow faithfully.... You will find still another class of man, – and a

3.3 Two Kinds of Justice?

class not to be despised, – who can be forced and driven to righteousness, who do not need a guide as much as they require someone to encourage and, as it were, to force them along. This is the third variety.[44]

Seneca's distinction is also echoed in a passage of Hermarchus' story of the emergence of culture, which will be discussed in more detail in Chapter 6 and which distinguishes between three kinds of agents according to their ability to learn.[45] Nevertheless, the Senecan passage makes abundantly clear that the Epicureans recognize the helpfulness of force in making agents act justly and so ultimately good.[46] Since the laws rely on the existence of agreements and in fact are their extension, contractual justice also becomes an indispensable part of Epicurean philosophy. Likewise, it is also clear that these laws will offer a protection to sages, for as Stobaeus reports, in the Epicurean view, "the laws are laid down because of sages, not so that they do not commit an injustice, but so that no injustice is done to them [οἱ νόμοι χάριν τῶν σοφῶν κεῖνται, οὐχ ὅπως μὴ ἀδικῶσιν, ἀλλ' ὅπως μὴ ἀδικῶνται]."[47]

In summary, then, aretaic justice and contractual justice work in tandem and complement each other in the Epicurean social theory, which accounts for not only ideal circumstances, but also nonideal ones. This will become even clearer in the subsequent chapter, in which the Epicurean theory of justice will be explored from the perspective of moral psychology.

---

[44] Seneca, *Moral Epistles* 52.3–4. Trans. Gummere. For a discussion of moral development in Epicureanism, see Bobzien 2006.
[45] See also the discussion in Chapter 4.
[46] This, of course, does not mean that the laws by themselves are sufficient for making agents good. It seems that this will also require teaching and adherence to Epicurean philosophy more broadly.
[47] Fr. 530 Usener (= Stobaeus, *Anthology* IV.90.7–8 Wachsmuth and Hense). Trans. mine.

CHAPTER 4

Moral Psychology

A key purpose of the laws and the punishments attached to them is to compel agents to act in accordance with the principles that motivate the laws (ideally, those of justice). If an agent could escape detection, would he violate a law? For the Epicureans, the answer seems prima facie to depend on which agent one has in mind, a virtuous or a nonvirtuous agent. In the case of a nonvirtuous agent, one who does not possess the virtue of justice, the answer seems to be that he would violate the law. After all, such an agent in Epicureanism is only motivated to obey the law by the fear of detection and the punishments associated with breaking the law. Once this fear and these punishments are taken away, there is nothing stopping the agent from violating the law. In the case of a sage, an ideal agent who possesses the virtue of justice, by contrast, the answer seems to be that he would not violate the law. After all, such an agent is not primarily motivated to obey the law by the fear of detection and of punishments, but because he has internalized certain patterns of behavior so that he will act according to these patterns regardless of whether there are laws telling him to act a certain way or not.

Now, interestingly, this is not quite the answer we find in the ancient texts. Plutarch reports that Epicurus *himself* raises the question in one of his works of "whether the sage who knows that he will not be found out will do certain things that the law forbids [εἰ πράξει τινὰ ὁ σοφὸς ὧν οἱ νόμοι ἀπαγορεύουσιν, εἰδὼς ὅτι λήσει]."[1] And Plutarch also supplies us with Epicurus' reply. Unfortunately, however, this reply is rather cryptic. Epicurus supposedly answers: "the unqualified predication is not free from difficulty [οὐκ εὔοδον τὸ ἁπλοῦν ἐστι κατηγόρημα]."[2] In other words, Epicurus answers "Maybe" and so does not straightforwardly deny that a

---
[1] Plutarch, *Against Colotes* 1127d. Trans. Einarson and De Lacy, modified.
[2] Ibid. Trans. Einarson and De Lacy. See also Westman 1955, 185–6, following Diano 1946, 147, who argues that "*epikatēgorēma*" has to mean "predicate."

sage would not violate a law under any circumstances. On the Epicurean view, then, there are some situations in which even a sage would violate a law. And so, the interpretive challenge posed by the passage in Plutarch is to explain what Epicurus meant by (1) specifying the circumstances in which a sage would violate a law and (2) arguing why the sage has good reasons to violate the law in such circumstances.

This chapter will take up the interpretive challenge, complementing the account of justice that has been given so far by a discussion of Epicurean moral psychology. It will argue that a sage will violate a law when the sage cannot fulfill his natural and necessary desires while obeying the law; in such a case, the law, however, will have ceased being just. Accordingly, a sage will under some circumstances violate a law, but will never commit an injustice.

The next section will briefly discuss Plutarch's explanations of the question of whether the sage would violate a law, knowing he will escape detection, setting the stage for an explanation of Epicurus' comment (Section 4.1). This explanation will then be developed in detail (Sections 4.2 and 4.3). The chapter will end with a discussion of three objections to the proposed explanation (Section 4.4).

4.1 Plutarch's Account of the Sage Violating a Law

In addition to reporting the question that Epicurus posed himself regarding a sage breaking the law and Epicurus' cryptic answer to this question, Plutarch also provides an interpretation of what Epicurus' answer might mean. Unfortunately, this answer is not at all charitable to Epicurus. Plutarch claims that the answer means that "I [the sage] shall do it [that is, violate the law], but I do not wish to admit it [πράξω μέν, οὐ βούλομαι δ' ὁμολογεῖν]."[3] This amounts to a dismissal of Epicurus' answer as untenable and to the thought that the sage is an immoral agent who is surreptitiously willing to harm others if he can. The context of the discussion in Plutarch is also wholly polemical. The passage is located at the end of *Against Colotes* where Plutarch tries to show that an Epicurean life is a life without any regard to the laws. Plutarch's reading is not surprising, though, given the general attitude thinkers of other schools had toward Epicureans.[4] In any

---

[3] Plutarch, *Against Colotes* 1127d. Trans. Einarson and De Lacy.
[4] Besides the treatise by Plutarch, Cicero's *On Ends* I–II is a great example of this as are some of the stories collected in Diogenes Laërtius' *Lives of Eminent Philosophers*. In this vein, for instance, it is reported that Epicurus, the philosopher of pleasure, vomited twice a day because he overindulged in food and drink (X.6). Cicero himself also discusses the likely Epicurean reaction to the Ring of Gyges thought experiment. See Appendix B for a detailed discussion.

case, the systematic dismissal of Epicurus' view influenced the opinions of notable scholars. In particular, early scholars writing on Epicurus often just accepted the view that the Epicureans do not have any means at all in their arsenal to answer the question of whether the Epicurean sage would violate a law if he knew that he would escape detection.[5] But if the passage really posed such a problem for the Epicurean theory, then it seems odd that Epicurus *himself* raises the question. Furthermore, Plutarch notes that Epicurus raises the question in his work *Problems* (Διαπορίαι). Unfortunately, this work has not come down to us, but from the surviving fragments in other authors, it seems that the work dealt with the life of the sage in regard to a series of contentious questions. In addition to dealing with the problem of obeying the law in all circumstances, we know, for instance, that Epicurus dealt with the question of whether the sage should marry in this work and perhaps also the problem of sexual desire in old age.[6] These questions may not have had simple, straight-forward answers.[7] Accordingly, it at least seems possible that the question of whether the sage would violate a law, if he could escape detection, also does not have an easy answer and requires a more charitable and sophisticated response than the one that Plutarch offers on Epicurus' behalf.

4.2 Moral Psychology and Justice

Let us begin to give an answer to whether the sage would violate a law, knowing that he will escape detection, by examining more closely the sage's motivations to act.[8] First, we must distinguish a negative and a positive reason why Epicurean agents might not violate a law.[9] The negative reason is the fear of being punished and the positive reason is that obeying a law will yield a benefit, namely, will be conducive to a state of freedom from mental distress.[10] Now, most Epicurean agents obey the

---

[5] See especially Taylor 1911, 94; and Zeller 2013 [1923], III.1, 463 [448], fn. 4. A version of this view is still found in Diano 1946, 147, who claims that the question as it is posed creates a double bind for Epicurus: if he answered that the sage would violate a law, this would mean that no one could in the end be safe. If he answered that the sage would not violate the law, he would admit that there is something just in itself, which flies in the face of Epicurean theory.
[6] See the texts collected in frr. 18–21 Usener.
[7] On the question of whether the sage should marry, see Arenson 2016 (with references to older literature).
[8] See Westmann 1955, 185–9; Müller 1972, 86, fn. 203; and Vander Waerdt 1987.
[9] Vander Waerdt 1987, 406 and 410.
[10] One could argue that both the positive and negative reason involve fear, since the Epicurean sage will pursue what is beneficial in order not to be plagued by the fear that results from living an unjust life. Nevertheless, there seems to be a difference between acting because there are certain external

law because they fear detection and punishment for their actions, but sages do not. They obey the law because they grasp its usefulness. In this vein, Stobaeus reports that for the Epicureans, "the laws are laid down because of sages, not so that they do not commit an injustice, but so that no injustice is done to them [οἱ νόμοι χάριν τῶν σοφῶν κεῖνται, οὐχ ὅπως μὴ ἀδικῶσιν, ἀλλ' ὅπως μὴ ἀδικῶνται]."[11] And Hermarchus writes:

Εἰ δὲ πάντες ἐδύναντο βλέπειν ὁμοίως καὶ μνημονεύειν τὸ συμφέρον, οὐδὲν ἂν προσεδέοντο νόμων, ἀλλ' αὐθαιρέτως τὰ μὲν εὐλαβοῦντο τῶν ἀπειρημένων, τὰ δὲ ἔμπραττον τῶν προστεταγμένων.

If everyone were equally able to observe and remember what is beneficial, they would have no need of laws in addition, but of their own choosing, they would steer clear of what is forbidden and do what is prescribed.[12]

In other words, then, laws protect the sage from other people's wrongdoing, but do not have the purpose of guiding the sage in his actions. Likewise, in Hermarchus, we also find the distinction between two different ways of obeying the law,[13] which roughly correspond to what Hart calls "being obliged" and "having an obligation."[14] According to the first way, the motivation for obeying the law is supplied by a system of punishment that is set up in order to deter people from "acting against public or private interest [τὸ μήτε κοινῇ μήτε ἰδίᾳ τὸ ἀλυσιτελὲς πράττειν]."[15] According to the second way, the motivation for obeying the law is an understanding of what is beneficial and of the fact that it is better to act on this understanding than not to act on it. The second understanding seems to be exactly the one that the sage possesses. In short, then, the main reason why a sage follows a law is because this law is beneficial, not because there are punishments in place that deter him from acting in a certain way.

Now, what kinds of beneficial things do Epicurean sages pursue? To answer this question, we must examine the desires agents – and

---

restraints in place (that is, sanction mechanisms) and acting because of a certain character disposition.
[11] Fr. 530 Usener (= Stobaeus, *Anthology* IV.90.7–8 Wachsmuth and Hense). Trans. mine.
[12] Fr. 34 Longo Auricchio (= Porphyry, *On Abstinence* I.8.4). Trans. mine. By contrast, Plutarch claims, "Epicurus does not believe that one has to keep from wrongdoing for any other reason than the fear of punishment [οὐ γὰρ Ἐπίκουρος ἄλλῳ τινὶ τῆς ἀδικίας οἴεται δεῖν ἀπείργειν ἢ φόβῳ κολάσεων]." Fr. 534 Usener = Plutarch, *That It Is Impossible to Live Pleasantly According to Epicurus* 1104b Trans. mine. However, this remark is contradicted by testimony in Epicurean authors, which thus supersedes the testimony in Plutarch.
[13] Fr. 34 Longo Auricchio (= Porphyry, *On Abstinence* I.8.4–5). [14] Hart 2012 [1961]: 82–91.
[15] Fr. 34 Longo Auricchio (= Porphyry, *On Abstinence* I.8.3).

specifically sages – cultivate. According to the Epicureans there are three kinds of desires:[16] First, there are natural and necessary desires. Second, there are natural and unnecessary desires. And third, there are unnatural and unnecessary desires. The first class of desires roughly consists of those desires that pertain to our basic needs. Natural and necessary desires are necessary for life, happiness, and freedom from pain, and their lack creates a pain that can be easily dissolved, even if it is in some way connected with an agent's nature. Hunger and thirst are examples of such desires. This contrasts with the second class of desires, the natural and unnecessary desires. These desires are not necessary for life, happiness, and freedom from pain. Natural and unnecessary desires merely vary the pleasure that an agent feels rather than dissolving any pain the agent experiences. The Epicureans include sexual desires in this class. Finally, the third and last class of desires are unnatural and unnecessary desires. These desires are those that are created as the result of empty opinions. They are without a limit, and as a result of this, can never be fully satisfied. The most common examples of these desires are the desire for fame, power, or wealth.

According to the Epicureans, the sage will focus on fulfilling his natural and necessary desires, partaking of natural and unnecessary desires only when he is sure that their objects can be obtained without any problem, and he will altogether avoid the pursuit of unnatural and unnecessary desires.[17] The reasons are quite simple: First, the sage has no interest in having unnatural and unnecessary desires because these desires are not conducive to freedom from bodily pain and mental distress.[18] On the contrary, if one pursues and acquires wealth, power, or fame, one will become concerned about losing these goods and as a consequence worry more.[19] One's soul will thus be disturbed and one cannot lead the life of *ataraxia*. Second, as the scholion to *KD* 29 states, only the satisfaction of natural and necessary desires directly removes the pain we feel as a result of our bodily constitution; neither satisfying unnatural and unnecessary nor natural and unnecessary desires will. Satisfying natural and unnecessary desires such as the desire to drink a particular drink, as the same scholion explains, only varies the pleasure we experience, but does nothing to

---

[16] Epicurus, *KD* 29 and 30; *SV* 21: *Letter to Menoeceus* 127–8; Cicero, *On Ends* I.45 and II.26; and the texts in fr. 456 Usener. For a detailed discussion of the Epicurean classification of desires, and references to further literature, see Robitzsch 2022a.
[17] *KD* 30 and *SV* 21.
[18] *SV* 81; *Letter to Menoeceus* 130–2; and Cicero, *On Ends* I.44 as well as I.59.
[19] See also fr. 582 Usener (= Clement of Alexandria, *Stromata* IV.22), where the sage is said not to commit an injustice "for some gain [*epi tini kerdei*]."

4.2 Moral Psychology and Justice

alleviate our pain.[20] Third, natural and necessary desires, in contradistinction to unnatural and unnecessary desires, are not unlimited desires.[21] Nature is set up in such a way that our basic human needs are easy to satiate.[22] And so, the Epicurean sage will have no problem satisfying natural and necessary desires; greediness (*pleonexia*) is not a problem for the Epicurean sage. Accordingly, a sage will not have a reason to commit an injustice, as Torquatus, the Epicurean spokesperson in *On Ends*, explicitly claims:

> et opes vel fortunae vel ingenii liberalitati magis conveniunt, qua qui utuntur, benivolentiam sibi conciliant et, quod aptissimum est ad quiete vivendum, caritatem, *praesertim cum omnino nulla sit causa peccandi.* quae enim cupiditates a natura proficiscuntur, facile explentur sine ulla iniuria, quae autem inanes sunt, iis parendum non est; nihil enim desiderabile concupiscent.
>
> For those who are well-endowed materially or intellectually, generosity is more appropriate. Those who are generous earn themselves the goodwill of others and also their affection, which is the greatest guarantor of a life of peace. *Above all there is never any reason to wrong.* Desires which arise from nature are easily satisfied without resort to wrongdoing, while the other empty desires are not be indulged since they aim at nothing which is truly desirable.[23]

In the same vein, the Epicureans claim that for the sage, living the life of pleasure is living the life of justice and living the life of justice is living the life of pleasure, as we saw in the previous chapter.[24] In short, then, since natural and necessary desires, which the sage exclusively cultivates, are easy to satisfy, and justice for the Epicureans consists in refraining from harming others, a sage can presumably most of the time easily fulfill his desire without needing to harm anyone. He will simply not have a motivation to be unjust because being unjust is not conducive to a life of pleasure.

It is interesting to note that this answer is in line with the answer that Democritus gives to the question of whether an ideal agent will always be just. Democritus stresses above all the negative consequences that committing an injustice will have for the agent's peace of mind (which also resembles the answer to the question of why one ought to be just that Plato gives in the *Republic*):

---

[20] "Natural and unnecessary desires are those that only vary the pleasure, but do not remove the pain [φυσικὰς δὲ οὐκ ἀναγκαίας δὲ τὰς ποικιλλούσας μόνον τὴν ἡδονήν, μὴ ὑπεξαιρουμένας δὲ τὸν ἄλγημα]." Trans. mine.
[21] *KD* 15. [22] *KD* 15 and 21. [23] Cicero, *On Ends* I.52–3. Trans. Woolf, emphasis added.
[24] *KD* 5. See also *Letter to Menoeceus* 132; Cicero, *On Ends* I.50–4 and I.57.

Ὁ μὲν εὔθυμος εἰς ἔργα ἐπιφερόμενος δίκαια καὶ νόμιμα καὶ ὕπαρ καὶ ὄναρ χαίρει τε καὶ ἔρρωται καὶ ἀνακηδής ἐστιν· ὃς δ' ἂν καὶ δίκης ἀλογῆι καὶ τὰ χρὴ ἐόντα μὴ ἔρδηι, τούτωι πάντα τὰ τοιαῦτα ἀτερπείη, ὅταν τευ ἀναμνησθῆι, καὶ δέδοικε καὶ ἑωυτὸν κακίζει.

The cheerful man who undertakes just and lawful deeds rejoices sleeping and waking, and is strong and free from care; he who disregards justice and does not do what needs be is distressed by all these things, whenever he remembers any of them, and is frightened and reproaches himself.[25]

However, Democritus also appeals to an inner moral law, consisting of feeling shame toward oneself, which is completely absent in Epicurus:

Μηδέν τι μᾶλλον τοὺς ἀνθρώπους αἰδεῖσθαι ἑωυτοῦ μηδέ τι μᾶλλον ἐξεργάζεσθαι κακόν, εἰ μέλλει μηδεὶς εἰδήσειν ἢ οἱ πάντες ἄνθρωποι· ἀλλ' ἑωυτὸν μάλιστα αἰδεῖσθαι, καὶ τοῦτον νόμον τῆι ψυχῆι καθεστάναι, ὥστε μηδὲν ποιεῖν ἀνεπιτήδειον.

One should not feel shame before others rather than oneself nor be more willing to do something bad, if no one will know it than if everyone will. Rather one should feel shame before oneself, and set up this law in one's heart, to do nothing unfitting.[26]

Now, being just and being lawful are not the same thing, however, and here Democritus and Epicurus may well part ways. Whereas both a Democritean ideal agent and an Epicurean sage will never commit an injustice, a Democritean sage is typically taken to be law-abiding as well.[27] An Epicurean sage, as we saw, might still violate a law. Let us therefore next turn to the question of whether the law that is to be violated is just in order to understand why the Epicurean sage might violate a law, knowing he can escape detection.

4.3 The Importance of a Just Law

In addition to the moral psychology of the sage, the second key factor to explain the question of whether the sage will violate a law is the circumstances in which laws are just or unjust, that is, circumstances in which violating a law is not equivalent to committing an injustice. This means adding a complication to the problem: not only are there different motivations regarding why an agent can perform a just action (the fear of

---

[25] DK 68 B 174 (= Stobaeus, *Anthology* II.9.3). Trans. Taylor, modified.
[26] DK 68 B 264 (= Stobaeus, *Anthology* IV.5.46). Trans. Taylor, modified.
[27] Procopé 1971, 245; and Paneris 1977, 57–62.

4.3 The Importance of a Just Law

detection and punishment, on the one hand, or grasping that an action is beneficial, on the other hand), but there are also different institutional configurations that result from the fact that the preconception of the just does or does not agree with the laws that are in place. Robert Philippson distinguishes between two scenarios:[28]

(1) The preconception of the just can agree with the things that are legislated (that is, the law in question is just).[29]
(2) The preconception of the just can disagree with the things that are legislated (that is, the law in question is unjust).

In the first case, Philippson argues that there is no reason for the sage to be unjust. Since justice and laws are in agreement and the sage is virtuous and so does what is just, there is no reason for the sage to do anything that is forbidden by the laws, even if he knew that he could do so and escape detection. The second case is thus the more interesting. Here the sage has reason to do something that is illegal, given that his allegiance to the preconception of justice might be thought to be greater than his allegiance to a law that has ceased to be just. According to Philippson, however, even in such a situation, the sage would not violate a law. Philippson argues that the sage, like Socrates in Plato's *Crito*, will adhere to the law of the state or else (unlike Socrates) choose to emigrate, which he backs up by referring to a passage in Philodemus:

Ὅσα δ' οὐκ ὄντα τοιαῦτα τεθεμάτισται παρ[ά] τισιν δι' ἀσδήποτ' αἰτίας, [κ]αὶ ταῦτα τηρεῖν ἀξιοῦντας ἢ μεταβαίνειν ἐκ τῶν τόπων, ἐὰν [μ]ὴ καλῶς ζ[ῆ]ν [οἴωνται·]

Whatever [agreements or laws] are not such [that is, are not just], but have been established by some for whatever reason, are also worthy of being observed or, if people do not think they can live well [there], they ought to move away from the place.[30]

In other words, according to Philippson's reading, obedience of the laws is valuable in and of itself for the Epicurean sage.[31]

---

[28] Philippson 1910, 302–3.
[29] See *KD* 37 and 38. For a more detailed discussion of the preconception of the just, see Chapter 6.
[30] Philodemus, *Rhetoric* I.259, col. XXIV.33–9 Sudhaus. Trans. mine. See also the discussion of the opening sentence of this passage in Chapter 6 as well as *Rhetoric* I.233, col. III.12–21, where Philodemus endorses a prima facie duty to obey the law.
[31] The same claim (that one should obey the laws even if they are unjust) is also made by Perelli (1967, 196), albeit on more dubious grounds. Referring to Hermarchus (Porphyry, *On Abstinence* I.9), Perelli writes: "Even if he proclaims the sage should abstain from public life, Epicurus affirms the utility and the convenience to obey the laws of the state; one can glean from Porphyry, just as for

The obvious problem with Phillipson's explanation is that it does not allow that the sage would at least in some circumstances violate a law, a consequence that, as was pointed out above, seems to be required to make sense of Epicurus' answer that "the unqualified predication is not free from difficulty." However, this issue is easily addressed by slightly modifying the explanation by allowing the sage to violate a law when a law has ceased to be just.[32] In such a case, breaking the law seems unproblematic; it does not imply that the sage also committed an injustice by violating a law.

This explanation has the merit that it takes Epicurus' reply seriously and it mainly differs from Philippson's in the assessment of whether obedience of the law as such has value for the Epicureans. In Epicureanism, human beings obey laws insofar as they are beneficial (*sumphera*). Accordingly, the just and, consequently, the things that have been legislated as just in accordance with the preconception of the just (the laws) are in *KD* 31 explicitly linked with what is beneficial. "Benefit" here first and foremost means the benefit of the individual agent. However, as we saw in Chapter 2, given the minimal content of justice as merely not harming and being oneself free from harm, there is no reason to suppose that the benefit of the group is incompatible with such a benefit. It follows, then, if there is no benefit (for an individual) to be obtained by obeying the law, in the sense that this does not lead to the harm of others and the agent is not himself harmed, then obeying the law is pointless. This could prima facie mean that a law is obeyed in some circumstances because it is better to have a law in place than to have no law at all. However, it could also mean that it is better for an agent to violate a law because he is focused on obtaining what is beneficial, not on what is just or lawful. In the same vein, Geert Roskam points out that a central tenet of Epicureanism is "conditional reasoning," that is, the dependence of the choice of action on

---

Socrates in the Crito, that obedience to the law is required even if the laws are not just [*Pur predicando per il sapiente l'astensione dalla vita pubblica, Epicuro afferma l'utilità e la convenienza di ubbidire alle leggi dello stato; da Porfirio si ricava che, come per Socrate nel* Critone, *l'obbedienza è dovuta anche quando le leggi non siano giuste*]." Note, however, that the passage in Porphyry does not discuss the obedience to an unjust law. At I.9, Hermarchus claims that even unintentional homicide (*ton akousion phonon*) was penalized by the first law-givers so as not to set a precedent for people to imitate such behavior unintentionally or negligently. (This is a strange claim; it seems rather unlikely that cases of (true) unintentional homicide will rise dramatically even if they are not penalized.) In Hermarchus, this act of legislation is, however, justified by referring to benefit: it is not beneficial to a society as a whole to have a high number of (unintentional or intentional) homicides occurring in it. It is therefore a just law, not an unjust law, as Perelli claims.

[32] See the comment on p. 313, fn. b of Einarson and De Lacy's edition of *Against Colotes*; see also Denyer 1983, 144–9; and Mitsis 1988, 90–1, fn. 75.

4.3 The Importance of a Just Law

whether it is conducive to benefit.³³ And Plutarch himself, in *Against Colotes*, shortly after discussing Epicurus on whether the sage would violate a law, quotes the no longer fully extant *Letter to Idomeneus* where Epicurus advises "not to live in servitude to the laws and to opinions, as long as they refrain from making trouble in the form of a blow administered by your neighbor [μὴ νόμοις καὶ δόξαις δουλεύοντα ζῆν, ἐφ' ὅσον ἂν μὴ τὴν διὰ τοῦ πέλας ἐκ πληγῆς ὄχλησιν παρασκευάζωσιν]."³⁴ This advice entails violating a law in some cases, namely, when an agent can escape detection. Finally, Philodemus himself writes elsewhere that agents should observe the laws, but only insofar as they do not conflict with exercising virtue: "it is necessary that all obey the laws and common customs *as long as they do not command anything impious* [[χρ]ὴ πάντα πείθεσ[θαι] τοῖς νόμ[οι]ς καὶ [τοῖ]ς ἐθισμοῖς ἕως [ἂν μ]ή τι τῶν ἀσεβῶν [προ]στάτ[τ]ωσιν]."³⁵ In other words, if there is a conflict between the laws and what is beneficial, an Epicurean agent may well do what is beneficial rather than obey the law. Epicurean agents do not need to observe a law at all costs, but rather will do so only if a utility calculation tells them to do so.

This brings us to the Philodemus passage that was quoted above and that Philippson adduces to support his view. Rather than understanding it as a general statement in favor of obeying the law, we might also understand it as a suggestion connected to leading a life free of mental distress and bodily pain: it is better for the sage to obey the laws of the state or else to migrate if he wants to live an unperturbed life.³⁶

What might be a scenario in which a sage will violate a law? The best candidate seems to be one in which there is a law that is at odds with the satisfaction of natural and necessary desires that sages have. To be any more specific is difficult, though, because such specificity depends on having a complete list of all desires Epicurus considers natural and necessary and because the scenarios themselves will have to be quite extreme to justify the violation of a law. Take, for instance, the case of sage deciding to steal in order to obtain food or drink to sustain himself, that is, fulfill his natural and necessary desires related to nourishment.³⁷ While prima facie a good candidate, such a scenario is problematic insofar as, according to Epicurean doctrine, nature is set up in such a way that the satisfaction of natural and necessary desires is by definition easy. Furthermore, Epicurean

---

³³ Roskam 2007; Roskam 2020.
³⁴ Plutarch, *Against Colotes* 1127d. Trans. Einarson and De Lacy, modified.
³⁵ Philodemus, *On Piety* I.1379–83 Obbink. Trans. mine, emphasis added.
³⁶ See Roskam 2012, 33. For additional criticism of Philippson, see Vander Waerdt 1987, 407, fn. 20.
³⁷ See Vander Waerdt 1988, 417–18.

agents are able to scale back their desires to a very large extent, to evade as much as possible being in the position of not being able to satisfy them. Therefore, by being content, for instance, with fewer and simpler things (eating a ration of beans instead of a four-course meal), Epicureans are well able to evade being in a situation in which they would be forced to violate a law (at least in the overwhelming majority of all cases).

Scholars have proposed four scenarios in which an Epicurean sage might violate a law: (1) to murder an enemy, (2) to kill a tyrant making the Epicurean life impossible, (3) to save a friend, and (4) to save the "institution of friendship." A more detailed discussion of these scenarios will allow us to clarify further why it is difficult to specify exactly what a special situation in which a sage would violate a law would look like, although in regard both to existential threats to Epicurean life (scenario 2) as well as to the network of friends (scenario 4), the Epicureans are likely to allow that a sage may violate a law.

Roskam suggests that a sage will violate a law to murder an enemy. Roskam gives the fictional (historicized) example of Epicurus killing Timocrates.[38] Timocrates was a member of the Epicurean school and the brother of Metrodorus. Unlike Metrodorus, who became one of Epicurus' most faithful and beloved disciples, Timocrates left the Epicurean school and attempted to refute core Epicurean beliefs, using his insider knowledge to launch a series of vitriolic attacks against Epicurus.[39] For all we know, Epicurus dealt with this situation, which certainly must have presented a great nuisance to him, in a composed manner: he himself engaged with Timocrates' allegations and ordered his disciples to do so as well.[40] Assuming that Timocrates greatly disturbed his *ataraxia*, would Epicurus have killed Timocrates if he knew that he could escape detection?

Roskam answers in the affirmative, laying out four conditions the sage will have to fulfill in order to perform such a deed. First, according to Roskam, the sage cannot act out of emotion. Second, the sage does not derive any pleasure from the act of killing itself. Third, the murder has to serve the interests of the Garden and not be based on unnatural and unnecessary desires. And four, it has to be certain that the sage's *ataraxia* is not disturbed by this act of killing. "In short, *if* Epicurus decided to kill Timocrates, he would do so in cold blood, in a premeditated way, and without the slightest remorse *post factum*."[41]

---

[38] Roskam 2012, 37–8.   [39] Diogenes Laërtius, *Lives of Eminent Philosophers* X.6.
[40] Ibid., X.23, 28, and 117; Cicero, *On the Nature of the Gods* I.93; and Plutarch, *Against Colotes* 1126c.
[41] Roskam 2012, 38. Emphasis in original.

4.3 The Importance of a Just Law

Roskam is certainly right that for the Epicureans even murder would in principle be subject to the same conditional reasoning that all acts are subject to according to Epicurean theory. *Pace* Roskam, however, it seems that *this particular scenario* will hardly be troubling enough for a sage like Epicurus who can overcome negative emotions and whose *ataraxia* will likely not be disturbed by it. Diogenes Laërtius explicitly writes: "Injuries are done by men either through hate or through envy or through contempt, all of which the sage overcomes by reasoning [βλάβας ἐξ ἀνθρώπων ἢ διὰ μῖσος ἢ διὰ φθόνον ἢ διὰ καταφρόνησιν γίνεσθαι, ὧν τὸν σοφὸν λογισμῷ περιγίνεσθαι]."[42] Roskam's scenario thus relies on ascribing a far simpler theory of moral reasoning to Epicurus than he in fact held.

This brings us to a second scenario, according to which the very possibility of living the Epicurean life is under threat by a tyrant, and killing the tyrant will with certainty avert this danger.[43] In certain ways, this example is similar to the previous one insofar as it also concerns murder, but the stakes are higher insofar as they concern the very practice of Epicureanism as such. The action that the sage is contemplating to undertake is what Fowler calls an "emergency action" and a "'heroic' existential choice."[44] Again, we might also rely on a historical example to flesh out this scenario: the plot against Caesar in 44 BCE, which involved Cassius as well as other senators who were affiliated with Epicureanism and who may have justified their involvement in the conspiracy by referring to the Epicurean beliefs.[45] The difficulty with this scenario, however, is that the conspirators were hardly sages; in fact, their precise commitment to Epicureanism is somewhat unclear and so is whether it was truly *Epicurean* beliefs that motivated them to action in *this* particular situation.[46] Likewise, there were also Epicureans at the time, for instance, Statilius, who refused to participate in the conspiracy explicitly because they thought that it was not worthy of an Epicurean to get caught up in unnecessary political turmoil.[47] Accordingly, in order for the scenario to count as one in which the sage would violate a law, we would have to assume that a senator like Cassius was an Epicurean sage and that the situation was indeed an existential one for everyone living under the dictator Caesar (that is, that an Epicurean like Statilius was wrong in his

---

[42] Diogenes Laërtius, *Lives of Eminent Philosophers* X.117. Trans. Bailey.
[43] See, for instance, Mitsis 1988, 90–1, fn. 75.   [44] Fowler 1989, 128.
[45] See Sedley 1997 and Canfora and Stringer 2007.
[46] Griffin 1997, 29–32. On Roman Epicureanism, see also Castner 1991 [1988]; Benferhat 2005; Sedley 2010 [2009]; Valchova 2018; and the papers by Gilbert and Volk in Yona and Davis 2022.
[47] Plutarch, *Brutus* 12.3.

assessment of the situation). Applying the principle of conditional reasoning to this case, then, it seems that a sage could arrive at the conclusion that it would be better to violate a law than not to do so. Certainly, the laws in this situation will have ceased to be beneficial, and so while the sage would then have violated a law by killing a dictator, he would thereby not have done anything unjust.

As an alternative to killing someone, Gerhard Seel has made the suggestion that a sage would violate a law to save a friend.[48] He gives no further argument for the plausibility of this scenario.[49] There are, however, at least some passages in the Epicurean corpus that could support the idea that the Epicurean sage would do far-reaching things to benefit his friend, even if not all of them are of the same quality.

First, Diogenes Laërtius at *Lives of Eminent Philosophers* X.121 writes: "sometimes [the sage] will die for a friend [ὑπὲρ φίλου ποτὲ τεθνήξεσθαι]." This arguably might also entail transgressing a law, although this is not explicitly stated in the text, and dying for a friend need not entail transgressing a law. Note also that a correct understanding of the pronouncement depends on the word "*pote*" ("sometimes" or "at some point in time"), which seems to mirror the same indeterminacy that Epicurus expresses in the Plutarch passage.

Second, there is also *SV* 56–7:

> Ἀλγεῖ μὲν ὁ σοφὸς οὐ μᾶλλον στρεβλούμενος <ἢ στρεβλουμένου τοῦ φίλου, καὶ ὑπὲρ αὐτοῦ τεθνήξεται· εἰ γὰρ προήσεται> τὸν φίλον ὁ βίος αὐτοῦ πᾶς δι' ἀπιστίαν συγχυθήσεται καὶ ἀνακεχαιτισμένος ἔσται.
>
> If the sage is tortured, he feels the same pain <as if his friend were tortured, and he would die for him. For if he betrays> the friend, his whole life will be demolished because of this treachery and it will be upset.[50]

As the angle brackets make clear, though, the main problem with this passage is that half of the text is supplied by a modern editor, Ettore Bignone. This makes the passage a difficult text to rely on by itself as a testimony of genuinely Epicurean ideas.

Third, we read at Diogenes Laërtius' *Lives of Eminent Philosophers* X.120 that an Epicurean sage "will never give up a friend [φίλον τε οὐδένα

---

[48] Seel 1996.
[49] The same is also true for Geert Roskam (2012, 35), who discusses and rejects the possibility that a sage would save the friend in such circumstances. Diaco 2022 defends a modified version of Seel's view and adduces the first two passages quoted below. Diaco's modified view is discussed in more detail below.
[50] Trans. mine.

4.3 The Importance of a Just Law

προήσεσθαι]." Yet it is not quite clear what "giving up" entails, that is, how far the allegiance to a friend extends for the Epicureans. Furthermore, the manuscript does not contain the word "give up [*proēsethai*]" at all, which is again an emendation proposed by Bignone, but rather "acquire [*ktēsesthai*]," which gives the sentence quite a different meaning.

This textual evidence aside, the fundamental problem with the suggestion that a sage would violate a law to benefit a friend is that it stipulates that a sage will be required to help a friend because this is the right thing to do. On the most basic understanding of the Epicurean view, however, justice consists only in an agreement to refrain from harming others, not in the duty of beneficence toward them, as was argued in detail in Chapter 2. In other words, then, helping a friend may not be a requirement *of justice* for the Epicureans.[51] Certainly, there are other obligations that agents have, and it may very well be, as we saw in Chapter 3, impossible to live well without friends on the Epicurean view.[52] Yet again, these requirements may not be directly related to justice.

In this context, we should also recall that a sage might not in the end be completely unsettled by what happens to any *particular* friend. In this vein, *SV* 66 advocates for the right attitude toward one's friends: "Let us show sympathy for friends not by lamenting but by having them in mind [Συμπαθῶμεν τοῖς φίλοις οὐ θρηνοῦντες ἀλλὰ φροντίζοντες]."[53] It is not clear, however, whether the passage means that the Epicurean should merely "have his friends in mind" (as translated above) and thus react calmly to bad news from his friends (rather than lament) or whether the Epicurean agent should adopt a mindful attitude ("mind" his friends) in a time when hardship has fallen upon them (rather than just lament their fate).[54] While friends in general are conducive to the sage's *ataraxia*, this does not entail the claim that having a specific person as one's friend will also be conducive to one's *ataraxia*. The understanding of the state of *ataraxia* that is required to give credence to *SV* 56–7 (in its emended form) and similar texts would make *ataraxia* appear to be a very volatile state. If a loss of any single friend means the loss of *ataraxia*, then this falsely portrays *ataraxia* as a

---

[51] An interesting case, however, would be one in which a sage sacrifices himself for a friend vis-à-vis a potential harm from a third party, for instance, a sage who breaks some law to avert harm from the friend. However, again, even if a sage decides to break the law in such a scenario, it is unclear whether this is really a requirement of justice on the Epicurean view.
[52] *PHerc.* 1251, col. XIV.1–8 Indelli and Tsouna-McKirahan.   [53] Trans. mine.
[54] In this context, see also fr. 213 Usener (= Plutarch, *It Is Impossible to Live Pleasantly According to Epicurus* 28, 1105d): "Sweet is the memory of a dead friend [ἡδὺ ἡ φίλου μνήμη τεθνηκότος]." Trans. mine.

rather volatile state, misconstruing the Epicurean view. It seems more likely, then, that the Epicurean sage will again rely on conditional reasoning to determine whether he will actually need to help a friend by violating the law. Consequently, it depends on the circumstances whether a sage will violate a law for a friend, even in a case in which the friend cannot be saved otherwise. Again, this is not to dismiss the importance of friends on the Epicurean view. However, we should be careful to overstate the importance of any *particular* friend and the obligation we have toward them.

An emendation of Seel's view, namely, that a sage would violate a law not to save a friend, but rather to save "the institution of friendship,"[55] which is a source of security and thus of *aponia* and *ataraxia*, thus seems more compelling than Seel's original proposal. This fourth and final suggestion increases the stakes involved, just as killing the tyrant Caesar had in comparison to killing a random nuisance like Timocrates. The case is no longer about a particular individual, but rather about the network of friends and the ability to live together with them and thus have a good life. Note, however, the following: (1) A scenario in which the very existence of the network of friends has to be saved by breaking a law will probably occur very, very rarely (just as one will not find oneself in the situation of having to decide whether to take action against an existentially oppressive dictator). (2) The principle of conditional reasoning will apply, which means that in the case that an agent decides that the action in question will not be necessary to preserve friendship as an institution, there is no need to break a law and occur a harm. (3) There is no reason to assume that the scenario of preserving friendship is in a privileged position compared with similar threats to natural and necessary desires. As was argued above, if any of the natural and necessary desires are forbidden by the law, then it seems that an Epicurean sage will have a reason to consider whether breaking the law will procure a greater benefit than adhering to the law.

4.4 Objections and Replies

After having specified what conditions have to be fulfilled for a sage to violate a law and having described potential scenarios that satisfy these conditions, the rest of the chapter will discuss three objections to the proposed solution. Let us begin with an objection concerning the role the "knowing that he will escape detection" clause plays for the solution just outlined. After all, one might think that on the solution proposed, a

---

[55] Diaco 2022, 332 and passim.

sage could also violate a law knowing that he will *not* escape detection. But if this is so, then one wonders whether this is a problem for the Epicurean view as it was presented.

Note that in reality not only are there the two scenarios that Philippson discussed, namely, whether the law in question is just or unjust, but, in fact, in each of these scenarios, the sage might or might not escape detection and also have knowledge of this fact. This gives us a total of six scenarios:

(1) The laws are just and the agent knows that he will escape detection.
(2) The laws are just and the agent knows that he will not escape detection.
(3) The laws are just and the agent does not know whether he will or will not escape detection.
(4) The laws are unjust and the agent knows that he will escape detection.
(5) The laws are unjust and the agent knows that he will not escape detection.
(6) The laws are unjust and the agent does not know whether he will or will not escape detection.

Since it has been argued that the sage will never commit an injustice, the first three scenarios can be dismissed immediately; if the sage will never commit an injustice, he will a fortiori never violate a just law. In regard to the fourth scenario, it was suggested that the sage will – under certain conditions – violate a law. This is the case that explains why Epicurus claims that "the unqualified predication is not free from difficulty." However, what about the fifth and sixth cases? Will the sage violate an unjust law if he knows that he will not escape detection or if he does not know whether he will or will not escape detection? If he will, then the answer proposed (namely, that the law in question is unjust) may seem to be insufficient to explain Epicurus' answer; it would be unclear what function of the escape-detection clause has for the question that Epicurus raises. Epicurus may have equally asked simpliciter whether the sage would violate a law, leaving aside the issue of detection and knowledge thereof. For instance, in a society that as a whole has agreed on outlawing Epicureanism, would it not be better for the Epicurean sage to violate this law and risk detection, since there are overwhelming hedonistic reasons to practice Epicureanism than not to do so?[56]

---

[56] The function of the detection clause and knowledge of detection is ignored in Diaco 2022, but her answer could be similar to the one given here.

In response to the above objection, one could reply that the detection clause above all has a rhetorical function. Epicurus might have chosen to raise the question in a less controversial form (Will the sage violate a law, knowing he will escape detection?) rather than in the more controversial form (Will the sage violate a law, even if he knows that he will not escape detection or if he does not know whether he will or will not escape detection?). After all, by looking at Plutarch's reaction in *Against Colotes*, one can already see what controversy the former version created. It is therefore not difficult to imagine how Epicurus' contemporaries would have reacted to the latter one. Alternatively, raising the issue of detection and the knowledge thereof is an easy way to recall the different motivations Epicurean agents have to be just (that is, being just because sanction mechanisms are in place or because an agent has a virtuous character). The invocation of the detection clause and the knowledge thereof may thus merely echo these different motivations. Again, then, in this case, the role of the detection clause would be mainly rhetorical. Whatever Epicurus' reasons may have been to include the detection clause, the Epicurean view also forces us to concede that in some circumstances, a sage would violate a law, knowing that he will not escape detection, or not knowing whether he will or will not escape detection. However, this does not make the solution presented less plausible, even if it means that it follows that a sage would also violate a law under some circumstances in which he did not know whether he will escape detection or even knew that he will not escape detection.

A second objection to the proposed solution concerns the account of moral psychology that it implicitly endorses. Raphael Woolf advances such an objection against Paul Vander Waerdt's account. And it also applies to the account advanced in this chapter insofar as it agrees with the reading of Epicurean moral psychology that Vander Waerdt advances, even if the solution advanced here differs from Vander Waerdt's insofar as it does not claim that an account of moral psychology on its own can explain under what circumstances the sage will violate a law.

Woolf's objection is part of a paper on the Ring of Gyges story and is briefly articulated in a footnote.[57] Woolf claims that, on the Epicurean view, thinking about pain and fear causes agents to cultivate certain desires that lead agents not to experience pain and fear. For instance, a sage will not commit an injustice, because committing such an injustice is connected with the fear of being found out and the pain of potential

[57] Woolf 2013, 809–10, fn. 29.

punishment. However, if the nondetection clause holds, then it seems that the sage in question will no longer experience the fear or the pain connected to potential punishment. He will thus no longer need to associate committing an injustice with fear and pain, which Woolf claims constituted the reason for not committing an injustice in the first place. As a result, the sage *would* now commit the injustice (if the injustice yielded some benefit) precisely because fear and pain would no longer hold him back.

In response to this objection, note first that Woolf slightly modifies the scenario in which the sage is said to be able to escape detection. Whereas the sage in the Plutarch passage is tempted to commit an injustice at a *specific* time, the sage in Woolf possesses the *permanent* capability to escape detection and commit injustices, as in the Ring of Gyges thought experiment, which is completely different in this regard from the scenario that Epicurus proposes.[58] In other words, the case Woolf has in mind is quite different from the case discussed by the Epicureans and their opponents.

Second, Woolf's objection is not focused on the status of the law that may or may not be violated, as the previous objection, but rather on the sage's commitment to being just. Addressing Woolf's objection thus allows us to clarify the process by which the sage comes to have knowledge of what is just and to make clear that the scenario that Woolf imagines is impossible on the Epicurean view. In order for his argument to work, Woolf seems to assume tacitly that a sage can be "dehabituated" and cease being just. This means that the sage can thus lose his status of being a sage if certain sanction mechanisms are not in place and temptation arises. However, this additional assumption is unwarranted, given the textual evidence.[59] The result of being a sage and possessing *ataraxia* in Epicureanism is precisely that one will not be tempted to be unjust, regardless of whether certain conditions that might favor committing an injustice hold. Accordingly, we read in Diogenes Laërtius that for the Epicureans, "he who has once become wise no longer assumes the opposite habit, not even in semblance, if he can help it [τὸν ἅπαξ γενόμενον σοφὸν μηκέτι τὴν ἐναντίαν λαμβάνειν διάθεσιν μηδὲ πλάττειν ἑκόντα]."[60] It is therefore irrelevant whether a sage, once he has truly become a sage, is subjected to desires that he would not have pursued otherwise; the sudden

---

[58] See also Appendix B.
[59] On the way agents learn in Epicureanism, see especially Rosenbaum 1996.
[60] Diogenes Laërtius, *Lives of Eminent Philosophers* X.117. Trans. Hicks, modified.

emergence of the possibility to commit an injustice will not "dehabituate" the sage to commit an injustice, as Woolf assumes.

Third, in claiming that a sage is motivated to act only in virtue of fear and punishment, Woolf offers a more simplified version of a sage's moral psychology than the one spelled out in this chapter. Sages are motivated to act according to the Epicurean view because they understand the benefit that is associated with a given action.

A final objection to the solution presented in this chapter is found in David Gill. He applies a different strategy than Woolf, but also targets the moral psychological explanation advanced by Vander Waerdt (and that is endorsed in this chapter) in his criticism. Unfortunately, Gill's paper was never published. As a result, we can only refer to the comments in Julia Annas' *Morality of Happiness* where Gill's critique is very briefly summarized:

> Gill ... argues that this [account of moral psychology required by the solution] cannot account for (1) Epicurus' repeated insistence on the impossibility of achieving complete security... nor for (2) the fact that Epicurus insists that the content of justice may vary with circumstances, so that the motivation to be just must be capable of explaining such differential behavior, whereas the lack of inappropriate desires would seem to explain the same behavior everywhere. Such an account, Gill argues, threatens to make the contractual account of justice applicable only to non-Epicureans, while good Epicureans will not need it; but this is difficult to reconcile with the totality of the evidence.[61]

Let us restate and then address this criticism. First, Gill claims that the account of moral psychology cannot plausibly explain the impossibility of achieving complete security. Since this claim is not spelled out further, it is unclear why this is an issue. After all, not all agents have the disposition to be a sage. As a result, one may very well acknowledge that even if sages do not commit injustices themselves, it is still possible that injustices may be committed against them and so that complete security is impossible on the Epicurean view.

Second, Gill contends that the account of moral psychology is deficient in assuming that the lack of certain desires explains just behavior. Since this lack would be the same everywhere where there is justice, the objection seems to state that the lack of desires merely explains why the same things would be just everywhere, but they would not explain why different

---

[61] Annas 1993a, 297, fn. 31.

things can be just in different circumstances. But this is precisely what the Epicureans claim in regard to the content of justice.

In regard to this point, one must distinguish between what is just and what is beneficial. The lack of certain desires explains why certain things are beneficial everywhere, but this lack does not explain why the same things are just in a given place. Justice depends on more than an objective fact about the world; it also depends on the social act of the agreement itself, which may vary from place to place, as we have seen. In other words, while not harming and being harmed is beneficial everywhere due to the constitution and structure of desires that agents have, what is just also depends on the particular circumstances unique to a specific community, that is, the agreements agents will make in order to obtain what is beneficial. So, while a certain set of behaviors may thus constitute just action in one place, another set of behaviors may constitute just action in another place, even if both sets of behavior are beneficial. In addition, we saw that the content of contractual justice is slightly wider than that of aretaic justice for the Epicureans: contractual justice has the additional function of solving coordination problems between different agents. If this is so, it is unclear why agreements would ever be superfluous on the Epicurean view or why they do not apply to certain agents, as Gill seems to assume.

In summary, then, a sage will violate a law in some circumstances, which are not easy to specify, but he will never commit an injustice. This is explained by the moral psychology of sages, which differs from those of regular agents, as well as by the fact that not all laws are just. Having thus investigated Epicurean justice from a political (Chapters 1 and 2) and an ethical perspective (Chapter 3 and this chapter), we can then in the next chapter examine Epicurean justice from the perspective of legal philosophy.

CHAPTER 5

Justice and Law

Having provided a detailed account of Epicurean justice in previous chapters, we can now turn to the precise relationship between morality and legality, between justice and the law, in Epicureanism, which has been the subject of some scholarly disagreement. In his 1910 paper, for instance, Robert Philippson squarely identifies Epicurus as an advocate of natural law theory.[1] By contrast, Reimar Müller and Victor Goldschmidt, in their respective books published in the 1970s, argue that justice is primarily a matter of agreement for the Epicureans. They thus both stress the conventional features of Epicurean theory.[2] Müller, for instance, points out that what is naturally just cannot be meant in the sense of something that is just in itself without recourse to human posits;[3] Epicurean natural law theory, for him, is very different from natural law theories that admit absolute, unchanging norms.[4] Goldschmidt, however, goes so far as to claim that Epicurus defends a kind of legal positivism:

> The objective of a legal theory is to protect human beings from each other, not to arouse their claims against the public power. In this sense, one can speak of "legal positivism.". . . Epicurus recognizes nevertheless that there can be an unjust law, that is, a harmful one. But in conformity with the general aspiration of his theory, the criterion of judgment will be derived neither from some natural law nor, even less, be left to the discretion of individuals: it will have to be found in the framework of positive law and, in fact, in the Attic law.[5]

---

[1] Philippson 1910, 292.
[2] See also Wilson 2019, 62, who emphasizes the conventional aspect of Epicurean theory.
[3] Müller 1972, 93. See also Goldschmidt 1977, 25–8.   [4] Müller 1972, 92.
[5] "L'obiettivo della teoria del diritto è di proteggere gli uomini gli uni dagli altri, e non di eccitare le loro rivendicazioni contro i poteri pubblici. In questo senso, si potrebbe parlare di 'positivismo giuridico.'. . . Epicuro riconosce, tuttavia, che può esserci un diritto ingiusto, cioè nocivo. Ma, in conformità con l'inspirazione generale della sua teoria, il criterio di apprezzamento non potrà discendere da un qualche diritto naturale né, tantomeno, essere lasciato all'arbitrio dei privati:

Antonina Alberti's 1995 contribution, by contrast, emphasizes the importance of distinguishing between justice, on the one hand, and the laws, on the other hand,[6] a position that is typically thought to be characteristic of legal positivism, and she regularly refers to H. L. A. Hart's seminal text of legal positivism *The Concept of Law* throughout her paper. However, she also pushes back on a purely positivistic reading, arguing that the Epicureans in certain ways are not defenders of a kind of legal positivism:

> [O]n the one hand [Epicureanism] anticipates the positivist thesis of the separation of law and justice, and on the other, by means of its conception of utility, rejects the thesis that law is conventional and arbitrary which might seem to be implied by this separation – the thesis which utilitarians and positivists like Bentham, Austin and Kelsen did later adopt.[7]

Finally, Pierre-Marie Morel is the latest author to have written explicitly on the relationship between justice and law in Epicureanism. Without directly stating whether the Epicurean view amounts to a kind of legal positivism or natural law theory, he, like Alberti, emphasizes that the Epicureans take up a kind of middle position, asking the rhetorical question: "Does Epicurus not precisely try to spell out the double theme of the variability and the contractual character of the just with a reflection on the conformity to nature?"[8]

The common deficiency of these contributions is that they often use the terms "legal positivism" and "natural law theory" without providing a clear definition of these terms. This chapter will remedy this defect of previous contributions and provide a characterization of the relationship between justice and law from the perspective of contemporary philosophy of law, arguing that Epicurean theory most closely resembles a natural law theory, although in certain ways it also prefigures elements that are associated with legal positivism. After offering an overview of the intellectual terrain (Section 5.1), this chapter will turn to classifying the Epicurean view (Section 5.2).

5.1 Natural Law and Legal Positivism

Natural law theory and legal positivism are generally considered to be the two main theories that describe the relationship between morality and

---

dovrà essere trovato nella cornice stessa del diritto positivo e, nella fattispecie, del diritto attico." Goldschmidt 1981, 309.

[6] But see also the remarks in Philippson 1910, 299.   [7] Alberti 1995, 172.
[8] "Épicure ne cherche-t-il pas précisément, à articuler le double thème de la variabilité et du caractère contractuel du juste avec une réflexion sur la conformité à la nature?" Morel 2000, 396. Trans. mine.

legality, between justice and law. To what each theory exactly amounts is contested among scholars and has been at the center of major debates of twentieth-century philosophy of law, as, for instance, the famous exchanges between H. L. A. Hart and Richard Dworkin or Lon Fuller show. In fact, some scholars even maintain that the two theories are not even opposed, as is generally assumed, but that they are complementary. On this reading, natural law theory is not another theory of legality on the whole as legal positivism is, but rather elaborates on legal positivism insofar as it provides a theory of nondefective legality.[9]

Rather than provide a comprehensive definition and discussion of the terms, which would exceed the scope of this chapter, this section will focus on two theses that are commonly used by contemporary authors to distinguish legal positivism from natural law theory: (1) the pedigree thesis and (2) the separation thesis. In what follows, each of these theses will be discussed briefly to develop a framework in which it will be possible to say that a certain theory leans more toward legal positivism or toward natural law theory.

5.1.1 *The Pedigree Thesis*

According to the pedigree thesis, legal positivism is characterized by the claim that law is a posit (hence the name "legal *positivism*"). Put differently, the existence of law depends on social facts, not on its merit. The classical statement of this thesis is found in John Austin: "The existence of law is one thing; its merit and demerit another. Whether it be or be not is one enquiry; whether it be or be not conformable to an assumed standard, is a different enquiry."[10] A social fact in this context is one that comes to be through the interaction of human beings. In other words, the idea behind this thesis is that human beings make the law and that this is the criterion of determining what law is in legal positivism.

If one glosses the pedigree thesis in this way, the difference between natural law theory and legal positivism is one of emphasis rather than of substance. After all, even natural lawyers will be able to accept the pedigree thesis insofar as human laws are indeed posits; that laws come into existence in this way is hardly news. Natural lawyers would emphasize, however, that this is not the full story, that by ignoring the connection between legality and morality, legal positivists miss out on what is truly

---

[9] Murphy 2007, 43–5 (with references to further literature).   [10] Austin 1998 [1832], 184.

important. It may thus be helpful to distinguish between the following two questions:

(1) Why are laws legitimate?
(2) Why are laws normative?

The question about legitimacy concerns the problem of how a law can be considered a law in the first place. This question does not ask whether a law is a good example of its kind, but rather how law comes to be at all. As we already saw, natural lawyers do not seem to differ much on this score from legal positivists insofar as both theorists are able to acknowledge the legitimizing function of the act of positing a law that makes a law a law. Accordingly, the pedigree thesis would provide something like a formal and functional perspective of how a law comes to be, which again, even natural lawyers can endorse.

In regard to the second question (what makes laws normative?), the pedigree thesis has nothing to contribute. The pedigree thesis leaves open whether morality can still factor into the law. Take, for instance, §4302 of the Pennsylvania Penal Code, which prohibits incest. This law against incest is a social fact insofar as lawmakers in the state of Pennsylvania who were mandated by the people created it. Yet whether the law came to be as a social fact or not, its content is arguably importantly formed by morality. It is not *merely* that people came together and created the law, but in making the law lawmakers and the people of the state had certain ideas about moral values that made their way into the written law. Put differently, the pedigree thesis is a thesis about the *origin* of law, but it leaves open whether the *content* of the law may or even should include moral ideas.

5.1.2 The Separation Thesis

The separation thesis states that legal positivism differs from natural law theory in that the latter, but not the former, argues that there is a necessary connection between what is moral and what is legal. Hart asserts in his seminal work *The Concept of Law*, for instance, that "we shall take Legal Positivism to mean the simple contention that it is in no sense a necessary truth that laws reproduce or satisfy certain demands of morality, though in fact they have often done so."[11] Put differently, the separation thesis states, according to a first approximation, that while legal systems may be

[11] Hart 2012 [1961], 185–6. See also Hart 1958.

connected with morality in some way, they do not need to exhibit such a connection in order to be legal systems.

While this thesis is perhaps the most famous thesis associated with legal positivism, legal positivists themselves today sometimes reject it as insufficient or confused.[12] Likewise, even some natural law theorists could accept the separation thesis in the gloss that was just given. After all, neither classical nor modern natural law theorists maintain that laws are simply read off moral norms or reproduce them one to one. A natural law theorist would only be committed to the separation thesis if she also maintained that a law is a law *only if* the law in question "reproduces or satisfies certain demands of morality." This is equivalent to saying that a law is only a law if it is, for instance, just. Yet most natural law theorists do not hold such a view, even if the contrary is often falsely attributed to them.[13]

We might therefore attempt to understand the separation thesis in a slightly different way, not merely as a thesis about the *actual separation* of what is lawful and what is moral, but rather about the study of law more broadly conceived. Understood in this way, the thesis aims at the claim of whether the law can and ought to be studied with or without a reference to morality. Accordingly, for the natural lawyer,

> [l]aw is best understood, at least in part, as a teleological concept: a concept or institution that can be properly understood only when the ultimate objective is kept in mind – here, the ultimate objective being a just society. This is in sharp contrast to the generally descriptive, largely empirical, morally neutral approach one finds among the legal positivists.[14]

Put differently, the legal positivist according to the separation thesis claims that law can be studied without reference to morality. This is perhaps most succinctly addressed in Hans Kelsen's pure theory of law, that is, a (positivistic) theory of law that focuses only on questions of legality, while setting aside completely questions of morality.[15] Natural lawyers, by contrast, claim that such a setting-aside of morality in the study of law misses out on essential questions: "Though the legal positivists might be able to offer what appears to be a simpler model of law..., a view of law that included more about the moral claims and moral aspirations of law would be a more complete, and therefore better, theory of law."[16]

---

[12] See, for instance, the discussion in Green 2008. The following discussion is also indebted to the comments in Green 2009.
[13] See Kretzmann 1988.   [14] Bix 2002, 76. Emphasis added.   [15] See Kelsen 2008 [1934].
[16] Bix 2002, 76.

5.1 Natural Law and Legal Positivism

Table 5.1 *Theories on the nature of law*

	Legal Positivism	Natural Law Theory
Pedigree Thesis		
Is law a social fact?	Yes → lean towards legal positivism	No → lean towards natural law theory
Separation Thesis		
Are justice and law actually separate?	Yes → lean towards legal positivism	No → lean towards natural law theory
Can justice and law be investigated completely separately?	Yes → lean towards legal positivism	No → lean towards natural law theory
Are there legal reasons to obey the law separate from moral ones?	Yes → lean towards legal positivism	No → lean towards natural law theory

An immediate practical upshot of these different attitudes toward the separation of morality and legality concerns the question of the authority of the law. "Authority of the law" here refers to the question of what obliges agents to obey the law. This is again a controversial topic in the philosophy of law, with some scholars arguing that agents do not have *legal* obligations to obey the law at all.[17] Yet insofar as we are here concerned with differences between natural law and legal positivism, it is interesting to note that legal positivists often argue that there are *legal* reasons for obeying, separate from moral reasons, and they allege that a failing of natural law theory is not to recognize this posit. According to this reading, natural lawyers are not able to furnish agents with reasons to obey the law in addition to the moral reasons that they may already have to do so.[18] After all, the standard of evaluating whether a law is good in natural law theory is whether it is moral, so a law is obeyed not because it is law, but because it is moral. If this is right, then natural lawyers reduce law to morality and so do not properly recognize law as an independent domain that can obligate agents in its own right. Put differently, in regard to the question of obeying the law, legal positivism and natural law theory could be said to differ from each other insofar as the former distinguishes between legal and moral reasons for obeying, whereas the latter theory does not make this distinction.

In conclusion, we may thus sum up the discussion as shown in Table 5.1. We should also note, again, though, that while in a certain way all of these questions can be used to distinguish legal positivism and natural law theory, the above discussion clearly showed that it is especially

---

[17] For a recent overview of the debate, see Green 2004. [18] Coleman and Leiter 1996, 243–4.

5.2 The Epicureans on the Relationship between Justice and Law

Having singled out theses that can be used to distinguish natural law theory and legal positivism, let us begin with the pedigree thesis and see whether the Epicureans would endorse it. As was shown in detail in previous chapters, the laws on the Epicurean view are created by preeminent individuals and then recognized by the many. This means that laws are social facts; they arise anew in different places and at different times. The Epicureans thus clearly support a version of the pedigree thesis. Nevertheless, as we saw in the previous section, the pedigree thesis does not directly help us to distinguish between legal positivism and natural law theory because it merely emphasizes the social origin of (human) positive law, which legal positivists and natural lawyers may agree on.

This thus brings us to the separation thesis. First, it is noteworthy – especially in the ancient context – that justice and law (the former of which can be seen as a stand-in for morality as a whole) for the Epicureans are indeed conceptually distinct entities, as has been repeatedly stressed in previous chapters.[19] The Epicureans are very careful to distinguish between the laws (*hoi nomoi*) and what is just (*to dikaion*), and they claim that the law is an extension of what is just. Accordingly, we can say that the Epicureans endorse the separation thesis in the first approximation that was distinguished above. This is noteworthy because a distinction between justice and law is not at all self-evident. English and Greek are in a privileged position here, since they clearly distinguish between justice and law. In other modern languages such as German and French, by contrast, the conceptual distinction between justice and law is often obscured. "*Recht*" and "*droit*" can refer to both what is just and what is lawful. And in addition to this, "*Recht*" and "*droit*" may also refer to a "right," which compounds the conceptual confusion. Be this as it may, even in the Greek context, there are examples for the conceptual confusion between what is just and what is lawful. At *Hippias Major* 284d, for instance, Socrates claims: "Then, when those who attempt to set down laws miss the good, they have missed the lawful and the law as well [Ὅταν ἄρα ἀγαθοῦ ἁμάρτωσιν οἱ ἐπιχειροῦντες τοὺς νόμους τιθέναι, νομίμου τε

---

[19] See also Alberti 1995.

5.2 Epicureans on the Relationship between Justice and Law

καὶ νόμου ἡμαρτήκασιν]."[20] Of course, in the context of this Platonic dialogue, Socrates' pronouncement may be rhetorical, and due to the nature of the text, it is not clear whether the view articulated here can also be reliably attributed to Plato. After all, one would need not only to endorse the theory that Socrates is always a reliable mouthpiece of Plato, but also to accept the authenticity of the *Hippias Major*. Nevertheless, the passage shows that in distinguishing between what is just and what is lawful, the Epicureans avoid the fault of crudely running together two ideas that should be conceptually separated but that are not always kept apart. Accordingly, one might say that in regard to this version of the pedigree thesis, Epicurean philosophy leans toward a kind of legal positivism.

As was argued above, however, the separation thesis understood in this sense is insufficient to distinguish natural law theory and legal positivism, since it can be endorsed by natural lawyers and legal positivists alike. Instead, the thesis ought to be understood not as a thesis on the actual separation of law and morality, but rather as one on the study of law as a domain independent of morality. Understood in this way, the thesis is a modern invention, however, and is not shared by the Epicureans. Recall here that Epicurean theory starts with the idea of benefit as a natural fact. This benefit, then, through agreements among contracting parties, becomes acknowledged as such and so is elevated to the rank of being just. Finally, then, the laws on the Epicurean view are created by preeminent individuals and then recognized by the many. While there can thus be laws on the Epicurean view that are not just, namely, when the preeminent individuals fail to aim at the common good in the endeavor of law-giving, there is no indication that the Epicureans ever consider laws independently of justice or benefit altogether. Instead, the categories of justice and benefit are also present in Epicurean discussions of the law and they are the standard to which all discussions make reference.

In the same vein and as an immediate upshot of the previous, the Epicureans do not acknowledge that there are separate legal reasons to obey the law for its own sake, as was shown in more detail in Chapter 4. The law is to be obeyed according to the Epicureans because it yields a

---

[20] Trans. mine. At *Laws* IV.715b2–4, the Athenian claims more carefully that "we say, I presume, that neither these [arrangements] are constitutions nor that those [laws] that have not been established for the good of the whole city-state are correct laws [ταύτας δήπου φαμὲν ἡμεῖς νῦν οὔτ' εἶναι πολιτείας, οὔτ' ὀρθοὺς νόμους ὅσοι μὴ συμπάσης τῆς πόλεως ἕνεκα τοῦ κοινοῦ ἐτέθησαν]." Trans. mine. In other words, the Athenian does not directly deny that not well-made laws are not laws at all.

benefit, but if it does not yield a benefit, it can be violated. Obedience to the law, in short, is, for them, merely a matter of calculation of the benefit associated with the obedience. In other words, Epicurean theory reduces legality to morality when it comes to obeying the law. This means that the Epicureans would not endorse the separation thesis in the stronger form that was distinguished above, and we could say that the Epicurean theory of law leans toward natural law theory.

If we were to classify the Epicurean theory as a kind of legal positivism, this would force us to focus on the law from a purely descriptive perspective and ignore the normative framework in which Epicurean theory is embedded. Modern-day legal positivism is characterized by its endorsement of the separation thesis in the stronger form, which states that the law can be investigated independently of justice. As should be abundantly clear at this point, however, the Epicureans would vehemently reject such an approach. Their theory of law cannot be meaningfully separated from the study of justice, just as there are no meaningful reasons for Epicurean agents to obey the law that are only legal reasons – as opposed to moral ones. The latter features of Epicurean theory thus decisively tip the scales. While again the Epicurean theory of law has some features that make it seem positivistic, a classification of the Epicurean theory as a kind of legal positivism is misleading.

Returning, then, to the opinions of the scholars cited at the beginning of this chapter, we can say that Reimar Müller's view is the closest to the one offered here. However, even Müller seems to be off-track insofar as he stresses that the change of moral norms themselves is a potential caveat to classifying Epicurean theory as a natural law theory. We have already discussed the dynamic conception of nature that the Epicureans offer in detail in Chapter 1. And again, what decisively characterizes Epicurean theory as a natural law theory is that according to the separation thesis, one will crucially miss out on understanding the law if one does not also take into account moral facts, that is, what is just and what is beneficial in the case of the Epicureans.

Robert Philippson, furthermore, is likewise right in classifying the Epicurean position as a natural law theory overall. His reasons for doing so, however, are not convincing. For one, his reading of the naturally just in *KD* 31 as something once and for all just is mistaken, as we saw in more detail in Chapter 2. Likewise, Phillipson also claims that

> [a] confirmation of our opinion [that Epicurus is a natural lawyer] will be supplied by Polystratus who (in response to his opponents' claim that the

existing moral concepts are to be considered artificial, not natural, because they are different everywhere) proves that the naturalness and validity of concepts is not rendered void by their relativity.[21]

This claim rests on a mistaken understanding of Polystratus' *On Irrational Contempt for Common Conceptions*. Polystratus does not argue that moral terms exist by nature, but rather only claims that those things that exist relative to something (*pros ti*), that is, moral terms, despite being only by convention (*tōi nomoi*), still have legitimacy and so cannot be ignored. (Put differently, Polystratus explicitly does not claim that moral terms exist by nature, as Philippson claims.)

Alberti's and Morel's readings, by contrast, are correct insofar as their approaches rightly emphasize that the Epicurean theory of justice and law anticipates legal positivistic ideas to some extent. Again, however, in the end, the Epicurean position is closer to a natural law theory. Finally, in regard to Goldschmidt's reading we can conclude the following. While Epicurean theory resembles legal positivism to some extent, such an understanding requires some explanation, elaboration, and caveats and ignores that in a decisive way, it is a natural law theory.

---

[21] "Eine Bestätigung unserer Auffassung wird uns Polystratus geben, der gegenüber der Behauptung seiner Gegner, die bestehenden Sittlichkeitsbegriffe seien als künstliche, nicht als natürliche zu betrachten, weil sie überall verschieden seien, beweist, dass durch die Relativität die Natürlichkeit und Gültigkeit von Begriffen nicht aufgehoben werde." Philippson 1910, 294.

CHAPTER 6

Ethical Naturalism

There are several competing kinds of naturalism in modern philosophy, and many of the definitions of naturalism that abound in ethics and other subdisciplines of philosophy are controversial.[1] The reader should note that here the term is used neither as a shorthand for materialism or physicalism, as it sometimes is, but rather as a stand-in for what Stephen Darwall, Allan Gibbard, and Peter Railton call a "continuity view," that is, a view that stresses a continuity between investigations in science and ethics, which contrasts with a "discontinuity view," that is, a view according to which investigations in science and ethics are radically different enterprises.[2] The chapter will argue that the Epicureans defend a kind of ethical naturalism in this sense.

In defending a kind of ethical naturalism, the Epicureans broadly align themselves with other thinkers of Greco-Roman antiquity who might also be described broadly as naturalist. In contradistinction to these other ancient thinkers who include nonsensible, supernatural, or divine entities as important explanatory principles in their respective ethical theories, the Epicureans adopt an approach that minimizes the explanatory role of the nonsensible, supernatural, or divine in the ethical domain. We thus do not find in Epicureanism an appeal to an invisible measure (Solon), a *logos* (Heraclitus, the Stoics), a nonsensible Form (Plato),[3] or the gods in general. Instead, the Epicurean approach explains what is moral by drawing only on the *empirical* investigation of nature. Recall here especially the bottom-up etiological explanation of the creation of the world from atoms and void in book V of Lucretius' *On the Nature of Things* and the rejection

---

[1] See, for instance, Sturgeon 2006; Dowell 2013; and Lenman 2014.
[2] Darwall et al. 1992, 128–30 and passim.
[3] Plato's case is complicated insofar as a Form as an "οὐσία ὄντως οὖσα" (*Phaedrus* 247c7), that is, the only truly existing entity, is a natural entity. Nevertheless, these natural entities, on the Platonic view, are grasped not by an empirical means but rather by reason.

of all supernatural causes as explanatory principles (for instance, the gods).[4] This need not mean that all explanations in Epicurean ethics should or do start with natural science and are straightforwardly reducible to it.[5] However, the mode of investigation in Epicurean ethics is modeled after the *empirical* mode of investigation in physics, which implies that Epicureans can always draw on the study of the natural world to refute rationalist metaphysical or religious assumptions that are to the detriment of a naturalistic ethical theory.

The Epicurean naturalist approach to ethics is much closer to Aristotle's approach than to those of other ancient schools.[6] According to Aristotle, one must first know what kind of beings human beings are before one can determine what their virtue (*aretē*) is. And this means that one must rely heavily on the empirical study of psychology to determine what is virtuous for human beings, that is, to know what capacities human beings have (in contrast to other beings), as the well-known function argument in Aristotle's *Nicomachean Ethics* makes clear. Now, Epicurus' ethics also importantly relies on psychology and, as we already saw, empirical means. However, it differs in substance from Aristotle's approach. In order to make clear how Epicurus' ethics is naturalistic, Nicholas Sturgeon's definition of ethical naturalism is a useful heuristic. According to Sturgeon, an ethical view is naturalistic if it fulfills two conditions, one metaphysical, the other epistemological:

> (a) that such ethical properties such as goodness of persons, character traits, and such things as the rightness and wrongness of actions, are natural properties of the same general sort as the properties investigated by the sciences, and (b) that they are investigated in the same general way that we investigate those properties.[7]

Using this definition as a guide, we will see in the following two sections that Epicurean naturalism meets the two conditions of ethical naturalism outlined by Sturgeon: (1) operating outside an Aristotelian substance-property ontology, the Epicureans understand justice to be a property just

---

[4] An interesting case in point is the Epicurean appropriation and secularization of the originally Platonic ideal of the assimilation to the divine (*homoiōsis theōi*). For a detailed discussion (and further references), see Hahmann and Robitzsch 2021. Likewise, the perception of the gods through a kind of sixth sense may at first seem like a nonnaturalist feature of Epicurean epistemology. However, even this feature is a thoroughly naturalized feature of Epicurean epistemology. See Robitzsch 2021.
[5] For some discussion, see Sedley 1988; Furley 1993; and O'Keefe 1997.
[6] On Aristotelian ethical naturalism, see Annas 2005 and Hursthouse 2013.
[7] Sturgeon 2006, 92. As Sturgeon goes on to note, much in the definition depends on what counts as a natural property. According to Sturgeon, this at the very least entails a rejection of the supranatural.

like other properties (Section 6.1) and (2) the Epicureans claim that justice can be known in the same way that other sensible properties are known, namely, via sense experience (Section 6.2).

6.1 The Ontology of the Moral: Justice as a Property

In order to classify the just from an ontological perspective on the Epicurean view, we need to review some key features of Epicurean ontology.[8] Starting from sense experience, the Epicureans argue that bodies are independently existing entities (*kath' heauta phuseis/ per se naturae*) in the world, that is, entities that do not depend on other entities for their existence.[9] Observing also that bodies move, they quickly add that movement requires the existence of the void, yielding the second basic entity of the world. Body is characterized by shape, weight, and size, while void is characterized by its nonresistance to body.[10] The Epicureans contend that there cannot be any third entity besides body and void; everything that exists in some way can be reduced to one of these two entities, which can each be described further, especially, body, with the help of a sophisticated atomic theory.

Given the Epicurean emphasis on body, one might first be tempted to assume that the just is also a kind of body, perhaps an atomistic one. On this view, an entity that is a cherry on the macroscopic/phenomenological level would be made up of many cherry atoms on the microscopic level.[11] However, the Epicureans explain the relationship between features of macroscopic and microscopic bodies in a different way. For them, it is the *properties* of atoms making up the cherry that determine the properties of the cherry on the macroscopic level, not the fact that the atoms are themselves microscopic cherries. The atoms of a cherry are, for instance, round and so glide more easily over the tongue than those of, say, a chili pepper, which are sharper. As a result, someone eating a chili experiences a

---

[8] For a more detailed account of Epicurean ontology, see Robitzsch 2020a.
[9] *Letter to Herodotus* 39–41 and 68. See also Lucretius, *On the Nature of Things* I.418–48.
[10] *Letter to Herodotus* 54 and Sextus Empiricus, *Against the Mathematicians* X.222. The exact relationship between body and void is contested among scholars: void might either be a simple complement to matter or, alternatively, it might be a kind of space, which matter occupies. For the different readings, see Sedley 1982 and Konstan 2014.
[11] This would be somewhat similar to the views of Anaxagoras of Clazomenae (fifth century BCE), who argues that the preponderance of certain component parts makes a certain thing the thing in question (even if unlike the Epicureans, Anaxagoras also assumes that traces of everything are contained in everything). Lucretius explicitly criticizes such a view at *On the Nature of Things* I.830–920.

6.1 The Ontology of the Moral: Justice as a Property

fiery sensation, whereas someone eating a cherry does not.[12] Put differently, shape, form, size, and arrangement of the atoms (which themselves do not have any further properties than the ones just mentioned) give rise to additional properties on the macroscopic level.[13] Accordingly, justice itself is not a type of atom or body on the Epicurean view.

Besides body and void, the Epicureans recognize the existence of properties, arguing for a kind of bundle theory by rejecting the substance-property ontology espoused by Aristotle.[14] In particular, they distinguish between *sumbebēkota/coniuncta*, on the one hand, and *sumptōmata/eventa*, on the other.[15] By the former, the Epicureans mean features that attach to entities and make the entity in question this particular entity, whereas by the latter, they mean features that attach to entities and that the entity can lose without ceasing to be the entity in question. For instance, from an ancient perspective, fire may not lose the feature of being hot and dry, since this makes fire fire. Without the *sumbebēkon* of being hot and dry, fire is extinguished. By contrast, a human being does not cease to be a human being if she loses a part or all of her hair. The feature of having hair is a *sumptōma*. In short, we may say that *sumptōmata* are accidental properties, whereas *sumbēbekota* are essential properties.

Lucretius provides us with several examples of accidental and essential properties on the Epicurean view: slavery, poverty, wealth, freedom, war, and concord are examples of the former, and heaviness in rocks, heat in fire, liquidity in water, touch in matter, and intangibility in void are examples of the latter.[16] The former series covers examples of properties in the human and sociopolitical sphere, while the later series covers examples from the nonhuman and natural life world sphere. Accordingly, it seems on the basis of the list that Lucretius provides that justice is most likely an accidental property, not an essential one.[17]

---

[12] Lucretius, *On the Nature of Things* II.730–841.
[13] While many Epicurean texts suggest that the reduction of higher-level phenomenal features to lower-level atomic ones is straightforward, there is also some evidence in regard to mixtures that points to a different view. Alexander of Aphrodisias reports that the Epicureans maintain that a mixture may have different properties than its constituent elements; that is, mixtures can have properties that are over and above the properties of the constituent ingredients. Fr. 290 Usener (= Alexander of Aphrodisias, *On Mixture* 214.28–215.8 Bruns).
[14] Betegh 2006, 279–82 *pace* Sorabji 1988, 47–8.
[15] *Letter to Herodotus* 68–71; see also Sextus Empiricus, *Against the Mathematicians* X.221–3.
[16] Lucretius, *On the Nature of Things* I.453–7.
[17] See also Glidden 1985, 212–13; and Alberti 1995, 180–5 (*pace* Morel 2000, 403–5, whose view will be discussed in more detail below).

The best positive, albeit indirect, evidence for the claim that justice is an accidental property on the Epicurean view is found in Polystratus' *On Irrational Contempt for Common Conceptions*. This text shows not only that there are normative properties but also that these normative properties are ontologically indistinguishable from nonnormative properties according to the Epicureans (which satisfies the metaphysical condition of Sturgeon's definition of ethical naturalism).[18]

Polystratus' discussion of normative properties occurs in the context of the refutation of the (admittedly somewhat absurd) view of an unnamed opponent who offers a kind of argument from disagreement. According to this argument, normative entities like the honorable (*kalon*) and shameful (*aischron*) do not exist at all on the grounds that they are relative to place and perceiver, which, for instance, "truly existing" natural kinds (that is, bodies) such as bronze and gold are not, since they are the same for everyone everywhere:

> [ο]ὐθὲν γὰρ τούτων εἶναι κατ' ἀλήθειαν· δεῖν γάρ, εἴπερ ἦν, ὥσπ[ερ] ὁ κατ' ἀλήθ[ε]ιαν χαλκὸ[ς ἢ χ]ρυσὸς πᾶσ[ι] καὶ πανταχ[οῦ] ὁμοίως ἐ[σ]τιν, καὶ οὐ τ[ῶι]δε μέν ἐστιν χαλκός, <τ>ῶιδε δ' οὔ, οὐδ' ἐμ μὲν <τ>ούτωι τῶι ἔθνει ἐστίν, [ἐ]ν δ[ὲ τοῖς] λοιποῖς οὐκέτι, [ἀλλὰ παν]ταχοῦ ὁμοίως, οὕ[τω κ]αὶ τὰ καλὰ καὶ τὰ ἀ[ισχρά, ε]ἴπερ κατ' ἀλήθ[ειαν ἦν], οὐ τῶ<ι>δε μὲν δι[ώ]κε[σθαι], τῶι[δε δ'] οὐκέ[τι] ὡ[μολ]ο[γῆσθαι].

> None of these [normative entities like the honorable and shameful] in fact truly exist. For it is necessary that if they were just as bronze and gold, which truly exist, the same everywhere and for everyone (and not for one [something] is bronze, for another it is not, nor for one people [something] exists and for another it does not, but it is in the same way everywhere), then also honorable and the shameful things, if they truly existed, would not be pursued by one person and not recognized by another person.[19]

In response, Polystratus denies the premise that the relativity of an entity entails its nonexistence. In doing so, he compares the honorable and the shameful to relative two-place predicates such as "*x* is bigger than *y*," arguing that because these predicates also change from place to place, yet are said to exist, it would be absurd to say that the honorable and shameful and similar entities, in virtue of the fact that they change from place to place, do not exist, either:

---

[18] On Polystratus' text, see, for example, Isnardi Parente 1971; Bett 1994; 144–8; Alberti 1996; Warren 2002, 142–9; and Giovacchini and Lemaire 2014.

[19] Polystratus, *On Irrational Contempt for Common Conceptions*, cols. XXI.27–XXII.18 Indelli. Trans. mine.

6.1 The Ontology of the Moral: Justice as a Property

ἐμποδὼν γὰρ ἑκάστωι δήπου συνορᾶν, ὡς οὐδὲ μεῖζον καὶ ἔλαττο[ν] τὸ αὐτὸ πανταχοῦ [κ]αὶ πρὸς πάντα τὰ μεγέ[θ]η ὁρᾶτα[ι, οὐδ'] ὡσαύ[τως τὸ] ἡδὺ [καὶ τὸ ἀηδὲς ... [lacuna] ...] ὡσαύτως [δὲ καὶ ἐ]πὶ τῶν βαρυτέρων καὶ κουφοτέρων συμβέβηκεν, καὶ ἐπὶ τῶν λοι[π]ῶν δ' ἁπλῶ[ς] δυνάμε[ν]ων τὸν αὐτὸν τρόπον ἔχει. οὔτε γὰρ ὑγιεινὰ ταὐτὰ πᾶσιν ὑπάρχει οὔτε θρεπτικὰ ἢ φθαρτικὰ οὔτε τὰ τούτοις ἐναντία, ἀλλὰ ταὐτὰ τοὺς μὲν ὑγιάζει καὶ τρέφει, τοὺς δ' ἐκ τ[ῶν ἐ]ναντίων διατίθησιν. ὥστε ἢ καὶ ταῦτα πάντα φατέον [[λ]] ψευδῆ εἶναι, ἃ περιφανῶς ἕκαστος θεωρεῖ ὃ ἐργάζεται, ἤ, μὴ βουλόμενον ἀναισχυντεῖν καὶ μάχεσθαι τοῖς φανεροῖς, οὐδὲ τὰ καλὰ καὶ τὰ αἰσχρὰ ἀρτέον ὡς ψευδῶς νομιζόμενα, ὅτι οὐ πᾶσι ταὐτά ἐστιν ὥσπερ λίθος ἢ χρυ[σὸ]ς ἢ [ἄλλ]ο [τι τῶν τοιούτων.]

It is evident to each person that the bigger and the smaller are not perceived the same everywhere and in regard to all magnitudes, and likewise the pleasant and the unpleasant [... lacuna ...] So too with the heavier and the lighter. And the same applies also to the other powers. For neither are the same [things] healthy for everyone nor nourishing nor fatal nor the opposites of these, but the very same entities are healthy and nourishing to some yet have the opposite effect on others. Therefore either they must say that these too are false – things whose effects are plain for everyone to see – or else they must refuse to brazen it out and to battle with what is evident, and not to abolish honorable and shameful [things] as falsely believed in as well, just because unlike stone and gold or [others that are such-like] they are not the same for all.[20]

We can put aside the question of whether Polystratus' defense is fully convincing and instead focus on a point of detail. In this text, Polystratus at least to some extent allows for the parallel treatment of entities like the honorable and the shameful, which are normative, and entities like larger and smaller, which are not (with health being an interesting middle case that might be understood descriptively or normatively). We should also note that in contradistinction to the examples in Lucretius discussed above, the text does not discuss largeness and smallness as such, but rather the relative properties of being larger and smaller, which would certainly not be essential properties on the Epicurean view, but rather accidental properties. Since larger, smaller, heavier, lighter, and so on are accidental properties, it follows that the passage claims that the honorable and the shameful, that is, normative properties, must be ontologically similar to them. Normative properties like the honorable and the shameful will thus turn out to be accidental properties. While Polystratus does not mention the just in his account, it seems that the just is of the same kind as the normative entities

---

[20] Ibid., cols. XXIV.8–XXV.15 Indelli. Trans. Long and Sedley, modified [= Long and Sedley 1987, 7C].

described in the passage. As a result, the just would also be an accidental property and it would be a property that is ontologically similar to other nonmoral accidental properties.

We should quickly add at this point that there is also no evidence to the contrary that normative properties ought to be treated differently in Epicureanism. Given the plethora of attacks on the Epicureans that have survived, it would be strange that hostile authors did not pick up on and did not take the Epicureans to task if they had endorsed what, in antiquity, would have been perceived as an unusual view. In general, it would very much fit into the state of the ancient debate if the Epicureans just like other schools treated moral and nonmoral properties alike from an ontological perspective. Recall, for instance, that while the exact scope of the Platonic theory of Forms is a matter of debate, at least according to some understanding thereof, the theory extends to both nonnormative entities like the tall as well as to normative ones such as the honorable, the beautiful, and the just.[21]

This, then, establishes the first, metaphysical condition of ethical naturalism laid out above, namely, that "ethical properties such as goodness of persons, character traits, and such things as the rightness and wrongness of actions, are natural properties of the same general sort as the properties investigated by the sciences,"[22] on the Epicurean view. However, it also leaves open the hard question of what exactly justice is an accidental property of. There is no direct textual evidence on this point, and it seems possible that the Epicureans may not have fully worked out a satisfying answer to the question. Nevertheless, before turning to the second, epistemological condition of Epicurean ethical naturalism in the next section, we will consider some potential solutions.

In regard to the ontological status of the accidental property of justice in Epicureanism, it will first be argued in what follows that justice comes to be by an agreement and that an agreement is an event, which in turn is best understood as an accidental property dependent on the bodies and space involved in the event. Furthermore, however, the Epicureans also claim that agreements can cease to be just. This means that the just is not simply identical with the agreement itself, but is a property of certain agreements. Nevertheless, Epicurus probably only thought that the just is an accidental property without specifying further that the just is an accidental property of an accidental property. Finally, Morel's suggestion that the just is an accidental as well as an essential property will be

---

[21] See, for instance, Plato, *Parmenides* 130a–d.   [22] Sturgeon 2006, 92.

6.1 The Ontology of the Moral: Justice as a Property 135

discussed and rejected, giving rise to a broader discussion of how different kinds of entities can be said to be just (and unjust) on the Epicurean view.

The obvious starting point for a discussion of the ontological status of justice is the observation that justice, on the Epicurean view, is an agreement. While we do not have a direct statement on the ontological status of agreements in Epicureanism, there is some evidence that agreements might be events and as such should be treated as accidental properties of the bodies that were involved in them and the space in which they occurred. This is precisely what Lucretius argues against unnamed opponents[23] who maintain that the Epicureans have to admit that past events exist independently (that is, like bodies and void on the Epicurean view and not as properties):

> denique Tyndaridem raptam belloque subactas
> Troiugenas gentis cum dicunt esse, videndumst
> ne forte haec per se cogant nos esse fateri,
> quando ea saecla hominum, quorum haec eventa fuerunt,
> inrevocabilis abstulerit iam praeterita aetas.
> namque aliud terris, aliud regionibus ipsis
> eventum dici poterit quod cumque erit actum.
> denique materies si rerum nulla fuisset
> nec locus ac spatium, res in quo quaeque geruntur,
> numquam Tyndaridis forma conflatus amore
> ignis Alexandri Phrygio sub pectore gliscens
> clara accendisset saevi certamina belli
> nec clam durateus Troianis Pergama partu
> inflammasset equus nocturno Graiugenarum;
> perspicere ut possis res gestas funditus omnis
> non ita uti corpus per se constare neque esse
> nec ratione cluere eadem qua constet inane,
> sed magis ut merito possis eventa vocare
> corporis atque loci, res in quo quaeque gerantur.

Again, when they assert that the rape of Tyndareus' daughter [= Helen] and the subjugation of the people of Troy "exist," beware of the possibility of being trapped by them into an acknowledgement that these exist in themselves [*per se esse*], simply because those generations of human beings, of whom they were accidental properties [*eventa*], have been swept away beyond recall by ages past. For it could be said that any action [*actum*] is an accidental property [*eventum*] of the whole earth or of the actual regions in which it occurred. Moreover, if there had been no material substance, and no place and space in which all things happen, the beauty of Tydareus'

---

[23] Robitzsch forthcoming c argues that these unnamed opponents are the Stoics.

daughter would never have fanned into flame the fire of passion smoldering deep in Phrygian Alexander's heart, so kindling the blazing strife of savage war; nor would the wooden horse, unknown to the Trojans, have discharged from its pregnant womb under cover of night the Greeks who filled Pergama with flames. From this you may clearly see that all events [*res gestae*] without exception have, unlike matter, no independent existence [*per se esse*], and cannot be said to exist in the same sense as void; rather you may with justification term them accidental properties [*eventa*] of matter, or of space in which all things happen.[24]

Although the focus of the passage is on past events (*res gestae*), the Epicureans can easily generalize the explanation and classify all events in the same terms. As a result, agreements of justice will also turn out to be accidental properties, being dependent on the bodies and the space where they occur.[25]

The problem with this explanation is that it will go only so far. While agreements themselves can be explained as accidental properties of the contracting parties involved in the agreement and the space in which the agreements occur, we also know that agreements can cease to be just. This means that the just cannot always be identical with the agreement, even if the agreement is the etiological origin of justice. Since an agreement will stay an agreement, even if it ceases to be just,[26] one might think that therefore justice is an accidental property of an agreement. Justice would thus turn out to be an accidental property of an accidental property.

The proposal might sound strange at first, but there is some evidence that the second-century BCE Epicurean Demetrius Lacon thought that time is precisely such an accidental property of an accidental property:

> συμπτώματα οὖν ταῦτ' ἐστιν οἷς χρόνος παρέπεται, φημὶ δὲ τήν τε ἡμέραν καὶ νύκτα καὶ ὥραν καὶ τὰ πάθη καὶ τὰς ἀπαθείας, κινήσεις τε καὶ μονάς. ἥ τε γὰρ ἡμέρα καὶ νὺξ τοῦ περιέχοντος ἀέρος εἰσὶ συμπτώματα, ὧν ἡ μὲν ἡμέρα κατὰ τὸν ἐξ ἡλίου φωτισμὸν συμβαίνει, ἡ δὲ νὺξ κατὰ φωτισμοῦ στέρησιν τοῦ ἐξ ἡλίου ἐπιγίνεται. ἡ δὲ ὥρα ἤτοι τῆς ἡμέρας ἢ τῆς νυκτὸς μέρος καθεστηκυῖα πάλιν σύμπτωμα γίνεται τοῦ ἀέρος, ὥσπερ καὶ ἡ ἡμέρα καὶ ἡ νύξ. ἀντιπαρεκτείνεται δὲ πάσῃ ἡμέρᾳ καὶ πάσῃ νυκτὶ καὶ ὥρᾳ ὁ χρόνος· ... τά τε πάθη καὶ αἱ ἀπάθειαι ἤτοι ἀλγηδόνες ἢ ἡδοναὶ ἐτύγχανον, διὰ δὲ τοῦτο οὐκ οὐσίαι τινὲς καθειστήκεισαν, ἀλλὰ συμπτώματα τῶν πασχόντων ἤτοι ἡστικῶς ἢ ἀλγεινῶς, καὶ

---

[24] Lucretius, *On the Nature of Things* I.464–81. Trans. Smith, modified.
[25] On the ontological status of events in Epicurean theory, see also Warren 2006b, 368–77.
[26] For instance, it was argued in detail in Chapter 5 in discussing Epicurean natural law theory that, on the Epicurean view, a law will remain a law, even if it is no longer just.

6.1 The Ontology of the Moral: Justice as a Property

συμπτώματα οὐκ ἄχρονα. πρὸς τούτοις καὶ ἡ κίνησις, ἔτι δὲ ἡ μονή, ὡς ἤδη παρεστήσαμεν, τῶν σωμάτων ἐστὶ συμπτώματα καὶ οὐ χωρὶς χρόνου· τὴν γοῦν ὀξύτητα καὶ βραδυτῆτα τῆς κινήσεως, ἔτι δὲ τὴν πλείονα καὶ ἐλάττονα μονὴν χρόνῳ καταμετροῦμεν.

Hence the things which time accompanies are accidental properties – I mean day, night, hour, presence and absence of feelings, motion and rest. For day and night are accidental properties of the surrounding air: day becomes its attribute because of its illumination from the sun, while night supervenes because of its deprivation of illumination from the sun. And the hour, being a part either of day or of night, is also an accidental property of the air just as day and night are. And coextensive with every day, night and hour is time.... As for presence and absence of feelings, these are either pains or pleasures, and hence they are not substances, but accidental qualities of those who feel pleasant or painful – and not timeless accidental properties. In addition, motion and likewise rest are also, as we have already established [immediately prior to the passage quoted, JMR], accidental properties of bodies and not timeless: for the speed and slowness of motion, and likewise the greater and smaller amount of rest, we measure with time.[27]

Sextus Empiricus, who reports Demetrius' views, introduces his account with the comment that Demetrius does not make an independent claim in the passage but "interprets [*exēgeitai*]" Epicurus. It is difficult to assess what this precisely means. It could mean that Epicurus really said what Demetrius is claiming he said. Alternatively, the passage could also be Demetrius' "interpretation" and development of Epicurean ideas.

The latter alternative seems to be, however, far more likely than the former.[28] First, when Epicurus discusses perception (*aisthēsis*) at *Letter to Herodotus* 64 as an accidental property, he notes that perception is such a property because the body has it not in virtue of itself but in virtue of its connection to the soul. However, he does not describe perception as an accidental property of an accidental or essential property (that is, of being ensouled). And in fact, there are no other extant discussions or examples of properties of properties in any Epicurean or in fact any non-Epicurean text of the time. This makes it rather unlikely that such properties were a generally accepted doctrine in Epicureanism. One would have to think that critics of Epicurean philosophy would have also picked up and commented on these ontological entities.

---

[27] Sextus Empiricus, *Against the Mathematicians* X.224–7. Trans. Long and Sedley, modified [= Long and Sedley 1987, 7D].
[28] See Robitzsch 2020a, 210–11.

Second, Epicurus' main interest was in setting out the outlines of his philosophical system that enabled agents to lead a life free from bodily pain and mental distress. In comparison to this goal, the exact ontological status of time is at best a subsidiary question. As such, however, it seems that the question could be the ideal sandbox for later (and lesser) Epicureans like Demetrius to introduce an innovation, working out in greater detail the Epicurean philosophical system.

In summary, then, while there is some evidence for the existence of accidental properties of accidental properties (that is, time), the explicit identification of such properties is the likely product of a later development in the school. Although the reading of time that Demetrius offers is compatible with other ideas in Epicureanism, it is not at all clear that Epicurus would have also classified time as an accidental property of an accidental property rather than simply an accidental property.

In contrast to the reading that justice is an accidental property, Pierre-Marie Morel has argued that justice is both an accidental and an essential property.[29] First, pointing to the term "*sustrophē*" that is used in *KD* 33 ("Justice is not anything in itself, but an agreement over not harming and not being harmed *en tais met' allēllōn sustrophais*"), Morel argues that this term is typically used in Epicurean physics to describe an aggregation of atoms of some kind.[30] Accordingly, while a human community is not identical with a body, it, like a body, can be said to have various properties, one of which is justice:

> It is striking to what extent the status of the *dikaion* [just] in *KD* 33 corresponds to that of *sumbebēkota* [essential properties]: it does not have an existence "by itself" and it constitutes an inseparable property of human groups [*groupements humains*]. What is more, according to *Letter to Herodotus* 69 *sumbebēkota* give a body its permanent nature, while accidents "do not have the nature of the whole which they describe."[31]

Yet while justice is first and foremost an essential property for Morel, there is also a further aspect to it, which Morel explains by likening the

---

[29] This view is most prominently defended in Morel 2000, 404. See also the discussion in Giussani 1896, 27–38.
[30] *Letter to Herodotus* 73 and 77 and Diogenes of Oenoanda, fr. 14.4 Smith. The LSJ cites *KD* 33 as the passage that is supposed to show that the term means "dealings."
[31] "Il est frappant de voir à quel point le statut du δίκαιον de la MC XXXIII correspond à celui des συμβεβηκότα: il n'a pas d'existence 'par soi' et il constitue une propriété inséparable et permanente des groupements humains. Plus encore, ce sont les συμβεβηκότα, d'après le paragraphe 69 de la Lettre a Herodote, qui donnent au corps sa 'nature' constante, alors que les accidents 'n'ont pas la nature du tout qu'ils caractérisent.'" Morel 2000, 404. Trans. mine. In this context, see also Fowler 1989, 145–8.

6.1 The Ontology of the Moral: Justice as a Property

property of justice to that of color. Not only is every body colored, that is, has the essential property of possessing some color or other, but it also has a determinate color that is not a necessary feature of the body in question, that is, is an accidental property of the body. On this proposal, justice, then, is understood to be an essential property of human groups, since a human group could not exist without justice, whereas the determinate way that a human group is just may be different from the way in which some other group is just, which is an accidental property of that human group.

This proposal is certainly interesting. However, it is unclear why justice needs to be an *essential* property of human groups. Recall that, by definition, an essential property is a property that an entity cannot lose without ceasing to be the entity in question. This means that when a human group loses the essential property of being just, it would also cease being a group. This does not seem plausible, though. While it seems right that in order for there to be a *real community* among human beings, for instance, a certain minimal amount of justice will be required, it is also right that the same human beings would still remain a group in some sense – a motley crew that one could identify – if they did not possess the property of being just. After all, such a reading would align much better with what we already observed in regard to agreements and laws than Morel's proposal: while agreements and laws are ideally just, they *do not* cease to be agreements or laws altogether when they become unjust on the Epicurean view.

Regarding the second part of Morel's proposal (that justice can also be understood as both an accidental property and an essential property), one should first note that it is not backed up by textual evidence. When Lucretius enumerates accidental properties at *On the Nature of Things* I.455–6, for instance, he does not indicate that the very same property can be understood as an *eventum* and *coniunctum* at the same time. And there is no example of any property that is both an accidental and an essential property of the same entity given anywhere in the entire corpus of Epicurean writings that has come down to us.[32] Second and more importantly, Morel seems to understand the distinction between *eventa* and *coniuncta* as the distinction between determinable and determinate properties (that is, being a color and being red or being just and being just in a specific way). Although there are some commentators who understand

---

[32] Being in movement is both an essential and accidental property of different bodies (an essential property of atomic bodies and an accidental property of macroscopic bodies), but note that being in movement is not an essential and accidental property of the very same body.

Aristotle's comments on the relation between genus and specific difference as a precursor to the distinction between determinable and determinate properties, most of the evidence that pertains to this distinction (including the explicit articulation of the distinction itself) is much more recent.[33] Furthermore, as is well known, Epicurus' access to Aristotelian ideas was likely not through Aristotle's own writings, but indirectly, through the writings of others at best;[34] accordingly, without further evidence to the contrary, we should be careful to think that Epicurus borrowed the distinction from Aristotle (or another ancient philosopher) and that it should be ascribed to him anachronistically. So while it is possible that Epicurus may have drawn the distinction between determinate and determinable properties, *pace* Morel, justice is thus more safely understood to be *only* an accidental property on the Epicurean view.

We have so far encountered just agreements and laws as well as just communities. It seems, though, that these entities are not just in exactly the same way. Just agreements are just with reference to what is beneficial, whereas laws, communities, people, and actions can only be called "just" in reference to agreements that are or were in place at some point and that are or were beneficial. Accordingly, it seems most probable that, on the Epicurean view, even Aristides the Just will not be essentially just, but only accidentally just with reference to what is agreed upon in certain agreements, and that a certain action will not be essentially just, but only just with reference to what is agreed upon in a certain agreement.

Finally, let us finish with some remarks on unjust agreements and laws. How can these arise? First, on the view advanced here, it is clear that agreements can arise that do not have the property of being just, namely, insofar as they do not aim at what is beneficial. Likewise, agreements can become unjust if they previously aimed at what is beneficial and if what is beneficial has changed. The case for laws is slightly more complicated. As we saw in Chapter 1, a law is a type of agreement that is distinct from the agreements of justice. Accordingly, there will already be agreements of justice in place when laws are first legislated. These laws will now be called "just" or "unjust" with reference to the agreements of justice that are or were in place. If they are in alignment with these agreements, then the laws will be called just; if they are not in alignment with these agreements, they

---

[33] See Wilson 2017.
[34] See the detailed discussion in Kamp 2001, 201–40 (with a focus on Epicurus' engagement with *On the* Soul); and Verde 2016.

will be called unjust. And given that what is just can change in the way described above, the laws may also gain or lose the property of being just.

6.2 Moral Epistemology

For the Epicureans, compound bodies, that is, the macroscopic bodies of human everyday life, emit a constant stream of images (*eidōla*).[35] These images are material, like the bodies that emit them; that is, they are three-dimensional hollow replicas of the things of which they are images. For instance, the cat lying on the couch, which has the typical form of a cat, emits very fine images or replicas of itself; these are themselves cat-shaped and perfectly reproduce its features. These cat images then travel through space. When they eventually reach a perceiver's sensory apparatus, it processes the images and gives the perceiver the impression (*phantasia*) of a cat. This impression, the Epicureans claim, is always true; error is introduced only if the image is processed incorrectly through some mental operation.[36] In this case, the mind inadvertently adds or subtracts something from the original image, which falsifies the testimony given by the senses. If the process of seeing is repeated, perceivers are able to learn: repeatedly seeing the same or similar objects, a cat or cats, allows them to form a kind of initial concept thereof, a so-called preconception (*prolēpsis*; pl. *prolēpseis*). This gives perceivers a functional understanding of the thing they perceived, enabling them to reliably recognize an object as the thing in question and act accordingly. In short, then, when it comes to how we come to having an understanding of the world around us, the Epicureans agree with the classical empiricist claim that there is nothing in the mind that was not previously in the senses.

For the purposes of this section, we can largely set aside all the miscellaneous problems that concern the details of the Epicurean account of perception. Instead, we can turn to the neglected question of what

---

[35] The most important passages to reconstruct the Epicurean theory of images are *Letter to Herodotus* 46–53; and Lucretius, *On the Nature of Things* IV.26–822. Also relevant is the discussion in Book II of *On Nature* (ed. Leone), although the state of the text is quite fragmentary. According to Diogenes Laërtius (*Lives of Eminent Philosophers* X.28), Epicurus wrote the treatises *On Images* (Περὶ εἰδώλων) and *On Impressions* (Περὶ φαντασίας), but these have not come down to us. On the Epicurean theory of knowledge, see Asmis 1984; Jürss 1991; and Hahmann and Robitzsch 2022. While the below focuses on vision, the account can be easily adapted to smell and hearing. Touch and taste rely not on images but instead on a direct contact with the object. Besides this difference, however, the below comments can easily explain these two senses as well.

[36] See Diogenes Laërtius, *Lives of Eminent Philosophers* X.31–2; and Lucretius, *On the Nature of Things* IV.479–521. The latter passage discusses the famous case of the square tower that appears round when seen at a distance.

consequences this standard account has for Epicurean moral epistemology. Do the Epicureans think that the moral case is analogous to the nonmoral case just sketched? In other words, do perceivers come to have an understanding that something is just in the same way that they learn that something is black? Some commentators simply do not discuss the question directly[37] or think that we cannot say anything definitive about the formation of the preconception of justice.[38] Others, by contrast, think that the preconception of justice is formed in a different way than other preconceptions are formed.[39] Finally, those commentators who are favorable to the view that the just is investigated in the same way that nonmoral properties are investigated typically content themselves to assert this view, without providing further support or elaboration.[40] This section aims to fill the lacuna. First, on the basis of some neglected direct evidence in Hermarchus, it will be argued that the Epicureans claim that even moral properties can be observed by the senses (Section 6.2.1). Second, by drawing on the Epicurean account of how preconceptions are formed, it will be shown by means of an additional, independent argument that what is just is directly perceived (Section 6.2.2).[41]

6.2.1 The Direct Perception of Justice

Much of Hermarchus' genealogy, which we already encountered in previous chapters, centers on the beneficial (*to sumpheron*), not on what is just. However, one may quickly add that the end of the passage preserved in Porphyry makes clear that the author also considers justice to be a kind of benefit:

> Εἰ μὲν οὖν ἠδύναντο ποιήσασθαί τινα συνθήκην ὥσπερ πρὸς ἀνθρώπους οὕτω καὶ πρὸς τὰ λοιπὰ τῶν ζώων ὑπὲρ τοῦ μὴ κτείνειν μήτε πρὸς ἡμῶν ἀκρίτως αὐτὰ κτείνεσθαι, καλῶς εἶχε μέχρι τούτου τὸ δίκαιον ἐξάγειν· ἐπιτεταμένον γὰρ ἐγίγνετο πρὸς τὴν ἀσφάλειαν. Ἐπειδὴ δὲ τῶν ἀμηχάνων ἦν κοινωνῆσαι νόμου τὰ μὴ δεχόμενα τῶν ζώων λόγον, διὰ μὲν τοῦ τοιούτου τρόπου τὸ συμφέρον οὐκ οἷόν τε κατασκευάσασθαι πρὸς τὴν ἀπὸ τῶν ἄλλων ἐμψύχων ἀσφάλειαν μᾶλλόν περ ἢ τῶν ἀψύχων.

---

[37] Fine 2014, 235–7.   [38] Manuwald 1972, 84–7.   [39] Asmis 2010 [2009], 87–90.
[40] Glidden 1985, 213; Longo Aurecchio 1988, 143–4; Armstrong 1997, 328–9; and Tsouna 2016, 170. A somewhat longer discussion is found in Müller 1987, 236–42, but even this is rather abbreviated.
[41] The rather difficult question of whether and how feelings (*pathē*) contribute to an understanding of what is just will be set aside here. On the relationship of perceptions and feelings as Epicurean criteria, see Robitzsch forthcoming b.

Now if people had been able to make an agreement with the rest of the animals as they did with human beings, not to kill and not to be killed indiscriminately by us, it would have been fine to push justice to that point, because it would tend to safety. But since it was an impossibility for animals that are not receptive of reason to share in law, this method could not be used to secure our advantage in respect of safety from other animate creatures, any more than from the inanimate.[42]

Furthermore, since other Epicurean texts make abundantly clear that what is just is merely a species of the beneficial, namely, what is beneficial in regard to the dealings with other human beings that has been codified by an agreement, as we already saw in previous chapters, it is possible to treat the beneficial as synonymous with the just in Hermarchus' genealogy. What is more, even if benefit were to differ substantially from justice, the beneficial, like the just, is a normative term. Accordingly, even if we were to take Hermarchus to claim only that what is beneficial can be directly perceived, such a reading would still establish a precedent, since it would show that the Epicureans think that at least one normative property can be perceived directly. This, again, would make it likely that the just, which is elsewhere understood as what is socially beneficial, can be perceived directly as well on the Epicurean view.

With this in mind, we can tackle the text directly, which addresses the issue of how agents come to learn what is beneficial. Hermarchus writes:

Διαμνημονεύοντες δέ τινες τῶν τότε χαριεστάτων ὡς αὐτοί τε ἀπέσχοντο τοῦ κτείνειν διὰ τὸ χρήσιμον πρὸς τὴν σωτηρίαν, τοῖς τε λοιποῖς ἐνεποίουν μνήμην τοῦ ἀποβαίνοντος ἐν ταῖς μετ' ἀλλήλων συντροφαῖς, ὅπως ἀπεχόμενοι τοῦ συγγενοῦς διαφυλάττωσι τὴν κοινωνίαν, ἣ συνήργει πρὸς τὴν ἰδίαν ἑκάστου σωτηρίαν. Οὐ μόνον δὲ χρήσιμον ἦν τὸ χωρίζεσθαι μηδὲ λυμαντικὸν ποιεῖν μηδὲν τῶν ἐπὶ τὸν αὐτὸν τόπον συνειλεγμένων πρὸς τὸ τῶν ἀλλοφύλων ἐξόρισμα ζῴων, ἀλλὰ καὶ πρὸς ἀνθρώπους τοὺς ἐπὶ βλάβῃ παραγιγνομένους. Μέχρι μὲν οὖν τινος διὰ ταύτην ἀπείχοντο τοῦ συγγενοῦς, ὅσον ἐβάδιζεν εἰς τὴν αὐτὴν κοινωνίαν τῶν ἀναγκαίων καὶ χρείας τινὰς παρείχετο πρὸς ἑκάτερον τῶν εἰρημένων· ἐλθόντος δὲ ἐπὶ πλέον τοῦ χρόνου καὶ τῆς δι' ἀλλήλων γενέσεως μακρὰν προηκούσης, ἐξωσμένων δὲ τῶν ἀλλοφύλων ζῴων καὶ τῆς παρασπάρσεως, ἐπιλογισμὸν ἔλαβον τινες τοῦ συμφέροντος ἐν ταῖς πρὸς ἀλλήλων τροφαῖς, οὐ μόνον ἄλογον μνήμην.

Some of the brightest people of that time, keeping in mind that they themselves abstained from killing because this is useful [*chrēsimon*][43] for

---

[42] Hermarchus, fr. 34 Longo Auricchio (= Porphyry, *On Abstinence* I.12.5–6). Trans. Clark, modified.
[43] "*Chrēsimon*" and "*sumpheron*" seem to be used as synonyms in Hermarchus.

security, reminded others what would result from their association with each other, so that abstaining from their kin they would safeguard the community, which was working for the individual security of each. Separating themselves out, and doing nothing to injure those who had gathered in the same place, was useful not only for excluding animals of other kinds, but also for dealing with human beings who came to do harm. For a time, then, they held back from their kinsman inasmuch as he was entering the same community for providing necessities and was making some contribution to both the purposes mentioned [that is, repelling threats from animals as well as from other human beings]. But as time went on and reproduction greatly increased, and other kinds of animals (and their dragging away of victims) had been driven out, some people acquired a reasoning [*epilogismos*] of what was beneficial [*sumpheron*] on their sustenance of each other, not just a nonrational memory [*alogos mnēmē*].[44]

In this passage, Hermarchus explicitly distinguishes between the brightest human beings who possess the capacity of "reasoning" (*epilogismos*) and those who merely have a "nonrational memory" (*alogos mnēmē*).[45] As we will see in more detail in the next section, a preconception is an *alogos mnēmē* as well: preconceptions are explicitly identified with memories and they are nonrational insofar as reason is not involved in any significant way in the process of their formation. Accordingly, it is tempting to suppose that Hermarchus' "nonrational memory" here is a preconception (even if it is not clear that *all* nonrational memories are also preconceptions for the Epicureans) and to think that the passage provides evidence for the fact that there are preconceptions as well as more elaborate concepts that involve further reasoning.

What exactly these more elaborate concepts are is somewhat unclear. Are these *ennoiai*, for instance, that are distinct from preconceptions as kinds of scientific concepts, or are they higher-level rational preconceptions? The latter claim has been made by Reimar Müller, who claims that the difference between the preeminent individuals and the others lies in the fact that the former have a second type of preconception, of higher generality, while the latter have preconceptions of lower generality.[46]

---

[44] Hermarchus fr. 34 Auricchio (= Porphyry, *On Abstinence* I.10.2–4). Trans. Clark, modified.
[45] What exactly "*epilogismos*" means is not quite clear. However, it may be a kind of comparative rational appraisal. For discussion, see Arrighetti 1952; De Lacy 1958; and especially Schofield 1996.
[46] See Müller 1987, 238. See also Jürss 1977, 221–2. Philodemus, *On Anger*, cols. XLIV.41–XLV.5 Armstrong and McOsker suggest that the Epicureans allowed that preconceptions are hierarchically structured; some preconceptions are more general than others: "It also pleases the leading men [= Epicurus, Hermarchus, Meterodorus, and Polyaenus] that the Sage does not become angry

We will discuss this alternative reading in more detail below, which is developed more systematically in Elizabeth Asmis' writings. For now, note merely that the passage claims (I) that there are lower and higher level understandings, some of which involve reasoning, some of which do not and (II) that what is beneficial can be an object of perception (more on this shortly).

In order to spell out Hermarchus' claims in more detail, let us consider the following passage, in which the above bipartite classification of perceivers is expanded to a tripartite schema. Hermarchus clearly distinguishes between (1) those who have knowledge (and who will be called "preeminent individuals"), (2) those who can obtain knowledge, but do not possess it yet (and who will be called "acolytes"), and (3) those who are ignorant (who will be called "ignoramuses"):[47]

> [A] Φρονήσει γὰρ ψυχῆς, οὐ ῥώμῃ σώματος καὶ δυναστευτικῇ δουλώσει τῶν ὄχλων διήνεγκαν οἱ τὰ τοιαῦτα τοῖς πολλοῖς εἰσηγούμενοι, [B] καὶ τοὺς μὲν εἰς ἐπιλογισμὸν τοῦ χρησίμου καταστήσαντες ἀλόγως αὐτοῦ πρότερον αἰσθανομένους καὶ πολλάκις ἐπιλανθανομένους, τοὺς δὲ τῷ μεγέθει τῶν ἐπιτιμίων καταπλήξαντες. [C] Οὐ γὰρ ἦν ἑτέρῳ χρῆσθαι φαρμάκῳ πρὸς τὴν τοῦ συμφέροντος ἀμαθίαν ἢ τῷ φόβῳ τῆς ἀφωρισμένης ἀπὸ τοῦ νόμου ζημίας.
>
> [A] Those who introduced such measures to the many excelled in practical wisdom of soul, not strength of the body or tyrannical enslavement of the masses. [B] They brought some people who previously perceived [*proteron aisthanomenous*] it, but without using reason [*alogōs*] and often forgetting it [*pollakis epilanthanomenous*], to reason about [*eis epilogismon*] the useful [*chrēsimon*], and the others they frightened by the severity of the punishments. [C] For no remedy could be used against ignorance [*amathia*] of what is beneficial [*sumpheron*] except the fear of the penalty laid down in the law.[48]

Hermarchus states that the preeminent individuals are those who bring certain people to reason about benefit, while they threaten others with punishment in (B). The acolytes are those who are brought to reason, and the ignoramuses are those who need to be threatened in (B) and (C). The epistemological vocabulary in the passage is quite striking, especially in

---

according to this preconception but according to a more general one [ἀρέσκει δὲ καὶ τοῖς καθηγεμόσιν οὐ τὸ κατ[ὰ] τὴν πρόληψιν [τ]αύτην θυμωθήσεσθαι τὸν σο[φ]όν, ἀλλὰ τὸ κατὰ τὴν κοι[ν]οτέραν]." Trans. mine.

[47] One should compare this passage with the comments on Epicurean moral development that are advanced in Seneca, *Moral Epistles* 52.3–4. But see also Giovacchini 2020, 55, as well as Chapter 4.

[48] Hermarchus, fr. 34 Longo Auricchio (= Porphyry, *On Abstinence* I.8.2–3). Trans. Clark, modified.

regard to the acolytes. They are said to *perceive* what is useful (just), and this perception, which the ignoramuses lack, is identified as a precondition for being able to calculate/reason out what is beneficial. However, the acolytes are also said to perceive the beneficial *without using reason* and they also often forget. Do the acolytes have an *alogos mnēme* of what is just? The text does not say this explicitly. However, it seems that they must have something in their mind so that there is something that can be the basis of them being brought to calculate and reason out.

In the same vein, consider the following passage, in which Hermarchus stresses that a full understanding of benefit is *only possible* after perceivers have had a "sufficient *perception* of it" (that is, of what is beneficial):

> οἱ μὲν παρακολουθήσαντες τῷ συμφέροντι τοῦ διορίσματος οὐδὲν προσεδεήθησαν ἄλλης αἰτίας τῆς ἀνειργούσης αὐτοὺς ἀπὸ τῆς πράξεως ταύτης, οἱ δὲ μὴ δυνάμενοι λαβεῖν αἴσθησιν ἱκανὴν τούτου τὸ μέγεθος τῆς ζημίας δεδιότες ἀπείχοντο τοῦ κτείνειν προχείρως ἀλλήλους.
>
> [S]ome people understood [*parakolouthēsantes*] the benefit of the decree, and required no other reason to keep them from this act; others, unable to achieve a sufficient perception of it [*hoi ... mē dunamenoi labein aisthēsin hikanēn*], refrained from readily killing each other because they feared the severity of the penalty.[49]

Unfortunately, Hermarchus does not spell out here what a sufficient perception is, and he does not comment on why certain people do not perceive what is just.[50] Possibly, the barriers to having an understanding of what is just are higher than those for seeing other objects, which might also explain why animals are not able to make agreements according to the Epicureans.[51] Be this as it may, the passages in Hermarchus imply that any perceiver who has an understanding of justice arrives at this understanding first and foremost through perception; recognizing what is just for the Epicureans truly means first and foremost recognizing what is before one's eyes.

One might object to the reading that "*aisthanomai*" and "*aisthēsis*" are used in Hermarchus in a figurative sense to mean "understand" and

---

[49] Hermarchus, fr. 34 Longo Auricchio (= Porphyry, *On Abstinence* I.7.3). Trans. Clark, modified.

[50] In regard to lacking the capacity to perceive what is beneficial or just, one might fill in the Epicurean account in different ways. For instance, some human beings simply do not have the hardware to have this perception (just like animals; see below). Alternatively, some human beings may not be capable given certain circumstances to perceive the just (perhaps there are no instantiations of the object in question in their phenomenal world).

[51] See *KD* 32 and the discussion in Chapter 2.

"understanding" rather than "perceive" and "perception." Unfortunately, the extant fragments of Hermarchus are not much of a help in addressing such a worry. However, an analysis of the extant writings of Epicurus, Philodemus, and Diogenes of Oenoanda provides evidence to the contrary.[52] In Epicurus, "*aisthanomai*" is used three times.[53] Except for *PHerc*. 176, where the meaning of the word is difficult to make out, the verb is clearly used in the sense of "perceive" and "sense" in the other two passages. The same is also true of Philodemus, who uses "*aisthanomai*" in three passages.[54] The verb is not used in a figurative sense in any of them. Diogenes of Oenoanda, by contrast, uses "*aisthanomai*" in a figurative sense in the *Letter to the Mother*,[55] but also in a nonfigurative sense elsewhere.[56] The noun "*aisthēsis*" is used by Epicurus in the *Letter to Herodotus*,[57] the *Letter to Pythocles*,[58] the *Letter to Menoeceus*,[59] *KD* 23 and 24 (two times in the latter maxim), and in some other passages.[60] In some of these passages, the term may mean "sense" rather than "perception." However, there is no clear case where the word has to mean "understanding" in a figurative sense. "Perception" is clearly the most dominant sense in which the word is used. This is also true of Philodemus[61] and Diogenes of Oenoanda[62] in regard to their usage of "*aisthēsis*": the word is typically used in the sense of "perception" or "sense," not "understanding" more broadly. In the overwhelming majority of instances, therefore, "*aisthanomai*" and "*aisthēsis*" have a nonfigural sense. When Hermarchus therefore claims that perceivers "perceive" what

---

[52] Since there is no database containing the current critical editions with the latest readings of Diogenes and Philodemus, the word indices of their respective writings were consulted. For Epicurus, the word index in Arrighetti's edition was consulted. If "*aisthanomai*" and "*aisthēsis*" were fully or partially added by an editor, these usages were not included here.
[53] *Letter to Herodotus* 66; Plutarch, *Against Colotes* 1100d: and fr. 59.1 Arrighetti (= *PHerc*. 176).
[54] Philodemus, *On Poems* II, col. CXCV.17–18 Janko; *On Piety* I.413–14 Obbink; and *PHerc*. 16/698, col. XXX.3–4 Monnet (this text is typically identified with Philodemus' *On the Senses*).
[55] Fr. 126.I.4. Smith.   [56] Fr. 43.I.13 Smith.
[57] 38, 39, 48, 55, 58, 59, 62, 63, 64, 65 (3x), 68 (2x), 71, and 82.   [58] 86, 90, and 91.   [59] 124.
[60] For instance, Diogenes Laërtius, *Lives of Eminent Philosophers* X.31 (2x) and 32 (3x); fr. 187 Usener (= *Gnomologicum Parisinum* 1168 f. 115 r.); as well as different papyri (= frr. 24.36.7, 24.48.3, 26.39.23, 26.42.8, 30.18 (2x), 31.5.3, 31.7.1, 31.8.8–9, and 36.11.4 Arrighetti).
[61] See, for instance, *On Death*, col. II.4 Henry; *On Methods of Inference*, cols. VI.3–4, XXIII.9, and fr. I.12 De Lacy and De Lacy; *On Music* IV, cols. XXVII.6, XXXIV.3–4, XXXIV.17, CXV.29, CXV.45 Delattre; *On Piety* I.138 Obbink; *On Poems* I, cols. LXXXVIII.21–2, CXXVIII.2 Janko; *On Poems* II, col. CLIX.6–7 Janko; *On Poems* V, cols. XXIII.25–6 and XXVIII.20 Mangoni; *Rhetoric* II.41, col. XLII.21 Sudhaus; *On the Gods* III, col. XIV.39 Diels; as well as *PHerc*. 19/698 (= Philodemus, *On the Senses*; multiple times). Philodemus, *On Frank Criticism*, fr. 29, Konstan et al. may be an exception, but note that most of the letters are supplied by the editors (see also the alternative way of reconstructing the passage offered by Philippson).
[62] Frr. 5.III.1, 10.I.13–14, 10.IV.12, and 147.13 Smith.

is beneficial or have a "perception" thereof, it is unlikely that this means merely that perceivers "understand" what is just if Hermarchus' usage of these terms is aligned with that of other Epicurean authors.

However, as is discussed in more detail in Appendix A, we cannot be entirely sure that the passage in Hermarchus is one in which Porphyry quotes Hermarchus verbatim. Accordingly, although this passage offers very strong support for the thesis that agents directly observe what is beneficial with the help of their sense perception, it would be imprudent to rely on this evidence alone, and in the next section we will turn to additional, independent evidence. Yet one should quickly add that a dismissal of Porphyry as a source for Hermarchus' view on this point, then, would more generally cast doubt on Hermarchus as a source for Epicurean ideas, which is a consequence that scholars of Epicureanism typically do not draw.

6.2.2 *The Preconception of Justice*

This section will offer an independent argument for the claim that perceivers can learn what is just in a similar way to how they learn other facts about the phenomenal world. It will discuss the way that preconceptions come to be according to the Epicureans, arguing that they are typically formed in a noninferential way. "Noninferentially" means that in forming a preconception, the mind *does not* draw an inference from a certain state of affairs to a more complex state of affairs as in an inference where premises are aggregated to obtain a certain conclusion.[63] This is equivalent to saying that reasoning (*epilogismos*) *is not involved in a substantive way* in the process of the formation of most preconceptions; rather, preconceptions are obtained in a way that is automatic and mechanical and truth-preserving, based on direct perceptions of the thing in question.

Because there is a preconception of justice and preconceptions typically come to be in a noninferential way according to the Epicureans, it follows that it is very likely that the just is also directly perceived on the Epicurean view. Put differently, the main argument of this section is as follows:

(P1) (Depending on the right circumstances,) perceivers are able to form a *prolēpsis* of justice.

(P2) A *prolēpsis* is a noninferential apprehension of an object.

(C1) (Depending on the right circumstances,) perceivers are able to form a noninferential apprehension of justice.

---

[63] See also Goldschmidt 2006 [1978], 159.

6.2 Moral Epistemology

(C2) Perceivers are able to come to know what is just in similar ways as they come to know other things in the phenomenological world.

P1 is established by *KD* 37 and 38.[64] This section will therefore focus on establishing P2 by drawing on Diogenes Laërtius' account of Epicurean teachings that establishes that preconceptions are noninferential apprehensions. Finally, at the end of the section objections to the argument will be addressed.

At *Lives of Eminent Philosophers* X.33, Diogenes Laërtius offers a detailed description of Epicurean preconceptions:

τὴν δὲ πρόληψιν λέγουσιν οἱονεὶ κατάληψιν ἢ δόξαν ὀρθὴν ἢ ἔννοιαν ἢ καθολικὴν νόησιν ἐναποκειμένην, τουτέστι μνήμην τοῦ πολλάκις ἔξωθεν φανέντος, οἷον τὸ τοιοῦτόν ἐστιν ἄνθρωπος·[65] ἅμα γὰρ τῷ ῥηθῆναι 'ἄνθρωπος' εὐθὺς κατὰ πρόληψιν καὶ ὁ τύπος αὐτοῦ νοεῖται προηγουμένων τῶν αἰσθήσεων. παντὶ οὖν ὀνόματι τὸ πρώτως ἐπιτεταγμένον ἐναργές ἐστι· καὶ οὐκ ἂν ἐζητήσαμεν τὸ ζητούμενον εἰ μὴ πρότερον ἐγνώκειμεν αὐτό· οἷον τὸ πόρρω ἑστὼς ἵππος ἐστὶν ἢ βοῦς;[66] δεῖ γὰρ κατὰ πρόληψιν ἐγνωκέναι ποτὲ ἵππου καὶ βοὸς μορφήν· οὐδ' ἂν ὠνομάσαμέν τι μὴ πρότερον αὐτοῦ κατὰ πρόληψιν τὸν τύπον μαθόντες. ἐναργεῖς οὖν εἰσιν αἱ προλήψεις.

They [the Epicureans] say that the preconception is like an act of apprehension [*katalēpsis*] or correct opinion [*doxa orthē*] or a conception [*ennoia*] or universal idea stored up [*katholikē noēsis enapokeimenē*], i.e., a memory [*mnēme*] of what has often appeared in the external world. For example, this sort of thing is "man." For as soon as "man" is uttered, immediately one has an idea of the general outline [*tupos*], according to our preconception, following the lead of the senses. Therefore, what is primarily denoted by every word [*onomati to prōtōs epitetagmenon*] is something evident [*enargeis*]; and we could have never inquired into an object if we had not been first aware of it. For example, is what is standing far off a horse or a cow? For one must at some time have been aware of the shape [*morphē*] of a horse and a cow according to a preconception. Nor would we have given a name to something if we had not first learned its general outline according to a preconception. Therefore, preconceptions are evident.[67]

---

[64] *KD* 37 and 38 are ambiguous insofar as the preconception of the passage is not explicitly identified as the preconception of justice; Epicurus could also merely have the preconception of benefit in mind. As we already saw, however, if this is so, it still follows that the beneficial – a different normative property – can be directly observed according to the Epicurean view.
[65] Leaving out the quotation marks that enclose τὸ τοιοῦτόν ἐστιν ἄνθρωπος in Dorandi's text.
[66] Leaving out the quotation marks that enclose τὸ πόρρω ἑστὼς ἵππος ἐστὶν ἢ βοῦς in Dorandi's text.
[67] Trans. Inwood and Gerson, modified.

This passage and Epicurean preconceptions more generally have received much scholarly attention, and a comprehensive review would exceed the scope of this chapter.[68] Instead, we can focus on some select features, namely, that preconceptions are "universal ideas stored up" and "memory of what has often appeared in the external world." Diogenes Laërtius does not provide a straightforward definition of preconceptions, but rather likens them to other technical terms of epistemological debates of the time.[69] To work out the significance of these select features, it is helpful to recall two competing accounts of concept formation. According to the Peripatetics and Stoics, conceptual knowledge stands at the last stage of a four-step process.[70] This process begins with isolated perceptions (*aisthēseis*) that are bundled in memories (*mnēmai*). Repeated memories then produce experience (*empeiria*), which, finally, depending on its object, yields scientific knowledge (*epistēmē*) or craft knowledge (*technē*), that is, different kinds of conceptual knowledge.

In contrast to Aristotle and the Stoics, the Epicureans do not explicitly discuss the role of experience in their account.[71] Nevertheless, the first two or three stages of the Aristotelian and Stoic accounts more or less map onto the Epicurean account, especially since Epicurus makes clear elsewhere that perceptions themselves do not involve memory:

> πᾶσα γάρ, φησίν, αἴσθησις ἄλογός ἐστι καὶ μνήμης οὐδεμιᾶς δεκτική· οὔτε γὰρ ὑφ' αὑτῆς κινεῖται οὔτε ὑφ' ἑτέρου κινηθεῖσα δύναταί τι προσθεῖναι ἢ ἀφελεῖν.

> Indeed, he [Epicurus] says, all perceptions are nonrational and not capable of receiving any memory because they neither move by themselves nor having been moved by another, are they capable of adding or subtracting something.[72]

---

[68] On preconceptions, see, for instance, Long 1971; Manuwald 1972; Jürss 1977; Glidden 1985; Goldschmidt 2006 [1978]; Goggins 2007; Morel 2008; Fine 2014, 226–56; and Tsouna 2016. The discussions in Sandbach 1930 and Dyson 2009, although their focus lies on Stoic *prolēpsis*, should also be consulted.
[69] See Asmis 1984, 61–6, for discussion.
[70] See Aristotle, *Posterior Analytics* II.19.100a3–9; and Aëtius, *Opinions of the Philosophers* IV.11.1–4 [= Long and Sedley 1987, 39E]. For differences between the Stoics and the Epicureans when it comes to preconceptions, see, for instance, Manuwald 1972, 14–16; Asmis 1984, 64; Goggins 2007; and Dyson 2009.
[71] The following discussion is heavily indebted to Dyson 2009, 115–19. "*Empeiria*" is used only twice in the extant texts of Epicurus (frr. 24.3.5 and 24.18.5 Arrighetti).
[72] Diogenes Laërtius, *Lives of Eminent Philosophers* X.31. Trans. mine. Leaving out the quotation marks in Dorandi's text.

6.2 Moral Epistemology

In summary, then, preconceptions are memories that have been formed as a result of multiple perceptions. It is unclear to what degree the resulting product is abstract. According to one view, preconceptions are like composite photographs.[73] The idea here is that preconceptions are to be understood as images that are themselves the result of a series of superimposed images. This would mean that at least to some degree, preconceptions abstract from the particular features of a singular perception insofar as the superimposition of the images emphasizes those features of the images that are shared among the images, while deemphasizing the features that are not. By contrast, according to an alternative view, a preconception is itself a representation of a mental particular that allows a perceiver to think of the universal, by focusing on a certain aspect of the particular.[74] On this reading, preconceptions would not be abstract at all.

As Voula Tsouna recently argued, in the process of acquiring preconceptions, the mind is in a receptive state.[75] In addition to her argument, we can add that at Diogenes Laërtius' *Lives of Eminent Philosophers* X.31, which was quoted above, perceptions, which are the basis from which preconceptions are formed, do not involve an inference of the mind if this is taken to mean that the mind in any way adds to or subtracts from the perceptions. Diogenes glosses this by saying that perceptions are nonrational (*alogos*). Again, falsehoods arise only on the level of opinion, as a result of the mind adding or subtracting something from a perception that it should not have on the Epicurean view. Just like perceptions, preconceptions, by contrast, as criteria of truth, can never be false. This makes it likely that they have not emerged as the result of a more substantive, additive, inferential process of the mind, either, but rather are situated somewhere between a perception and an opinion.

The noninferential character of preconceptions is furthermore confirmed by Diogenes of Oenoanda, who seems to describe the physical process of how the mind is altered when preconceptions are formed in the following passage:

---

[73] Bailey 1964 [1928], 245; see also Taylor 1911, 47. Kamtekar 2021, 216, seems to endorse the same view, even if she does not use Bailey's composite image metaphor. For criticism of the metaphor, see above all Glidden 1971, 171–3. For a discussion of Glidden's criticism, see, in turn, Obi 1993, 98–104.
[74] Fine 2014, 229–31; and Asmis 2020, 200.
[75] Tsouna 2016, 186–93. By contrast, there is also the *epibolē tēs dianoias* that accompanies mental acts as a kind of awareness. While this awareness constitutes an activity of the mind, the important point is that this activity does not contribute substantively to the process of preconception formation, as is argued in more detail below. For a recent account of *epibolē*, see Robitzsch 2021.

Τὰ οὖν ἀπὸ τῶν πραγμάτων ῥέοντα εἴδωλα, ἐνπείπτοντα ἡμῶν ταῖς ὄψεσιν, τοῦ τε ὁρᾶν ἡμᾶς τὰ ὑποκείμενα αἴτια γείνεται καὶ, εἰς [... lacuna ...] ἐνπτ[ώσεις μὲ]ν ο[ὖν] τὰ ὑπὸ τῶν ὄψεων βλεπόμενα ἡ ψυχὴ παραλαμβάνει· μετὰ δὲ τὰς τῶν πρώτων ἐνπτώσεις εἰδώλων ποροποιεῖται ἡμῶν οὕτως ἡ φύσις ὥστε, καὶ μὴ παρόντων ἔτι τῶν πραγμάτων ἃ τὸ πρῶτον εἶδεν, τὰ ὅμοια τοῖς πρώτοις τῇ διανοίᾳ δεχθῆναι.

Now the images that flow from objects, by impinging on our eyes, cause us both to see the things underlying [the images] and, [... lacuna ...] that the soul receives in turn the things seen by the eyes; and after the impingement of the first images, our nature is rendered porous in such a manner that, even if the objects which we first saw are no longer present, images similar to the first ones are received by the mind.[76]

The passage suggests that it is the images *themselves* that alter the human mind physically and so make perceivers susceptible of recognizing the same object again in the future (which is precisely the role of preconceptions). *Reasoning (epilogismos) or any other additive intervention of the mind does not play a role in the process.*

In the context of the discussion of how human beings come to have an understanding of something, an important upshot of this analysis is that Epicurean preconceptions are the most basic form of cognition that perceivers can have. In other words, preconceptions are not *ennoiai* or *epinoiai* if one means by this the concepts that are acquired by science or craft.[77] Accordingly, to elucidate the way preconceptions function in Epicurean theory, Diogenes Laërtius, in the passage quoted above, gives the example of identifying an unspecified object in the distance as either a horse or a cow. This is not a case of a preconception being employed as an initial concept in a scientific inquiry, but rather a case in which a preconception is used as an everyday conceptual device to classify a perception. Nevertheless, the passage describes the kind of understanding a perceiver has when she has a preconception: she can classify objects she has perceived and so has a *functional understanding* of the thing in question rather than scientific knowledge thereof, which would require more elaborate reasoning.[78]

---

[76] Fr. 9.II.9–III.14 Smith. Trans. Smith, modified.
[77] Contrast Aristotle's view at *Metaphysics* I.1.980a20–982a3 here, according to which an agent with experience only knows how to handle a particular case and, unlike an agent who has knowledge, does not know the reason why something is the case and is unable to teach a third party.
[78] One should here compare Epicurus' remarks about preconceptions with his ideas on definitions. On the latter, see Besnier 1994; Mansfeld 1994; and Giovacchini 2003. On the idea of outline accounts (*hupographē*) in Epicureanism, which in a certain way replace definitions, see *Letter to*

Now, if (1) preconceptions really are typically noninferential concepts, that is, are produced merely as a result of multiple perceptions without any substantive intervention of the mind in the way just described, and (2) there is a preconception of what is just, then it follows that, on the Epicurean view, (3) perceivers have direct perceptions of what is just.

In contrast to what has been argued up to this point, Elizabeth Asmis, among others, has suggested that the process in which some preconceptions are formed is different from the way that other preconceptions are formed.[79] In particular, she maintains that there are higher-level preconceptions that come to be by a more substantive involvement of the mind. Moreover, Asmis distinguishes between basic preconceptions of qualities, more complex ones of individuals and kinds, and the most complex, which comprise entities such as the good property manager, justice, and cause. To make her case, Asmis points to Philodemus' *On Methods of Inference*, which mentions a special kind of inference called "transition by similarity [*kath' homoiotēta metabasis*]." Since Cicero[80] and Sextus[81] seem to link this inference with our conception of the gods, Asmis concludes that there are at least some preconceptions that are formed with the help of rational inferences.[82]

It is not possible to fully review and discuss Asmis' view here. However, one may note that some details of her reading are controversial. First, note that Philodemus' *Methods of Inference* largely deals with judgments. Preconceptions are not mentioned frequently in the text, and it is not quite clear how the inferences discussed in Philodemus' work map onto the discussion of preconceptions. Likewise, it is not quite clear whether Philodemus' view is identical with Epicurus' or already presents a doctrinal development. In regard to the passage in Cicero, note that, as Asmis herself notes, there is some controversy about whether the words "*similitudine et transitione*" translate the Epicurean technical term "transition by similarity" and whether the *metabasis* described in Sextus is the same as the one described by Philodemus.[83] Most importantly, however, even if we were to

---

Menoeceus 123 along with the comments in Manuwald 1972, 55–68; Asmis 1984, 42–7; and Fine 2014, 237–41.
[79] Asmis 2009, 281–2; and Asmis 2010 [1999], 87–9. See also Jürss 1977, 221–2; Asmis 1984, 61–80; Voelke 1986, 70–2; and Müller 1987, 238.
[80] Cicero, *On the Nature of the Gods* I.105.
[81] Sextus Empiricus, *Against the Mathematicians* IX.45–6.
[82] Asmis also refers to *On the Nature of Things* V.1169–79 where Lucretius comments that perceivers reflect on the images of the gods that they receive. The below comments can also be taken to explain this passage.
[83] For a recent alternative reading, see Piergiacomi 2017, 183–5.

accept Asmis' proposal that some preconceptions are formed with the help of reasoning, while others are not, it does not follow that there is a three-tiered view of preconceptions as Asmis suggests. There is no textual evidence for this claim. However, in regard to justice, the passage in Hermarchus that was quoted above might be taken to distinguish between a perceptual nonrational preconception and a higher-level rational preconception of justice, as on Müller's reading. But this does not spell trouble for the idea that justice is directly perceived. After all, there would still be a *perceptual nonrational preconception* of justice on the Epicurean view, and so justice would still be experienced in the same way that other things are.

Furthermore, it is unclear why the lower-level preconception of justice would not be sufficient as a criterion of truth, as outlined in *KD* 37 and 38. Given that the higher-level preconception of justice would involve reasoning of some kind and reasoning is a potential source of error, the perceptual nonrational preconception of justice prima facie seems like a much more promising candidate as a criterion of truth than its higher-level counterpart.

In the same vein, even in the case of the preconception of justice that involves reasoning, independent evidence in Philodemus suggests that this preconception of justice is not formed by reasoning about prior concepts alone, but rather that a direct perception of some kind plays a major role in obtaining the higher-level preconception:[84]

> Τὰ μὲν γὰ[ρ δίκαια καὶ] ἀγαθὰ κα[ὶ καλ]ὰ ταὐ[τὰ] τοῖς ὑπὸ τῶν πολλῶ[ν] νοουμένοις [ε]ἶναί [φα]σιν [οἱ] καθ' ἡμᾶς φιλο[σο]φοῦ[τε]ς αὐτῶι μόνον παρα[λλά]ττοντες ἐκε[ί]νων [τῶι μ]ὴ παθητικῶς μόνον ἀλλ' [ἐ]πιλογ[ι]στικῶς αὐτὰ κατανοεῖν καὶ μὴ πολλάκις αὐτῶν λήθην λαμ[βά]νειν.

> For those who philosophize according to us [Epicureans] say in agreement with the thoughts of the many that just and good and honorable things are the same, differing from them alone in that they do not apprehend these things by the senses alone, but by reasoning, and do not forget them many times.[85]

While the passage does not explicitly say that the perception from which the higher-level preconception of justice is formed is a perception of what is

---

[84] See also Aoiz and Boeri 2023, 173, fn. 50.
[85] Philodemus, *Rhetoric* I.254, col. XX.25–36 Sudhaus. Trans. mine. Again, it does not seem quite clear that the passage claims that the understanding the Epicureans arrive at at the end is a preconception rather than some kind of higher-level concept. Be this as it may, even on the slightly modified reading that the preconception of justice is formed with the help of reasoning in some way, it must be clear that the contribution of reasoning cannot be substantive in the sense that reasoning adds or subtracts anything from the original perception. This would lead to potential falsifications. The preconception of justice, by contrast, is supposed to be a criterion of truth that guides perceivers as a kind of infallible classification device.

just or beneficial (that is, a moral property), it would seem odd if it were not. After all, there should also be the perceptual noninferential preconception that must start with a direct perception of justice, as we saw above. Accordingly, it would prima facie be strange if the higher-level perception of justice were ultimately grounded on an entirely different perception than the one that the perceptual, noninferential preconception is grounded on.

This brings us to a different objection against the main argument of this chapter. One might contend that the preconception of the just is not quite formed in the same way as other preconceptions are, this time on the basis of Cicero's *On the Nature of the Gods* I.43. Some readers have taken this passage to show that the Epicureans argue that some preconceptions are innate. Accordingly, the preconception of justice might also be innate.

Let us examine this text:

> Solus enim vidit primum esse deos, quod in omnium animis eorum notionem inpressisset ipsa natura. quae est enim gens aut quod genus hominum quod non habeat sine doctrina anticipationem quandam deorum, quam appellat πρόληψιν Epicurus, id est anteceptam animo rei quandam informationem, sine qua nec intellegi quicquam nec quaeri nec disputari potest. quoius rationis vim atque utilitatem ex illo caelesti Epicuri de regula et iudicio volumine accepimus. quod igitur fundamentum huius quaestionis est, id praeclare iactum videtis. cum enim non instituto aliquo aut more aut lege sit opinio constituta maneatque ad unum omnium firma consensio, intellegi necesse est esse deos, quoniam insitas eorum vel potius innatas cognitiones habemus; de quo autem omnium natura consentit, id verum esse necesse est; esse igitur deos confitendum est.

> For he [Epicurus] alone saw, first, that the gods existed, because nature herself had imprinted the conceptions of them in the minds of everyone. For what human nation or race does not have, without instruction, some preconception of the gods? Epicurus' word for this is "*prolēpsis*," that is, what we may call a delineation of a thing, preconceived by the mind, without which understanding, inquiry and discussion are impossible. The power and value of this reasoning we have learnt from Epicurus' heaven-sent book on the yardstick and criterion. Thus you see the foundation of the inquiry admirably laid. For since belief has not been established by any convention, custom or law, and retains unanimous consent, it must necessarily be understood that there are gods, given that we have ingrained, or rather innate, knowledge of them. But that on which everyone's nature agrees must be necessarily true. Therefore it must be conceded that there are gods.[86]

---

[86] Long and Sedley 1987, 23E. Trans. Long and Sedley, modified. See also Lucretius, *On the Nature of Things* V.1047–8, where human beings are said to have an "*insita notities . . . utilitatis*," and V.182,

In this passage, the Epicurean spokesperson Velleius argues for the existence of gods by referring to the preconception that human beings have in their minds. Because these preconceptions are universally agreed upon and because what is universally agreed upon must be true, Velleius claims that the existence of the gods is necessary.[87] Furthermore, Velleius repeats that preconceptions are the first terms in an investigation and adds that they are "imprinted [*inpressisset*]" in us and that they are "ingrained, or rather innate, knowledge [*insitas ... vel potius innatas cognitiones*]." In other words, Velleius seems to claim that at least some preconceptions are innate ideas,[88] which would make it possible that the preconception of the just might also be an innate idea rather than an empirically acquired understanding.

However, such a reading of the passage is mistaken.[89] Important in this context is above all the observation that "*innatus*" does not have to mean "innate."[90] One can say about a plant, for instance, that it is implanted in a field ("*innascitur agro*") without having to assume that it is inborn in or innate to the field. Likewise, then, the Cicero passage does not have to mean that preconceptions are innate, but that they arise naturally because of the impressions that caused them. In other words, such a reading would understand "*innatus*" as "*insitus*" and regard the two words as synonyms, posing no problems for an empiricist reading of concept formation in Epicureanism.

In addition, it is also clear that from the perspective of the human species as a whole, moral beliefs and knowledge are not innate for the Epicureans, either. We already saw this in Chapter 1. In his discussion of the original state, Lucretius observes: "Nor could they [primitive human beings] look to the common good, nor did they know to make mutual use of any moral norms or laws [*nec commune bonum poterant spectare neque ulllis | moribus inter se scibant nec legibus uti.*]."[91] This comment indicates that primitive human beings as a whole lacked moral beliefs and

---

where the gods are said to have a "*notities hominum ... insita.*" Note, however, that the passages in Lucretius might use "*notities*" in a more generic sense ("knowledge/cognition") than Epicurus does (but for the contrary view, see Rover 2022). At *On Ends* I.31, finally, Cicero also claims that the idea that pleasure is to be sought and pain to be avoided "is almost a natural and innate concept in our minds [*quasi naturalem atque insitam in animis nostris inesse notionem*]." Trans. mine.

[87] On the argument from universal agreement, see especially Obbink 1992 and the reply in Brittain 2005.

[88] DeWitt 1954, 142–50.

[89] See, for instance, Kleve 1963, 23–34; Manuwald 1972, 11–16; Asmis 1984, 66–73; and Jürss 1991, 94–5, fn. 72. On the passage as a whole, see also Tsouna 2016, 174–85.

[90] As is already suggested by Roorda in an article in 1822 (quoted in Tohte 1874, 17).

[91] Lucretius, *On the Nature of Things* V.958–9. Trans. mine.

knowledge, which means that moral beliefs and knowledge as a whole needed to be acquired and so cannot have been innate.

According to yet another objection, the main argument of this section goes wrong in assuming that justice is ontologically the same kind of thing as cows or horses.[92] Because cows and horses can be directly experienced by sense perception, but justice cannot, perceivers will necessarily have to come to understand justice in a different way than they come to know cows or horses. In other words, this objection maintains that there must be another way that preconceptions are formed in the case of "nonsensual" entities like justice.[93]

In response, one may point to entities that are nonmanifest (*adēla*) according to the Epicurean view, that is, are not accessible to direct sense perception. The standard example for such entities is void, which, like other nonmanifest entities, is known through the complex epistemological procedure of non-counter-witnessing (*antimaturēsis*).[94] On the strength that they cannot be directly experienced by the senses, several scholars have argued there is no preconception of what is *adēlon*.[95] In doing so, these scholars invoke the same principle invoked above, namely, that there are only preconceptions of things that were antecedently experienced by the senses. In short, if justice were nonsensual altogether (like objects that are *adēla*), we would also not expect it to have a preconception. However, as *KD* 37 and 38 make clear, justice in fact has a preconception associated with it, and so cannot be "nonsensual" in the way just described.

Alternatively, when using the term "nonsensual," the above objection that justice is ontologically a different kind of thing may simply mean that justice is something "nonbodily." This points to a different, but related problem. We saw in the previous section of this chapter that justice is to be understood as an (accidental) property on the Epicurean view, not a body. Understood in this way, the objection alleges that perceivers have understandings of (accidental) properties in a different way than understandings of bodily entities. After all, the case of perceiving what is just is analogous to perceiving that something is sweet or smooth, not to perceiving a cow.

---

[92] DeWitt 1954, 144.
[93] The Epicureans might also admit preconceptions of entities like oratory (Philodemus, *Rhetoric* II.189, fr. III.6–8 and II.266, col. XIa.2–7 Sudhaus) and cause (Epicurus, *On Nature* XXV, 34.28 Arrighetti). These preconceptions pose similar issues as the preconception of justice does, since generally such entities are not believed to be objects of direct sensory perception.
[94] For a recent overview of different readings of this technical term of Epicurean epistemology, see Bakker 2016, 15–31.
[95] Sedley 2011, 42; and Fine 2014, 236.

However, in response to this way of stating the objection, one may say that it is unclear why, in absence of other evidence, preconceptions of properties ought to be obtained by a rational inference of some kind, whereas preconceptions of bodies are not obtained in this way. We have only limited and basically uniform evidence of the process of how preconceptions are formed. Why could the preconception of the color red (if there is one) not be obtained by multiple perceptions of what is red without an additional rational inference just as in the case of a preconception of a cow?

Finally, the critic could understand the objection in yet another way. She could have in mind that justice is different from other attributes insofar as it is a normative property, while, say, being smooth is clearly a nonnormative one. However, this way of framing the objection presupposes a distinction between what is normative and nonnormative that is un-Epicurean as well as foreign to ancient philosophy more broadly, as we already saw in more detail in the previous section of this chapter, in regard to Polystratus' *On Irrational Contempt for Common Conceptions*. There does not seem to be sufficient evidence to conclude that the Epicureans deal with the perception of moral properties in a different way than they deal with the perception of nonmoral properties.

Admittedly, it is difficult to imagine what a preconception, perception, or even *eidōlon* of justice will look like and so to provide a more detailed account of what it means for a perceiver to perceive what is just via images. There is no direct textual evidence for how this is supposed to work.[96] *POxy.* 5077, fr. II, col. II.3–11, may contain the very fragmentary remains of a letter by Epicurus, critiquing the perhaps Platonic idea that justice is reducible to a mathematical form:

> το ἐπὶ τῶν σχ[ημάτων ἐνάρ]γημα, ὥσπε[ρ ἐπὶ τοῦ τετραγώ]νου σχή[ματος ἐσ]τι, καὶ ἡ τοῦ [δι]κ[αίου] καὶ ἄλλ[α] ἔστι σχήματα τ[ῆι] αὐτῆι [μ]ωροσοφία<ι>, πό[τε]ρον κατὰ συνήθειαν τ[ῆς] φωνῆς αὐτῆς. ἂν μὲν εἴπη<ι> τις τὸ τετρ[άγωνον σχῆ]μα ἢ σῶμα ...
>
> How could there be a shape of justice owing to the vividness in the figures, just as there is in the figure of a square – and that of the just and the rest of the figures is through this same ridiculous "wisdom." Whether through the habit of voicing it, one could say that the square was a figure or a body ...[97]

---

[96] For some discussion, see Hahmann and Robitzsch 2022 (*pace* Glidden 1971, 173; and Striker 1974, 71–2).
[97] Trans. Obbink and Schorn.

6.2 Moral Epistemology

Such a critique, however, does not mean that justice for the Epicureans does not have a perceptible form of any kind. Likewise, the Democritean atomistic theory of perception very clearly claims that normative properties are perceived with the help of images. Let us thus conclude the chapter by considering a final passage in Plutarch that reports Democritus' view on moral perception that will further support the view that moral properties are likely perceived in the very same way as nonmoral properties are on the Epicurean view:

> οὐ μόνον ἔχοντα μορφοειδεῖς τοῦ σώματος ἐκμεμαγμένας ὁμοιότητας (ὡς Ἐπίκουρος οἴεται μέχρι τούτου Δημοκρίτῳ συνεπόμενος, ἐνταῦθα δὲ προλιπὼν τὸν λόγον), ἀλλὰ καὶ τῶν κατὰ ψυχὴν κινημάτων καὶ βουλευμάτων ἑκάστῳ καὶ ἠθῶν καὶ παθῶν ἐμφάσεις ἀναλαμβάνοντα συνεφέλκεσθαι, καὶ προσπίπτοντα μετὰ τούτων ὥσπερ ἔμψυχα φράζειν καὶ διαγγέλλειν τοῖς ὑποδεχομένοις τὰς τῶν μεθιέντων αὐτὰ δόξας καὶ διαλογισμοὺς καὶ ὁρμάς, ὅταν ἐνάρθρους καὶ ἀσυγχύτους φυλάττοντα προσμίξῃ τὰς εἰκόνας.

> [The atomic images] not only have the impressed likeness of the body in form – so far Epicurus agrees with Democritus, though he drops the subject at this stage – but they include with them impressions of each person's mental movements, resolutions, moral character, and emotions. And entering the mind with them, [the atomic images] speak, as if they were alive, and report to those that receive them the very opinions and considerations and impulses of those from whom they escape, whenever the images are preserved whole and undistorted until contact is made.[98]

The passage makes clear that for Democritus, the atomic images of all objects carry information about normative properties; these are directly perceived on Democritus' view.[99] However, Plutarch also notes in the passage that Epicurus "drops the subject at this stage [*entautha de prolipōn ton logon*]," that is, does not explicitly discuss the role of nonmoral properties in regard to the images of perception. However, this can merely mean that the Epicurean treatise that Plutarch is basing his ideas on does not discuss the matter explicitly. It does not need to mean that the Epicureans did not discuss the matter at all. Evidence in Hermarchus as well as on the general process of preconception formation in Epicureanism

---

[98] Plutarch, *Table Talk* VIII.10.2.735a–b. Trans. Minar, modified.
[99] According to a stronger, alternative reading of the Democritean view, images not only are likenesses of the thing of which they are an image but also *themselves* have perceptions, feelings, and so on. See, for instance, Diogenes of Oenoanda, frr. 10.IV.10–V.6 and 43.I.12–II.14 Smith. This may well be a misrepresentation of the Democritean position, which may be similar to the Epicurean one; see Warren 2006a, 96–9.

makes it very likely that when pressed, the Epicureans may have to endorse an account according to which agents come to know moral properties like what is just in the same way that they come to know other properties, namely, by direct sense perception.[100]

In summary, then, we can conclude that the Epicurean theory of justice is naturalistic not only insofar as it does not deal with the supernatural, but also because it fulfills the following two conditions for the Epicureans: (1) a moral property like the just is not fundamentally different from a nonmoral property in regard to its ontological status and (2) agents come to know moral facts such as what is just in the same way that they come to know nonmoral facts.

---

[100] Warren 2006a, 98, points to Lucretius' *On the Nature of Things* III.370–95, where it is argued that the Democritean soul differs from the Epicurean one insofar as the former is dispersed throughout the whole body, including the skin, whereas the latter is not. This would furnish the Epicureans a physiological reason why internal states are not expressed in images (while they are for Democritus). However, this observation about Epicurean physiology does not completely rule out that *eidola* cannot transport any information on moral properties, as was argued above. In addition to the passage in Plutarch discussed above, the skepticism in regard to what information about moral properties perception may carry is also evident in Philodemus, who at *Rhetoric* II.41, col. XLII.7–21 Sudhaus, criticizes Epicurus' Democritean teacher Nausiphanes for holding the view that a politician does not have a direct perception of political matters. See also Porter 2002, 153–9.

CHAPTER 7

Conclusion

In advancing their ideas about justice, the Epicureans develop a sophisticated theory, one – this book has argued – that articulates an interesting middle position between conventional Sophistic *nomos* theories of justice, on the one hand, and the *phusis* theories of the other major philosophical schools, on the other hand, and that prefigures distinctly modern positions like legal positivism, while still significantly differing from them.

At the center of the Epicurean theory are agreements. These agreements regulate the relationship of the contracting parties to each other and bring about justice. However, these agreements may also include others in their purview: women and children and perhaps the disadvantaged more generally. The goal of the agreements of justice is to procure a benefit: security. Security, on the Epicurean view, is an important good that contributes to the highest goal in life, freedom from mental distress and bodily pain.

A key principle of Epicurean philosophy is that the development of every social achievement is layered: it appears first in primitive forms, but then reappears in more sophisticated forms at later stages of cultural development. Human beings make rudimentary arrangements with each other already in their original state of existence by trading fruits for sexual favors, for instance. And likewise, they take care of animals in exchange for certain benefits that these animals bestow on them, again developing arrangements with them. Such arrangements prefigure the agreements of justice whose content is what is beneficial in the mutual dealings of human beings, even if they are not equivalent to them. The agreements of justice themselves, on the Epicurean view, are not the latest form of development, though. The Epicureans also emphasize the importance of more codified laws, which through people's consent also resemble the agreements of justice, in obtaining the same end as the more informal moral agreements that bring about justice, namely, the benefit of security.

From the perspective of the ancient *nomos-phusis* debate, according to which a given entity is either artificial/human-made or natural, the

Epicurean view can be said to mediate between the two extreme positions of the debate insofar as the Epicureans agree with the defenders of *nomos* that justice and the laws come to be as the historical result of agreements and thus are conventional. However, they also side with the defenders of *phusis* insofar as they insist that justice and the laws are not merely the result of a convention, but rather are firmly (but not deterministically) grounded in the things that are beneficial for everyone.

From the perspective of legal philosophy, insofar as the Epicureans stress conventional features by emphasizing the historical emergence of the law, their account might be said to prefigure a kind of legal positivism. Again, however, the Epicurean view is more subtle. As a result of their commitment to what is beneficial, as expressed in their commitment that the law cannot be meaningfully studied by itself, without a reference to the category of benefit, and in their lack of recognition that there are separate legal reasons that obligate agents to act, Epicurean theory on the whole is much closer to a natural law theory.

While defenders of *nomos* typically stress conventionality without a robust virtue of justice, and defenders of *phusis* typically stress virtue without the agreements, Epicurean theory again takes a middle route insofar as, on their view, agreements are at the center of the account but there is also a virtue of justice. This creates the puzzle of how aretaic justice and contractual justice are related to each other. According to the most plausible account, the former is nested in the latter; that is, contractual justice is slightly more expansive in content, and it forms the foundation on which agents can (ideally) develop aretaic justice. The practical upshot of this idea is furthermore that the goal of Epicurean social theory is to develop agents who are aretaically just by relying as far as possible on friendships to procure security. This diminishes the need for laws and mitigates the negative consequences of their existence, even if some agreements need to be in place that can solve coordination problems between different agents. We may imagine an Epicurean community of friends as a prime example of such an approach. However, the Epicureans realize that a withdrawal from the many may not always be possible. Especially in these circumstances, the laws play an important role in keeping agents secure, emphasizing that nonideal theorizing (that is, contingency planning) is an important part of Epicurean social and political philosophy.

In the same vein, whereas defenders of *phusis* typically have no problems insisting that agents should always be just and obey the laws, defenders of *nomos* are typically taken to struggle to explain why agents should obey the laws or be just if sanction mechanisms fall away. The Epicurean view again splits the difference insofar as it reasonably suggests that one should never be unjust, but that there are occasions when it is all right to violate a law (even if actual scenarios, in which Epicureans will violate the law and it will be impossible to satisfy natural and necessary desires, will likely be rare).

Finally, from the perspective of contemporary metaethics, Epicurean theory, like other ancient ethical theories, is naturalistic. First, it is naturalistic insofar as it rejects supernatural explanations. Second, however, it is also naturalistic insofar as it explains and investigates nonmoral entities in continuity with the entities that are investigated in the sciences. This means that it fulfills both ontological and epistemological requirements: what is just, according to the Epicureans, is best understood as an accidental property that is not different from nonmoral properties such as what is sweet or smooth. From an epistemological perspective, moreover, Epicurean justice is most likely directly perceived by perceivers just as bodies or at least their properties are perceived.

In antiquity, what one might call theories of justice that focus first and foremost on character development and virtue rather than agreements, the *phusis* theories of Plato and Aristotle as well as of the Stoics of the Hellenistic period and Neoplatonic authors of late antiquity, dominated the discussion. These schools flourished, whereas the Epicurean school all but died out by the third century CE.[1] During the medieval period, Epicurus was stylized as a defender of bodily pleasure and thus inimical to Christian teachings.[2] The social and political ideas of the school were little discussed, as not only did this area of philosophy receive less attention in general during the Middle Ages, but the writings of Epicurus, Lucretius, and other Epicurean authors became inaccessible to an intellectual public that spoke Latin, not Greek. Accordingly, the sophisticated Epicurean theory was all but forgotten. During the fifteenth century, this situation changed: Poggio Bracciolini rediscovered Lucretius' *On the Nature of Things* in a German monastery,[3] and Ambrose Traversari translated into Latin Diogenes Laërtius' *Lives of Eminent Philosophers*, whose tenth book is an important source on Epicureanism.[4] The availability of both texts prepared the ground for a reception of Epicurean ideas, first and foremost by Pierre Gassendi and Thomas Hobbes.[5] And Hobbes, in particular, also revived the Epicurean ideas of the social contract in his writings, even if, as we saw, he also importantly diverged from them, for instance, in regard to

---

[1] For some of the later history of the Epicurean school, see Fleischer 2016, 23–211.
[2] For a detailed account, see Kaiser 2019. [3] Greenblatt 2011. [4] Kaiser 2019, 225–317.
[5] Ludwig 2005; Wilson 2008; and Paganini 2020.

his understanding of human beings in general as well as of the description of the original condition of human beings that precedes the social contract. Twenty-first-century attempts to revive Epicurean thinking, especially in regard to society and politics, are rare. However, David Gauthier's *Morals by Agreement* is a neo-Hobbesian account of the social contract that at least stands in the tradition that can be traced back to Epicurus and his followers.[6] As a result, there is much room today to appreciate the Epicurean middle position as a genuine theoretical alternative to other views about justice and law that have been advanced.

---

[6] See also Fitzpatrick 2018.

APPENDIX A

Oikeōsis

At *On the Nature of Things* V.1021–3, Lucretius remarks that at a certain point in the coming to be of communities, human beings agree to take care of weaker members of the community. Some commentators take Lucretius at this point of the account to introduce a motive separate from the benefit of not harming and being harmed. Such a view was already discussed in Chapter 1. However, there are also some commentators who think that Lucretius engages with the doctrine of *oikeiōsis* in this passage, which during the Hellenistic period is typically associated with the Stoics.[1] This claim will be the topic of this appendix. In what follows, the Stoic doctrine of *oikeiōsis* will be briefly characterized. Then the discussion will turn to the Epicurean texts that seem to deal with *oikeiōsis*, that is, passages in Lucretius and Hermarchus.[2] It will be argued that if the Epicureans are indeed taken to engage with the Stoic doctrine – which is not at all clear, but in the case of Lucretius possible – they must have given *oikeiōsis* a radically different interpretation, one firmly based on the calculation of

---

[1] See especially Pigeaud 1984, 137–42; and Algra 1997.
[2] Algra 1997, 146–7, also finds traces of the *oikeiōsis* doctrine in Epicurus' own writings (see also Aoiz and Boeri 2023, 28). However, there is no need to read the respective passages in this way. First, Diogenes Laërtius, *Lives of Eminent Philosophers* X.120, merely stresses that there is a community of friends. Second, *KD* 40 and *SV* 61 show there is value to having close friends. Both these claims are independent of a doctrine of appropriation. Third, finally, Algra argues that *KD* 39 shows that the Epicureans recognize different degrees of appropriation: "The one who has made the best arrangements for confidence about external threats is he who has made the manageable things akin to himself, and has at least made the unmanageable things not alien to himself. But he avoided all contact with things for which not even this could be managed and he drove out of his life everything which it profited him to drive out ['Ο <τὰ ἑαυτοῦ πρὸς> τὸ μὴ θαρροῦν ἀπὸ τῶν ἔξωθεν ἄριστα συστησάμενος, οὗτος τὰ μὲν δυνατὰ ὁμόφυλα κατεσκευάσατο, τὰ δὲ μὴ δυνατὰ οὐκ ἀλλόφυλά γε· ὅσα δὲ μηδὲ τοῦτο δυνατὸς ἦν, ἀνεπίμεικτος ἐγένετο καὶ ἐξηρείσατο ὅσα <πρὸς> τοῦτ' ἐλυσιτέλει πράττειν]." Trans. Inwood and Gerson. Note, however, that here the degrees of appropriation do not concern different people, but different things (note the neuter plurals) that are more and less familiar. Furthermore, the passage makes clear that there are limits to appropriation insofar as some things will always be alien.

what is beneficial, and not understood it as a natural affinity that human beings feel for their fellow human beings.

While the details of the Stoic doctrine are much disputed,[3] the basic idea behind *oikeiōsis* is that human beings exhibit a natural tendency to show concern, which means that they seek out what is appropriate for themselves. This takes two forms. First, there is the tendency to care for one's own self-preservation (personal *oikeiōsis*) and, second, there is the tendency to care for the well-being of other human beings (social *oikeiōsis*). The exact relationship between the two forms of *oikeiōsis* is unclear in Stoic theory. Perhaps these forms of *oikeiōsis* are completely distinct; perhaps, though, at least in some Stoic authors, social *oikeiōsis* is understood as an extension of personal *oikeiōsis*. On this model, self-concern is gradually extended to a concern vis-à-vis close family members, neighbors, and others, ultimately leading to social *oikeiōsis*, or the concern for the human race as a whole. This leads to the famous Stoic doctrine of cosmopolitanism.[4]

At *On the Nature of Things* V.1020, Lucretius employs language that suggests that he could be replying to or borrowing from the Stoics. In particular, the verb "*commendo*" is also one of the terms employed by Cicero to render the Greek verb "*oikeioumai*" into Latin:

> Simul atque natum sit animal (hinc enim est ordiendum), ipsum sibi conciliari et commendari ad se conservandum et ad suum statum eaque quae conservantia sunt eius status diligenda, alienari autem ab interitu iisque rebus quae interitum videantur afferre. id ita esse sic probant, quod ante quam voluptas aut dolor attingerit, salutaria appetant parvi aspernenturque contraria, quod non fieret nisi statum suum diligerent, interitum timerent. fieri autem non posse tut appeterent aliquid nisi sensum haberent sui eoque se diligerent. ex quo intelligi debet principium ductum esse a se diligendo.
>
> Every animal, as soon as it is born (this is where one should start), is concerned with itself and takes care to preserve itself [*commendari ad se conservandum*]. It favors its constitution and whatever preserves its constitution, whereas it recoils from its destruction and whatever appears to promote its destruction. In support of this thesis, the Stoics point out that babies seek what is good for them and avoid the opposite before they ever

---

[3] On *oikeiōsis* in the Stoics, see, for instance, Klein 2016 (with references to older literature).
[4] In addition to *On Ends* III, a selection of which is quoted below, the key texts for Stoic *oikeiōsis* are Arius Didymus' epitome of Peripatic ethics as well as Diogenes Laërtius, *Lives of Eminent Philosophers* VII.85–6; Plutarch, *On Stoic Self-contradictions* 1038b; Hierocles' *Elements of Ethics*; as well as Stobaeus, *Anthology* IV.671.7–673.11 Wachsmuth and Heinse (= Long and Sedley 1987, 57G).

feel pleasure or pain. This would not happen unless they valued their own constitution and feared destruction. But neither could it happen that they would seek anything at all unless they had self-awareness and thereby self-love. So one must realize that it is self-love which provides the primary motivation.[5]

In addition to Lucretius, Hermarchus explicitly uses the term "*oikeiōsis*" in his account of cultural development as one of the reasons why human beings should abstain from killing animals:[6]

> Οἱ δὲ ἀπὸ τοῦ Ἐπικούρου ... φασὶν ὡς οἱ παλαιοὶ νομοθέται, ἀπιδόντες εἰς τὴν τοῦ βίου κοινωνίαν τῶν ἀνθρώπων καὶ τὰς πρὸς ἀλλήλους πράξεις, ἀνόσιον ἐπεφήμισαν τὴν ἀνθρώπου σφαγὴν καὶ ἀτιμίας οὐ τὰς τυχούσας προσῆψαν. τάχα μὲν καὶ φυσικῆς τινος οἰκειώσεως ὑπαρχούσης τοῖς ἀνθρώποις πρὸς ἀνθρώπους διὰ τὴν ὁμοιότητα τῆς μορφῆς καὶ τῆς ψυχῆς εἰς τὸ μὴ προχείρως φθείρειν τὸ τοιοῦτον ζῷον ὥσπερ ἕτερόν τι τῶν συγκεχωρημένων· οὐ μὴν ἀλλὰ τὴν γε πλείστην αἰτίαν τοῦ δυσχερανθῆναι τοῦτο καὶ ἀνόσιον ἐπιφημισθῆναι τὸ μὴ συμφέρειν εἰς τὴν ὅλην τοῦ βίου σύστασιν ὑπολαβεῖν.

> The followers of Epicurus ... say that the ancient lawgivers, having considered human life in community and people's dealings with each other, declared that the slaughter of a human being is a sacrilege, and imposed exceptional penalties.[7] Perhaps there is also [*taxa men kai*] a natural appropriation [*oikeiōsis*] of human to human, because of their likeness of appearance and of soul, which inclines them away from readily destroying such an animal as if it were one or other of those it is acceptable to kill. But the main reason [*tēn pleistēn aitian*] for indignation at this act, and its being declared

---

[5] Cicero, *On Ends* III.16. Trans. Woolf. Note that social *oikeiōsis* is discussed later in the text, at III.62–4, and that here Cicero also uses "*conciliare*" as a synonym of "*commendare*."
[6] On *oikeiōsis* in Hermarchus, see Vander Waerdt 1988. See also Cole 1990 [1967], 84, fn. 10 (with references to further literature).
[7] That the text religiously sanctions killing (it is declared "*anhosion*") is perhaps surprising and could be thought to be unusual for an Epicurean author. However, given comments in the *PHerc.* 1251 (col. XII.4–19 Indelli and Tsouna-McKirahan), an Epicurean ethical treatise whose author is unknown, but is now generally believed to be Philodemus, this might not be unorthodox: "[The many] are rather led to right conduct by the laws which threaten with death, and with punishments coming from the gods, and with pains which are considered intolerable, and with the privation of some things which are supposedly hard to procure. This is partly on account of what was said at the beginning, partly because these things threaten men who are foolish and who cannot be persuaded by the true precepts; and the only thing that is achieved through them [that is, the laws] is deterrence for a short period of time [κ[αὶ μ]ᾶλ[λ]ον εἰς ὀρθ[ο]π[ρ]αξίαν ὑ[πὸ] τῶν νόμων ἄγονται θάνατον ἀνατ[εινομέ]νων καὶ τιμωρία[ς ἐ]κ θε[ῶ]ν καὶ πόνους ὡς δυσ[εκπο]νήτους καὶ στρήσε[ις] ἐνίων ὡς δυσπορίστων, τὸ μὲν ἐκ τῶν κατὰ τὴν ἀρχὴν εἰρημένων, τὸ δ' ἐκ τοῦ πρὸς ἄφρονας ταῦτ' ἀνατ[είνε]σθαι καὶ μὴ δ[υ]ναμένους ὑπὸ τῶν ἀλη[θι]νῶν πείθεσθαι παραγγε[λ]μάτων καὶ μόνον ἐπισχέσεις δι' αὐτῶν γίνεσθαι πρὸς ὀλίγον χρόνον]." Trans. Indelli and Tsouna, modified. See also Schmid 1943, 40–2; and Müller 1972, 76 and fn. 166.

168   Appendix A: *Oikeōsis*

sacrilege, is that it was not beneficial [*mē sumpherein*] for the general organization of life.[8]

There are some problems with attributing the *oikeiōsis* doctrine to the Epicureans without any reasonable doubt, although the reasons against attributing the doctrine to Hermarchus are more conclusive than the ones against attributing it to Lucretius.

Let us begin with the passage in Hermarchus. First, there is some question whether the passage, which is found in Porphyry's *On Abstinence*, is a direct quotation of a text by the second head of the Garden or is instead Porphyry's summary.[9] Anthony Long and David Sedley have suggested that "*oikeiōsis*" is an interpolation by Porphyry,[10] and Eleni Kechagia argues for a similar view by pointing out that there are good reasons pertaining to the content of the text not to assume that Hermarchus is advancing an anti-Stoic polemic.[11] After all, the text does not seem like an explicit critique of another thinker.

Second, the passage is typically presumed to have been taken from Hermarchus' treatise *Against Empedocles*. However, the relationship between the Stoics and Empedocles was different from the relationship between the Stoics and Socrates. While Socrates was clearly an authority for the Stoics, Empedocles was not. As Kechagia points out, the Stoics had views on natural affinity conflicting with those of Empedocles. For Kechagia, this suggests, then, that the passage is part of an anti-Stoic polemic and so the use of the term "*oikeiōsis*" by Hermarchus is quite unlikely.

Third, and perhaps most importantly, there are also serious chronological issues in ascribing to Hermarchus a robust conception of *oikeiōsis* that in some way reacts to the Stoics.[12] Hermarchus and Epicurus were roughly the same age. After Epicurus' death in 270 BCE, Hermarchus succeeded him as head of the Garden. Generally, Hermarchus is thought to have died around 250 BCE. Given the status of Epicurus in the Garden, Hermarchus thus could have introduced such a significant innovation as the doctrine of *oikeiōsis* without Epicurus' explicit consent only after 270 BCE, and, in fact, such a rather late date would give the Stoics some time

---

[8] Hermarchus, fr. 34 Longo Auricchio (= Porphyry, *On Abstinence* I.7.1–2). Trans. Clark, modified.
[9] In favor of direct quotation are, for instance, Philippson 1923, 5; and Vander Waerdt 1988, 94–5. Against direct quotation are, for instance, Krohn 1921, 5–6; Müller 1972, 74; and Kechagia 2010, 144–5 as well as fn. 46.
[10] Long and Sedley 1987, II.137.   [11] Kechagia 2010, 143–6.
[12] As Vander Waerdt 1988 wants to do. See also the reply to his argument in Roskam 2007, 76–9; and the brief comment in Sedley 1997, 46, fn. 33.

to develop their doctrine. In this case, though, one would still have to assume that the *oikeiōsis* doctrine was well developed before the time of Chrysippus (279–206 BCE), who is generally considered to be the most important early Stoic author.[13]

On Abstinence I.7–12 is, as already noted, usually taken to be an excerpt from Hermarchus' *Against Empedocles*, and one can infer from fr. 29 Longo Auricchio that *Against Empedocles* was written during Epicurus' lifetime or rather, more precisely, that it was written before 301 BCE (before Epicurus wrote *On Nature* XII, which may have contained Epicurus' own culture story).[14] If this date is right, Epicurus must have known and endorsed Hermarchus' ideas about *oikeiōsis*. Otherwise, Hermarchus' treatise would have been quite heterodox. What is more, if we assume that *On Nature* XII or a later book of this work contained Epicurus' own account of cultural development, this means that even before writing his own culture story in systematic form, Epicurus already had Hermarchus' account to draw on. This is not to say that Hermarchus did not truly come up with a response to the *oikeiōsis* doctrine in Epicureanism, but it means that, if he did, this likely happened with the explicit endorsement of Epicurus, given the status of the school head. In any case, on this suggestion, there is not much time for the Stoics to develop their doctrine of *oikeiōsis*, which – again – seems problematic.

Alternatively, one might, of course, doubt that *On Abstinence* I.7–12 really stems from Hermarchus' *Against Empedocles* and so claim that the excerpt in question is from another work that was written after Epicurus' death.[15] This would give the Stoics more time to develop their doctrine, although Chrysippus' involvement would still be a problem insofar as Hermarchus is typically taken to have died around the time that Chrysippus would have been only twenty-nine years old (which would not give him much time to develop the *oikeiōsis* doctrine and Hermarchus to respond to it). In short, then, the chronology of a supposed debate on *oikeiōsis* between the Epicureans and the Stoics in the third century BCE is difficult to piece together.

In the Lucretian passage, by contrast, there are issues neither in regard to the authenticity nor in regard to dating. However, one may wonder whether Lucretius is not an outlier among Epicurean authors in his use

---

[13] Porphyry reports at *On Abstinence* III.19.2 that the doctrine was already developed by the followers of Zeno, but this seems unlikely, if this means Zeno himself rather than the Stoics more generally.
[14] On dating the different books of Epicurus' *On Nature*, see Sedley 1998b, 128–32.
[15] See Longo Auricchio 1988, 137–9.

of *oikeiōsis*. In general, it is contested among scholars to what extent Lucretius engaged with contemporary positions when writing *On the Nature of Things* and to what extent he mechanically follows Epicurus' writings,[16] but his version of Epicureanism differs from the orthodox version of Epicurus in some regards. For instance, we already encountered Lucretius' stance toward animals, which is much more favorable than that of Epicurus and other Epicurean authors.[17] Accordingly, one might also think that Lucretius is engaging with the Stoics at *On the Nature of Things* V.1021–3 and trying to fit a non-Epicurean technical concept into the Epicurean framework, which could explain the oddness of the passage.

In this context, it is also interesting to note that Lucretius uses "*commendare*" at V.861, when discussing the "agreements" with animals. If "*commendare*" implies *oikeiōsis*, as some scholars suggest, then V.861 could be taken to suggest that for Lucretius, there is a natural affinity between animals and human beings. Such a conclusion would be denied not only by other Epicurean authors, but also of course by the Stoics as well, who limit *oikeiōsis* to human beings. It would thus seem that even if we were to accept that Lucretius is merely reporting an older Epicurean position, according to which human beings feel a natural affinity for other human beings, he would certainly go beyond this older position by referring to an affinity with animals (which in turn establishes that at minimum in regard to animal *oikeiōsis* Lucretius goes beyond what any other author claims).

Finally, even if we assume that the Epicureans (or more specifically Lucretius) defended a version of the *oikeiōsis* doctrine in their (his) writings, it seems unlikely that this version of the doctrine is identical to the Stoic one. After all, as especially Hermarchus makes clear, *oikeiōsis* would be at best an additional, subsidiary motive that is introduced in the account ("perhaps there is also"), while the determination of what is benefit is "the main reason" why human beings act the way they do. Likewise, we already saw in Chapter 1 that the feeling of pity is not a feeling that grounds a certain behavior in Lucretius, but rather that this feeling is sanctioned by the agreements of justice; ultimately, the reason why the feeling of pity is sanctioned is that it is beneficial for everyone to do so. In short, then, we can conclude that even if the Epicureans were using the *oikeiōsis* doctrine in their writings, they would be adapting it to their philosophy and specific argumentative needs.

---

[16] For the former view, see Schmidt 1990; Lévy 1999; and Schrijvers 1999, 167–82. For the latter view, see Sedley 1998b.
[17] See Chapter 2.

APPENDIX B

Cicero, the Epicureans, and the Ring of Gyges

Cicero's *On Duties* contains a brief discussion that is related to Plutarch's report of the law-breaking Epicurean sage. Cicero does not directly address Plutarch's question, namely, whether the sage will violate a law, knowing he will escape detection. Instead, Cicero discusses the response "certain philosophers [*philosophi quidam*],"[1] who are often identified with the Epicureans, give to the challenge posed by the Ring of Gyges thought experiment.[2] In this well-known story, which is found in Plato's *Republic*,[3] a shepherd finds a ring that gives him the power to become invisible whenever he wishes. This allows him to perform any action he wants without any consequences, including actions that would be considered immoral. The challenge raised by the story is thus to identify reasons for being just, although there are no societal sanctions to be feared by committing an injustice. The scenario developed in the Ring of Gyges thought experiment, however, differs from the scenario described by Plutarch insofar as the latter imagines a scenario in which the violation of the law is a one-time event, whereas in the Ring of Gyges story, the person with the ring has a permanent capacity to become invisible and so indulge in wrongdoing. Furthermore, while the scenario in Plutarch involves a sage, an ideal agent, the protagonist at the center of the Ring of Gyges story is not such an ideal agent, but a regular agent.

The third book of *On Duties*, where Cicero's brief discussion is found, in general deals with the relationship between the honorable (*honestum*) and the beneficial (*utile*). Accordingly, the Ring of Gyges story is introduced as a challenge of how the pursuit of pleasure can entail the exercise

---

[1] Cicero, *On Duties* III.39. Trans. mine.
[2] By contrast, Stephen White suggests that the passage may reflect a second-century debate between the Stoics and Academics. See Dyck 1996, 541.
[3] Plato, *Republic* II.359c–360d. See also Woolf 2013.

of virtue on the Epicurean view. According to Cicero, who is greatly annoyed about such stubbornness, the Epicureans

> fictam et commenticiam fabulam prolatam dicunt a Platone, quasi vero ille aut factum id esse aut fieri potuisse defendat. haec est vis huius anuli et huius exempli: si nemo sciturus, nemo ne suspicaturus quidem sit, cum aliquid divitiarum, potentiae dominationis libidinis causa feceris, si id diis hominibusque futurum sit semper ignotum, sisne facturus? negant id fieri posse. quamquam potest id quidem, sed quaero, quod negant posse, id si posset, quidnam facerent. urgent rustice sane. negant enim posse et in eo perstant, hoc verbum quid valeat non vident. cum enim quaerimus, si celare possint, quid facturi sint. Non quaerimus, possintne celare.
>
> declare that the story related by Plato [about the Ring of Gyges] is fictitious and imaginary. As if he affirmed that it was actually true or even possible! But the force of this ring and this example is this: if nobody were to know or even suspect the truth, when you do anything to gain riches or power or sovereignty or sensual gratification – if your act should be hidden forever from the knowledge of gods and men, would you do it? They deny that it is possible. But my question is, if that were possible which they declare to be impossible, what they would do? They press their point with right boorish obstinacy: they deny that it is possible and they insist on it; they refuse to see the meaning of my words. For when we ask what they would do, if they could escape detection, we are not asking whether they can escape detection.[4]

There are at least two possible different readings of the Epicurean response. On a first reading, the Epicureans outright deny that there are such situations as the one described in the Ring of Gyges story; that is, they simply say it is impossible to have a ring that grants an agent the superpower of invisibility.[5] On a second reading, by contrast, they acknowledge that there are such scenarios as described in the Ring of Gyges story, but claim that in such cases, it is impossible that agents would escape detection. In other words, on this second reading, the impossibility here does not relate to the thought experiment's stipulation of having the superpower of invisibility at all, but rather to the fact that even if the superpower were granted to an agent, the agent in question would escape detection.

On the first reading, their denial of the impossibility of the Ring of Gyges thought experiment could be seen as a general critique of this and

---

[4] Cicero, *On Duties* III.39. Trans. Miller, modified.
[5] For this reading, see also Roskam 2012, 24–6.

Appendix B: *Cicero, the Epicureans, and the Ring of Gyges* 173

similar thought experiments in philosophy (may they involve a floating man, a swamp man, or even a zombie) that make use of assumptions that do not have any grounding in reality. After all, it is indeed completely impossible in this world to use a ring to become invisible because there is no such ring and thus no way to become invisible. Such a reading gains further support by the fact that the Epicureans overall defend a naturalistic philosophy.[6]

The second reading has textual support insofar as some Epicurean texts explicitly mention the *impossibility* of ever being able to escape detection when one commits an injustice:

> Ἀδικοῦντα λαθεῖν μὲν δύσκολον, πίστιν δὲ λαβεῖν ὑπὲρ τοῦ λαθεῖν ἀδύνατον.
>
> It is hard to commit an injustice and escape detection, but to be confident of escaping detection is impossible.[7]

In *KD* 35, furthermore, the impossibility of escaping detection is noticeably connected with repeated wrongdoing ("he will escape detection ten thousand times"), which is one key difference between the Ring of Gyges thought experiment and the puzzle in Plutarch, which is also limited to ideal agents, sages. Accordingly, *KD* 35 could be exactly the kind of passage Cicero has in mind in *On Duties*:

> Οὐκ ἔστι τὸν λάθρα τι ποιοῦντα ὧν συνέθεντο πρὸς ἀλλήλους εἰς τὸ μὴ βλάπτειν μηδὲ βλάπτεσθαι πιστεύειν ὅτι λήσει, κἂν μυριάκις ἐπὶ τοῦ παρόντος λανθάνῃ· μέχρι γὰρ καταστροφῆς ἄδηλον εἰ καὶ λήσει.
>
> It is impossible for someone who secretly does something which men agreed [not to do] in order to avoid harming one another or being harmed to be confident that he will escape detection ten thousand times. For until his death it will be uncertain whether he will continue to escape detection.[8]

---

[6] See Chapter 6. However, we should also quickly add that the Epicureans are not completely opposed to thought experiments in their philosophy. The most famous example is perhaps the spear argument used to argue against the infinity of the universe. Lucretius, *On the Nature of Things* I.968–83. And Lucretius discusses personal identity through time with the help of a palingenesis thought experiment at *On the Nature of Things* III.843–61.

[7] *SV* 7. Trans. Inwood and Gerson. There are of course many more Epicurean texts that establish a link between fear and escaping notice: "Injustice is not a bad thing in itself, but [only] because of the fear produced by the suspicion that one will not escape the notice of those assigned to punish such actions ['Η ἀδικία οὐ καθ' ἑαυτὴν κακόν, ἀλλ' ἐν τῷ κατὰ τὴν ὑποψίαν φόβῳ, εἰ μὴ λήσει τοὺς ὑπὲρ τῶν τοιούτων ἐφεστηκότας κολαστάς]." *KD* 34. Trans. Inwood and Gerson, modified. "Let nothing be done in your life which will cause you to fear if it is discovered by your neighbor [Μηδέν σοι ἐν βίῳ πραχθείη ὃ φόβον παρέξει σοι, εἰ γνωσθήσεται τῷ πλησίον]." *SV* 70. Trans. Inwood and Gerson.

[8] *KD* 35. Trans. Inwood and Gerson.

Which of these two readings is to be preferred? On the basis of the available evidence, the question is difficult to decide. In either case, it would have been helpful to have the Epicurean answer as to why it is impossible to escape detection – either in the form of the said metaphilosophical critique or in the form of the different examples of how wrongdoers have given themselves away, for instance, in their sleep.[9] That we lack this explanation could be due to Cicero, who as a hostile source might simply omit the true explanation that the Epicureans give. Alternatively, if the Epicureans really merely insisted that it is impossible to escape detection without giving any explanation as to why this is the case, they would certainly turn out to be rather obtuse interlocutors. Be this as it may, we should note that both answers given here are completely compatible with the answer that Epicurus is supposed to have given to the question of whether a sage will violate a law, knowing he will escape detection. On the first reading, the Epicureans would not be giving an answer to Plutarch's question, but rather denying the possibility of the Ring of Gyges thought experiment. On the second reading, by contrast, they would engage with the Ring of Gyges thought experiment, claiming that agents in general cannot escape detection, which motivates them to act justly. However, this is of course compatible with the ideas that *sages*, which are the focus of the Plutarch passage, are motivated differently than regular agents and that *sages* may violate a law in some circumstances (and in these cases do not perform an unjust action).

---

[9] See, for instance, Lucretius, *On the Nature of Things* IV.1018–19.

Bibliography

Classical Authors

Anonymous/Collections of Works by Multiple Authors

Diels, Hermann, and Kranz, Walter (eds.) 1951–2. *Die Fragmente der Vorsokratiker*, 6th ed., 3 vols., Berlin: Weidmannsche Buchhandlung

Inwood, Brad, and Gerson, Lloyd (eds.) 1997. *Hellenistic Philosophy: Introductory Readings*, 2nd ed., Indianapolis: Hackett

Lefkowitz, Mary R., and Fant, Maureen B. (eds.) 2016. *Women's Life in Greece and Rome: A Sourcebook in Translation*, 4th ed., Baltimore: Johns Hopkins University Press

Long, Anthony, and Sedley, David (eds.) 1987. *The Hellenistic Philosophers*, 2 vols., New York: Cambridge University Press

Aristotle

Bywater, John (ed.) 1894. *Aristotelis Ethica Nicomachea*, Oxford: Clarendon

Jaeger, Werner (ed.) 2010 [1957]. *Aristotelis Metaphysica*, Oxford: Oxford University Press

Minio-Paluello, Luigi (ed.) 2008 [1949]. *Aristotelis Categoriae et Liber de interpretatione*, Oxford: Oxford University Press

Reeve, C. D. C. 1998. *Aristotle: Politics*, Indianapolis: Hackett

Ross, W. D. (ed.) 1957. *Aristotelis Politica*, Oxford: Clarendon

 (ed.) 1964. *Aristotelis Analytica priora et posteria*, Oxford: Clarendon

 (ed.) 2009 [1950]. *Aristotelis Physica*, Oxford: Clarendon

Cicero

Annas, Julia (ed.) 2001. *Cicero: On Moral Ends*, New York: Cambridge University Press

Miller, Walter (ed.) 2005 [1913]. *Cicero: On Duties*, Cambridge, MA: Harvard University Press

Rackham, Harris (ed.) 1942. *Cicero: On the Orator Book 3*, Cambridge, MA: Harvard University Press

(ed.) 1951. *Cicero: On the Nature of the Gods Academics*, Cambridge, MA: Harvard University Press
Reynolds, L. D. (ed.) 1998. *M. Tulli Ciceronis De finibus bonorum et malorum*, Oxford: Clarendon
Winterbottom, Michael (ed.) 1994. *M. Tulli Ciceronis De officiis*, Oxford: Clarendon

Demetrius Lacon

Puglia, Enzo (ed.) 1988. *Aporie testuali ed esegetiche in Epicuro (PHerc. 1012)*, Naples: Bibliopolis

Democritus

Taylor, C. C. W. (ed.) 1999. *The Atomists: Leucippus and Democritus*, Toronto: University of Toronto Press

Diogenes Laërtius

Dorandi, Tiziano (ed.) 2013. *Diogenes Laeritus: Lives of Eminent Philosophers*, New York: Cambridge University Press
Hicks, R. D. (ed.) 2005 [1931]. *Diogenes Laeritus: Lives of Eminent Philosophers*, 2 vols., Cambridge, MA: Harvard University Press

Diogenes of Oenoanda

Hammerstaedt, Jürgen, and Smith, Martin Ferguson (eds.) 2014. *The Epicurean Inscription of Diogenes of Oinoanda: Ten Years of Discoveries and Research*, Bonn: Habelt
Smith, Martin Ferguson (ed.) 1993. *Diogenes of Oinoanda: The Epicurean Inscription*, Naples: Bibliopolis

Epicurus

A. Complete Works

Arrighetti, Graziano (ed.) 1973. *Epicuro: Opere*, 2nd ed., Turin: Einaudi
Bailey, Cyril (ed.) 1979 [1926]. *Epicurus: The Extant Remains*, Westpoint: Hyperion Press
Bignone, Ettore (ed.) 1964 [1920]. *Epicuro: Opere, frammenti, testimonianze sulla sua vita*, Rome: "L'Erma" di Bretschneider
Bollack, Jean (ed.) 1975. *La pensée du plaisir: Épicure: Textes moraux, commentaires*, Paris: Éditions de Minuit
Diano, Carlo (ed.) 1946. *Ethica Epicuri*, Florence: Sansoni
Hessler, Jan Erik (ed.) 2014. *Epikur: Brief an Menoikeus*, Basel: Schwabe

Usener, Hermann (ed.) 1887. *Epicurea*, Leipzig: Teubner
Verde, Francesco (ed.) 2010. *Epicuro: Epistola a Erodoto*, Rome: Carocci

B. Papyri

Laursen, Simon 1995. "The Early Parts of Epicurus, *On Nature*, 25th Book," *Cronache ercolanesi* 25: 5–109
   1997. "The Later Parts of Epicurus, *On Nature*, 25th Book," *Cronache ercolanesi* 27: 5–82
Leone, Giuliana (ed.) 2012. *Epicuro: Sulla natura, libro II*, Naples: Bibliopolis
Obbink, Dirk, and Schorn, Stefan 2011. "5077. Epicurus (et al.), *Epistulae ad familiares*," *Oxyrhynchus Papyri* 76: 37–50

Eusebius

Helm, Rudolf (ed.) 1956. *Die Chronik des Hieronymus*. Berlin: De Gruyter

Gaius

Gordon, W. M., and Robinson, O. F. (eds.) 1988. *The Institutes of Gaius*, London: Duckworth

Hermarchus

Auricchio, Francesca Longo (ed.) 1988. *Ermarco: Frammenti*, Naples: Bibliopolis
Krohn, Karl (ed.) 1921. *Der Epikureer Hermarchos*, Berlin: Weidmannsche Buchhandlung

Herodotus

Godley, A. D. (ed.) 2000 [1938]. *Herodotus: The Persians Wars, Books III–IV* [= *Histories*], Cambridge, MA: Harvard University Press

Hierocles

Ramelli, Illaria (ed.) 2009. *Hierocles: Elements of Ethics, Fragments and Excerpts*, Atlanta: Society of Biblical Literature

Lucretius

Bailey, Cyril (trans.) 1936 [1910]. *Lucretius: On the Nature of Things*, Oxford: Clarendon
   (ed.) 1947. *Titi Lucreti Cari De rerum natura libri sex*, 3 vols., Oxford: Clarendon

Smith, Martin Ferguson (trans.) 1969. *Lucretius: On the Nature of Things*, Indianapolis: Hackett

Philodemus

Angeli, Anna (ed.) 1988. *Filodemo: Agli amici di scuola (PHerc. 1005)*, Naples: Bibliopolis
Armstrong, David, and McOsker, Michael (eds.) 2020. *Philodemus: On Anger*, Atlanta: Society of Biblical Literature
De Lacy, Phillip Howard, and De Lacy, Estelle Allen (eds.) 1978. *Philodemus: On Methods of Inference*, Naples: Bibliopolis
Delattre, Daniel (ed.) 2007. *Philodème de Gadara: Sur la musique: Livre IV*, 2 vols., Paris: Les Belles Lettres
Diels, Hermann (ed.) 1916. *Philodemos, Über die Götter, Erstes Buch*, Berlin: Verlag der königlichen Akademie der Wissenschaften
  (ed.) 1917. *Philodemos, Über die Götter, Drittes Buch*, 2 vols., Berlin: Verlag der königlichen Akademie der Wissenschaften
Dorandi, Tiziano (ed.) 1982. *Filodemo: Il buon re secondo Omero*, Naples: Bibliopolis
Henry, W. Benjamin (ed.) 2009. *Philodemus: On Death*, Atlanta: Society of Biblical Literature
Hubbell, Harry (trans.) 1920. *The Rhetorica of Philodemus*, New Haven, CT: Yale University Press
Indelli, Giovanni, and Tsouna-McKirahan, Voula (eds.) 1995. *[Philodemus] [On Choices and Avoidances]*, Naples: Bibliopolis [= *PHerc* 1251]
Janko, Richard (ed.) 2000. *Philodemus: On Poems, Book 1*, Oxford: Oxford University Press
  (ed.) 2011. *Philodemus: On Poems, Book 3–4*, Oxford: Oxford University Press
  (ed.) 2020. *Philodemus: On Poems, Book 2*, Oxford: Oxford University Press
Konstan, David, et al. (eds.) 1998. *Philodemus: On Frank Criticism*, Atlanta: Society of Biblical Literature
Mangoni, Cecilia (ed.) 1993. *Filodemo: Il quinto libro della Poetica (PHerc. 1425 e 1538)*, Naples: Bibliopolis
Monnet, Annick 1996. "[Philodème, *Sur les sensations*] Pherc. 19/698," *Cronache ercolanesi* 26: 27–126
Obbink, Dirk (ed.) 1996. *Philodemus: On Piety, Part 1*, Oxford: Clarendon
Sudhaus, Siegfried (ed.) 1892. *Philodemi Volumina rhetorica*, 2 vols., Leipzig: Teubner
Tsouna, Voula (ed.) 2012. *Philodemus: On Property Management*, Atlanta: Society of Biblical Literature

Plato

Burnet, John (ed.) 1900–7. *Platonis Opera*, 5 vols., Oxford: Clarendon
Cooper, John (ed.) 1997. *Plato: Complete Works*, Indianapolis: Hackett

Eigler, Günther (ed.) 2005 [1971]. *Platon: Werke*, Darmstadt: Wissenschaftliche Buchgesellschaft

Plutarch

Cherniss, Harold (ed.) 1976. *Plutarch's Moralia Moralia XIII, Part II*, Cambridge, MA: Harvard University Press

Einarson, Benedict, and De Lacy, Phillip (eds.) 1967. *Plutarch's Moralia XIV*, Cambridge, MA: Harvard University Press

Minar, Edwin L., Jr., et al. (eds.) 1961. *Plutarch's Moralia IX*, Cambridge, MA: Harvard University Press

Perrin, Bernadotte (ed.) 1918. *Plutarch's Lives VI*, London: William Heinemann

Polystratus

Indelli, Giovanni (ed.) 1978. *Polistrato: Sul disprezzo irrazionale delle opinioni popolari*, Naples: Bibliopolis

Porphyry

Bouffartigue, Jean, and Patillon, Michel (eds.) 1979. *Porphyre: De l'abstinence*, 3 vols., Paris: Les Belles Lettres

Clark, Gillian (trans.) 2000. *Porphyry: On Abstinence of Killing Animals*, London: Duckworth

Seneca

Hummere, Richard M. (ed.) 1953. *Seneca: Ad Lucilium epistulae morales*, 3 vols., Cambridge, MA: Harvard University Press

Sextus Empiricus

Bury, R. G. (ed.) 1936. *Against the Physicists Against the Ethicists* [= *Against the Mathematicians* IX–XI], Cambridge, MA: Harvard University Press

Zenon

Angeli, Anna, and Colaizzo, Maria (eds.) 1979. "I frammenti di Zenone Sidonio," *Cronache ercolanesi* 9: 47–133

Post-Classical Authors

Alberti, Antonina 1995. "The Epicurean Theory of Law and Justice," in Laks, André, and Schofield, Malcom (eds.), *Justice and Generosity: Studies in*

Hellenistic Social and Political Philosophy – Proceedings of the Sixth Symposium Hellenisticum, Cambridge: Cambridge University Press, 191–212

1996. "Polistratos e il realismo etico epicureo," in Giannantoni, Gabriele, and Gigante, Marcelo (eds.), *Epicureismo greco e romano*, 2 vols., Naples: Bibliopolis, vol. II, 527–47

Algra, Keimpe 1997. "Lucretius and the Epicurean Other: On the Philosophical Background of DRN v.1011–1027," in Algra, Keimpe, et al. (eds.), *Lucretius and His Intellectual Background*, Amsterdam: Royal Netherlands Academy of the Sciences, 141–50

Annas, Julia 1981. *An Introduction to Plato's Republic*, Oxford: Clarendon

1992. *Hellenistic Philosophy of Mind*, Berkeley: University of California Press

1993a. *The Morality of Happiness*, New York: Oxford University Press

1993b. "Epicurus on Agency," in Brunschwig, Jacques, and Nussbaum, Martha (eds.) *Passions & Perceptions: Studies in Hellenistic Philosophy of Mind*, New York: Cambridge University Press, 53–71

2005. "Virtue Ethics: What Kind of Naturalism," in Gardiner, Stephen (ed.) *Virtue Ethics, Old and New*, Ithaca, NY: Cornell University Press, 11–29

2016 [2002]. "Democritus and Eudaimonism," in Graham, Daniel, and Caston, Victor (eds.) *Presocratic Philosophy: Essay in Honour of Alexander Mourelatos*, London: Routledge, 169–82

Aoiz, Javier, and Boeri, Marcelo D. 2023. *Theory and Practice in Epicurean Political Philosophy*, London: Bloomsbury

Arenson, Kelly 2016. "Epicureans on Marriage as Sexual Therapy," *Polis* 33: 291–311

2023. "Ancient Women Epicureans and Their Anti-Hedonist Critics," in O'Reilly, Katharine, and Pellò, Caterinà (eds.) *Ancient Women Philosophers: Recovered Ideas and New Perspectives*, Cambridge: Cambridge University Press, 77–95

Armstrong, John 1997. "Epicurean Justice," *Phronesis* 42, no. 3: 324–34

Arrighetti, Graziano 1952. "Sul valore di ΕΠΙΛΟΓΙΖΟΜΑΙ, ΕΠΙΛΟΓΙΣΜΟΣ, ΕΠΙΛΟΓΙΣΙΣ nel sistema epicureo," *Parola del passato* 7: 119–44

Asmis, Elizabeth 1984. *Epicurus' Scientific Method*, Ithaca, NY: Cornell University Press

1991. "Philodemus's Poetic Theory and 'On the Good King According to Homer,'" *Classical Antiquity* 10, no. 1: 1–45

2001. "Basic Education in Epicureanism," in Too, Yun Lee (ed.) *Education in Greek and Roman Antiquity*, Leiden: Brill, 209–39

2008. "Lucretius' New World Order: Making a Pact with Nature," *Classical Quarterly* 58, no. 1: 141–57

2010 [1999]. "Epicurean Epistemology," in Algra, Keimpe, et al. (eds.) *The Cambridge History of Hellenistic Philosophy*, New York: Cambridge University Press, 260–94

2010 [2009]. "Epicurean Empiricism," in Warren, James (ed.) *The Cambridge Companion to Epicureanism*, New York: Cambridge University Press, 84–104

2020. "Psychology," in Mitsis, Phillip (ed.) *Oxford Handbook of Epicurus and Epicureanism*, Oxford: Oxford University Press, 189–220
Atherton, Catherine 2009 [2005]. "Lucretius on What Language Is Not," in Frede, Dorothea, and Inwood, Brad (eds.) *Language and Learning: Philosophy of Language in the Hellenistic Age*, Cambridge: Cambridge University Press, 101–38
Austin, John 1998 [1832]. *The Providence of Jurisprudence Determined and the Uses of the Study of Jurisprudence*, Indianapolis: Hackett
Bailey, Cyril 1964 [1928]. *The Greek Atomists and Epicurus: A Study*, New York: Russell and Russell
Bakker, Frederik 2016. *Epicurean Meteorology: Sources, Method, and Organization*, Leiden: Brill
Benferhat, Yasmina 2005. *Cives epicurei: Les épicuriens et l'idée de monarchie à Rome et en Italie de Sylla à Octave*, Brussels: Éditions Latomus
Beresford, Adam 2013. "Fangs, Feathers, & Fairness: Protagoras on the Origins of Right and Wrong," in van Obhuijsen, Johannes M., et al. (eds.) *Protagoras of Abdera: The Man, His Measure*, Leiden: Brill, 139–62
Besnier, Bernard 1994. "Épicure et la definition," in Jerphagnon, Lucien, et al. (eds.) *Ainsi parlaient les anciens*, Lille: Presses Universitaires de Lille, 117–30
Betegh, Gabor 2006. "Epicurus' Argument for Atomism," *Oxford Studies in Ancient Philosophy* 30: 261–84
Bett, Richard 1994. "Sextus 'Against the Ethicists: Scepticism, Relativism, or Both?,'" *Apeiron* 27, no. 2: 123–61
Bix, Brian 2002. "Natural Law Theory: The Modern Tradition," in Coleman, Jules, and Shapiro, Scott (eds.) *Oxford Handbook of Jurisprudence and Philosophy of Law*, Oxford: Oxford University Press, 61–103.
Blickman, Daniel 1989. "Lucretius, Epicurus, and Prehistory," *Harvard Studies in Classical Philology* 92: 157–91
Bobzien, Susanne 2006. "Moral Responsibility and Moral Development in Epicurus' Philosophy," in Reis, Burkhard, and Haffmanns, Stella (eds.) *The Virtuous Life in Greek Ethics*, Cambridge: Cambridge University Press, 206–29
Boyancé, Pierre 1963. *Lucrèce et l'Épicurisme*, Paris: Presses Universitaires de France
Brittain, Charles 2005. "Common Sense: Concepts, Definition and Meaning in and out of the Stoa," Frede, Dorothea, and Inwood, Brad (eds.) *Language and Learning: Philosophy of Language in the Hellenistic Age*, New York: Cambridge University Press, 164–209
Brown, Eric 2002. "Epicurus on the Value of Friendship ('Sententia Vaticana' 23)," *Classical Philology* 97, no. 1: 68–80
2010 [2009]. "Politics and Society," in Warren, James (ed.) *The Cambridge Companion to Epicureanism*, New York: Cambridge University Press, 179–96
Brunschwig, Jacques 1986. "The Cradle Argument in Epicureanism and Stoicism," in Schofield, Malcom, and Striker, Gisela (eds.) *The Norms of*

Nature: Studies in Hellenistic Ethics, Cambridge: Cambridge University Press, 113–44

Campbell, Gordon 2002a. "Lucretius 5.1011–27: The Origins of Justice and the Prisoner's Dilemma," *Leeds International Classical Studies* 1: https://web.archive.org/web/20141201223704/http://lics.leeds.ac.uk/2002/200203.pdf

2002b. "Lucretius and the Memes of Prehistory," *Leeds International Classical Studies* Discussion Paper 1: https://web.archive.org/web/20141129231755/http://lics.leeds.ac.uk/discussion/2002dp1.pdf

2003. *Lucretius on Creation and Evolution*, New York: Oxford University Press

2008. "'And bright was the flame of their friendship' (Empedocles B130): Humans, Animals, Justice, and Friendship in Lucretius and Empedocles," *Leeds International Classical Studies* 7: https://web.archive.org/web/20141201221416/http://lics.leeds.ac.uk/2008/200804.pdf

Canfora, Luciano, and Stringer, Julian 2007. "Epicureans in Revolt?," in Canfora, Luciano (ed.) *Julius Caesar: The People's Dictator*, Edinburgh: University of Edinburgh Press, 296–305

Carnes, Thomas 2021. "Keeping the Friend in Epicurean Friendship," *Apeiron* 54, no. 3: 385–410

Castner, Catherine J. 1991. *Prosopography of Roman Epicureans from the Second Century B.C. to the Second Century A.D.*, Frankfurt: Peter Lang

Clay, Diskin 1998. *Paradosis and Survival: Three Chapters in the History of the Epicurean School*, Ann Arbor: University of Michigan Press

Cole, Thomas 1990 [1967]. *Democritus and the Sources of Greek Anthropology*, Atlanta: Scholars Press

Coleman, Jules, and Leiter, Brian 1996. "Legal Positivism," in Patterson, Dennis (ed.) *A Companion to Philosophy of Law and Legal Theory*, Malden, MA: Blackwell, 241–60

Darwall, Stephen, et al. 1992. "Towards *Fin de Siècle* Ethics: Some Trends," *Philosophical Review* 101, no. 1: 115–89

De Lacy, Phillip 1958. "Epicurean Epilogismos," *American Journal of Philology* 79, no. 2: 179–83

Delattre, Daniel 2003. "Les figures du sage et du philosophe au travers de quatres livres étiques de Philodème," *Cronache ercolanesi* 33: 229–41

Denyer, Nicholas 1983. "The Origins of Justice," in Gigante, Marcelo (ed.) ΣΥΖΗΤΗΣΙΣ: *Studi sull' Epicureism greco e romano*, Naples: Gaetano Macchiaroli, 133–52

De Sanctis, Dino 2010. "φρόνησις e φρόνιμοι nel giardino," *Cronache ercolanesi* 40: 75–86

Detel, Wolfgang 1975. "Αἴσθησις und Λογισμός: Zwei Probleme der epikureischen Methodologie," *Archiv für Geschichte der Philosophie* 57, no. 1: 21–35

DeWitt, Norman 1954. *Epicurus and His Philosophy*, Minneapolis: University of Minnesota Press

Diaco, Sara 2022. "Epicureans and the City's Laws," *Archiv für Geschichte der Philosophie* 104, no. 2: 312–34

Dierauer, Urs 1977. *Tier und Mensch im Denken der Antike*, Amsterdam: Grüner

Dixon, Suzanne 1992. *The Roman Family*, Baltimore: Johns Hopkins University Press
Dowell, J. L. 2013. "Ethical Naturalism," in LaFollette, Hugh (ed.), *The International Encyclopedia of Ethics*, Chichester: Wiley-Blackwell, 3532–42
Dyck, Andrew R. 1996. *A Commentary on Cicero, De Officis*, Ann Arbor: University of Michigan Press
Dyson, Henry 2009. *Prolepsis and Ennoia in the Early Stoa*, Berlin: De Gruyter
Erler, Michael 1994. "Epikur – Die Schule Epikurs – Lukrez," in Flashar, Helmut (ed.) *Grundriss der Geschichte der Philosophie*, vol. IV.1, Basel: Schwabe, 29–490
  2020. *Epicurus: An Introduction to His Practical Ethics and Politics*, Basel: Schwabe
Essler, Holger 2016. "Zusammenhang bei Einzelsätzen: Zum assoziativen Aufbau der epikureischen κύριαι δόξαι," in Männlein-Robert, Irmgard, et al. (eds.) *Philosophus Orator: Rhetorische Strategien und Strukturen in philosophischer Literatur*, Basel: Schwabe, 145–60
Evans, Matthew 2004. "Can Epicureans Be Friends?," *Ancient Philosophy* 24, no. 2: 407–24
Farrar, Cynthia 1988. *The Origins of Democratic Thinking: The Invention of Politics in Classical Athens*, New York: Cambridge University Press
Farrington, Benjamin 1953. "Second Thoughts on Epicurus," *Science & Society* 17, no. 4: 326–39
Fine, Gail 2014. *The Possibility of Inquiry: Meno's Paradox from Socrates to Sextus*, New York: Oxford University Press
Fish, Jeffrey 2011. "Not All Politicians Are Sisyphus: What Roman Epicureans Were Taught about Politics," in Fish, Jeffrey, and Sanders, Kirk (eds.) *Epicurus and the Epicurean Tradition*, Cambridge: Cambridge University Press, 72–104
  2018. "Some Critical Themes in Philodemus' *On the Good King According to Homer*," in Klooster, Jacqueline, and van den Berg, Baukje (eds.) *Homer and the Good Ruler in Antiquity and Beyond*, Leiden: Brill, 141–56
Fish, Jeffrey, and Sanders, Kirk (eds.) 2011. *Epicurus and the Epicurean Tradition*, Cambridge: Cambridge University Press
Fitzpatrick, Tony 2018. *How to Live Well: Epicurus as a Guide to Contemporary Social Reform*, Cheltenham: Edward Elgar
Fleischer, Kilian 2016. *Dionysios von Alexandria De Natura (περὶ φύσεως): Übersetzung, Kommentar und Würdigung*, Turnhout: Brepols
Fowler, Don 1989. "Lucretius and Politics," in Griffin, Miriam, and Barnes, Jonathan (eds.) *Philosophia Tolgata: Essays on Philosophy and Roman Society*, Oxford: Clarendon, 120–50
Furley, David 1978. "Lucretius the Epicurean," *Entretiens Hardt* 24: 1–27
  1993. "Epicurus and Democritus on Sensible Qualities," in Brunschwig, Jacques, and Nussbaum, Martha (eds.) *Passions and Perceptions: Studies in Hellenistic Philosophy of Mind*, New York: Cambridge University Press, 72–94

Gallo, Italo 1985. "Ermarco e la polemica epicurea contro Empedocle," in Cosenza, Paolo (ed.) *Esistenza e destino nel pensiero greco arcaico*, Naples: Edizioni Scientifiche Italiane, 33–50
Garbo, Guido 1936. "Società et stato nella concezione di Epicuro," *Atene e Roma* 3, no. 4: 243–62
Gatz, Bodo 1967. *Weltalter, Goldene Zeit und sinnverwandte Vorstellungen*, Hildesheim: Georg Olms
Giovacchini, Julie 2003. "Le refus épicurien de la définition," *Les Cahiers philosophiques de Strasbourg* 15: 71–89
  2019. "La *tetrapharmakos*: Formule authentique ou résumé simpliste de l'éthique épicurienne? Quelques élements sur le statut des abrégés et des florilèges dans la pédagogie du Jardin," *Philosophie antique* 19: 29–56
  2020. "La confusion du juste chez Épicure, Hermarque et Lucrèce: Une inégalité intellectuelle des citoyenes?," *Fons* 5, 39–59
Giovacchini, Julie, and Lemaire, Juliette 2014. "La philosophie populaire de Polystrate l'Épicurien," in Cournet, Jean-Michel (ed.) *Philosophie et langage ordinaire: De l'antiquité à la renaissance*, Louvain: Peeters, 57–82
Giussani, Carlo 1896. *Studi Lucreziani*, vol. I, Turin: Ermano Loescher
Glidden, David 1971. "The Epicurean Theory of Knowledge," PhD thesis, Princeton University
  1985. "Epicurean Prolēpsis," *Oxford Studies in Ancient Philosophy* 3: 175–218
Goggins, Rory 2007. "Preconceptions and Epistemic Priority," *Ancient Philosophy* 27, no. 2: 371–90
Goldschmidt, Victor 1977. *La doctrine d'Épicure et le droit*, Paris: Vrin
  1981. "La teoria epicurea del diritto," *Elenchos* 2: 290–316
  2006 [1978]. "Remarques sur l'origine épicurienne de la 'prénotion,'" in Brunschwig, Jacques (ed.), *Les Stoïciens et leur logique*, Paris: Vrin, 41–60
Gordon, Pamela 2012. *The Invention and Gendering of Epicurus*, Ann Arbor: University of Michigan Press
Gough, John Wiedhofft 1957. *The Social Contract: A Critical Study of Its Development*, Oxford: Clarendon
Green, Jeffrey 2015. "Solace for the Frustrations of Silent Citizenship," *Citizenship Studies* 19, no. 5: 492–506
Green, Leslie 2004. "Law and Obligations," in Coleman, Jules, et al. (eds.) *The Oxford Handbook of Jurisprudence and Philosophy of Law*, Oxford: Oxford University Press, 514–47
  2008. "Positivism and the Inseparability of Law and Morals," *New York University Law Review* 84, no. 4: 1–23
  2009. "Legal Positivism," in Zalta, Edward (ed.) *The Stanford Encyclopedia of Philosophy* (Fall 2009 edition), http://plato.stanford.edu/archives/fall2009/entries/legal-positivism/.
Greenblatt, Stephen 2011. *The Swerve: How the World Became Modern*, New York: W. W. Norton

Griffin, Miriam 1997. "Philosophy, Politics, and Politicians at Rome," in Griffin, Miriam, and Barnes, Jonathan (eds.) *Essays on Philosophy and Roman Society,* Oxford: Clarendon Press, 1–37
Grilli, Alberto 1953. *Il problema della vita contemplativa nel mondo greco-romano,* Milan: Fratelli Bocca
  1996. "Considerazioni sul fr. 555 Us. di Epicuro," in Giannantoni, Gabriele, and Gigante, Marcelo (eds.) *Epicureismo greco e romano,* Naples: Bibliopolis, vol. I, 377–86
Guthrie, W. K. C. 2003 [1971]. *The Sophists,* Cambridge: Cambridge University Press
Hahmann, Andree, and Robitzsch, Jan Maximilian 2021. "Epicurus' Divine Hedonism," *Mnemosyne* 74: 401–22
  2022. "Epicurus' Non-Propositional Theory of Truth," *Mnemosyne* 75: 739–58
Hardach, Karl von 2007. "'Nicht hungern, nicht dürsten, nicht frieren': Zum Lebensstandard der Athener zu Zeiten Epikurs," in Hardach, Karl von (ed.) *Wirtschaftshistorische Studien: Festgabe für Othmar Pickl,* Frankfurt: Peter Lang, 75–115
Hart, H. L. A. 1958. "Positivism and the Separation of Law and Morals," *Harvard Law Review* (1958): 593–629
  2012 [1961]. *The Concept of Law,* Oxford: Oxford University Press
Haussleiter, Johanes 1935. *Der Vegetarismus in der Antike,* Berlin: Töpelmann
Heinimann, Felix 1945. *Nomos und Physis: Herkunft und Bedeutung einer Antithese im griechischen Denken des 5. Jahrhunderts,* Basel: Friedrich Reinhardt
Held, Katharina 2007. *Hēdonē und Ataraxia bei Epikur,* Paderborn: Mentis
Hoffmann, Klaus Friedrich 1997. *Das Recht im Denken der Sophistik,* Leipzig: B.G. Teubner
Horky, Phillip Sydney 2021. "Laws and Justice among the Socratics: Contexts for Plato's *Republic*," *Polis* 38, no. 3: 399–419
Horn, Christoph 2021. "Normative Naturalism in Aristotle's Political Philosophy," in Adamson, Peter, and Rapp, Christoph (eds.) *State and Nature: Studies in Ancient and Medieval Philosophy,* Berlin: De Gruyter, 59–80
Huby, Pamela 1967. "The First Discovery of the Freewill Problem," *Philosophy* 42, no. 162: 353–62
  1978. "Epicurus' Attitude towards Democritus," *Phronesis* 23, no. 1: 80–6
Hursthouse, Rosalind 2013. "Neo-Aristotelian Ethical Naturalism," in LaFollette, Hugh (ed.) *The International Encyclopedia of Ethics,* Chichester: Wiley-Blackwell, 3571–80
Isnardi Parente, Margherita 1971. "L'epicureo Polistrato e le Categorie," *Parola del passato* 26, no. 4: 280–9
Jürss, Fritz 1977. "Epikur und das Problem des Begriffs (Prolepse)," *Philologus* 121: 211–25
  1991. *Die epikureische Erkenntnistheorie,* Berlin: Akademie

Kaerst, Julius 1909. "Die Entstehung der Vertragstheorie im Altertum," *Zeitschrift für Politik* 2: 505–38
Kahn, Charles 1981. "The Origins of Social Contract Theory," in Kerferd, G. B. (ed.) *The Sophists and Their Legacy*, Wiesbaden: Franz Steiner, 92–108
  1985. "Democritus and the Origins of Moral Psychology," *American Journal of Philology* 106, no. 1: 1–31
Kaiser, Christian 2019. *Epikur im lateinischen Mittelalter*, Turnhout: Brepols
Kamp, Andreas 2001. *Philosophiehistorie als Rezeptionsgeschichte: Die Reaktion auf Aristoteles' De Anima-Noetik. Der frühe Hellenismus*, Amsterdam: B. R. Grüner
Kamtekar, Rachana 2021. "Experience and Preconception in Epicurus' Refutation of Determinism," *Oxford Studies in Ancient Philosophy* 60: 203–37
Kechagia, Eleni 2010. "Rethinking a Professional Rivalry: Early Epicureans against the Stoa," *Classical Quarterly* 60, no. 1: 132–55
Kelsen, Hans 2008 [1934]. *Reine Rechtslehre*, Tübingen: Mohr Siebeck
Kerferd, G. B. 1981. *The Sophistic Movement*, Cambridge: Cambridge University Press
Klein, Jacob 2016. "The Stoic Argument from *oikeiōsis*," *Oxford Studies in Ancient Philosophy* 50: 143–200
Kleve, Knut 1963. *Gnosis Theōn: Die Lehre von der natürlichen Gotteserkenntnis in der epikureischen Theologie*, Olso: Universitetsforlaget
Konstan, David 2008. *A Life Worthy of the Gods: The Materialist Psychology of Epicurus*, Las Vegas: Parmenides
  2014. "Epicurus on Void," in Ranocchia, Graziano, et al. (eds.) *Space in Hellenistic Philosophy: Critical Studies in Ancient Physics*, Berlin: De Gruyter, 83–99
Kraut, Richard 1992. "The Defense of Justice in Plato's *Republic*," in Kraut, Richard (ed.) *Cambridge Companion to Plato*, New York: Cambridge University Press, 311–37
  2002. *Aristotle: Political Philosophy*, New York: Oxford University Press
Kretzmann, Norman 1988. "Lex iniusta non est lex," *American Journal of Jurisprudence* 33, no. 1: 99–122
Lathière, A. M. 1972. "Lucrèce traducteur d'Épicure," *Phoenix* 26, no. 2: 123–33
Laursen, Simon 1988. "Epicurus' *On Nature* XXV (Long-Sedley 20, B, C and j)," *Cronache ercolanesi* 18: 7–18
Lenman, James 2014. "Moral Naturalism," in Zalta, Edward (ed.) *The Stanford Encyclopedia of Philosophy* (Sprung 2014 edition), http://plato.stanford.edu/archives/spr2014/entries/naturalism-moral/
Lévy, Carlos 1999. "Lucrèce et les Stoïciens," in Poignault, Rémy (ed.) *Présence de Lucrèce. Actes du colloque tenu à Tours (3–5 décembre 1998)*, Tours: Centre de recherches A. Piganiol, 87–98
Liebich, Werner 1960. "Aufbau, Absicht und Form der Pragmateiai Philodems," PhD thesis, Humboldt University of Berlin

Long, Anthony 1971. "Aisthesis, Prolepsis, and Linguistic Theory in Epicurus," *Bulletin of the Institute of Classical Studies* 18: 114–33
  1985. "Pleasure and Social Utility: The Virtues of Being an Epicurean," *Entretiens Hardt* 32: 283–324
Lovejoy, Arthur Oncken, and Boas, George (eds.) 1965 [1935]. *Primitivism and Related Ideas in Antiquity*, New York: Octagon Books
Ludwig, Bernd 2005. "Cicero oder Epikur? Über einen 'Paradigmenwechsel' in Hobbes' politischer Philosophie," in Boros, Gábor (ed.) *Der Einfluß des Hellenismus auf die Philosophe der Frühen Neuzeit*, Wiesbaden: Harrassowitz Verlag, 159–79
Mansfeld, Jaap 1994. "Epicurus Peripateticus," in Alberti, Antonina (ed.) *Realtà e ragione*, Florence: Olschki, 29–47
Manuwald, Anke 1972. *Die Prolepsislehre Epikurs*, Bonn: Rudolf Habelt
Manuwald, Bernd 1980. *Der Aufbau der lukrezischen Kulturentstehungslehre (De Rerum Natura 5,925-1457)*, Wiesbaden: Franz Steiner
  2014. "Bürger als politische Akteure: Überlegungen zur allgemeinen Politikkompetenz bei Platon und Aristoteles," *Hyberboreus* 20: 225–43
Masi, Francesca 2006. *Epicuro e la filosofia della mente: Il XXV libro dell'opera Sulla natura*, Sankt Augustin: Academia
McConnell, Sean 2010. "Epicureans on Kingship," *Cambridge Classical Journal* 56: 178–98
  2017a. "Demetrius of Laconia and the Debate between the Stoics and the Epicureans on the Nature of Parental Love," *Classical Quarterly* 67, no. 1: 149–62
  2017b. "The Epicurean Virtue of μεγαλοψυχία," *Classical Philology* 112, no. 2: 175–99
McKirahan, Richard 2010. *Philosophy Before Socrates*, 2nd ed., Indianapolis: Hackett
Mehl, David 1999. "The Intricate Translation of the Epicurean Doctrine of ψυχή in Book 3 of Lucretius," *Philologus* 143, no. 2: 272–87
Mejer, Jørgen 2004. "Democritus and Democracy," *Apeiron* 37, no. 1: 1–9
Merlan, Philip 1950. "Lucretius: Primitivist or Progressivist," *Journal of the History of Ideas* 11, no. 3: 364–8
Miller, Fred 1995. *Nature, Justice, and Rights in Aristotle's Politics*, Oxford: Clarendon
Mitsis, Phillip 1988. *Epicurus' Ethical Theory*, Ithaca, NY: Cornell University Press
  2020. "Friendship," in Mitsis, Phillip (ed.) *Oxford Handbook of Epicurus and Epicureanism*, Oxford: Oxford University Press, 250–81
Mitsis, Phillip, and Piergiacomi, Enrico 2018. "Edonismi: Epicurei e Cirenaici a confronto," in Mitsis, Phillip, and Piergiacomi, Enrico (eds.) *La libertà, il piacere, la morte: Studi sull' Epicureismo e sulla sua influenza*, Rome: Carocci, 107–52
Moore, Stanley 1988. "Democracy and Commodity Exchange: Protagoras versus Plato," *History of Philosophy Quarterly* 5, no. 4: 357–68

Moraux, Paul 1957. *À la recherché de l'Aristote perdu: Le dialogue "Sur la justice,"* Leuven: Publications universitaires de Louvain
Morel, Pierre-Marie 2000. "Épicure, l'histoire et le droit," *Revue des études anciennes* 102, no. 3: 393–411
  2008. "Method and Evidence on Epicurean Preconception," *Proceedings of the Boston Area Colloquium in Ancient Philosophy* 23: 25–48
  2010. "Prudence aristotélicienne et prudence épicurienne," in Silbeira, Denis Coitinho, and Hobuss, João (eds.) *Virtudes, Direitos e Democracia*, Pelotas: Editora Universitária UFPL, 11–30
  2019a. "Épicure et la *phronēsis*: Une autre sagesse pratique," in Masi, Francesca, et al. (eds.) *Ēthikē theōria: Studi sull' Etica Nicomachea in onore di Carlo Natali*, Rome: Edizioni di Storia e Letteratura, 365–84
  2019b. "Sexe, amour et politique chez Lucrèce," *Philosophie antique* 19: 57–84
Mulgan, R. G. 1979. "Lycophron and Greek Theories of Social Contract," *Journal of the History of Ideas* 40, no. 1: 121–8
Müller, Reimar 1972. *Die epikureische Gesellschaftstheorie*, Berlin: Akademie
  1980. "Le rapport entre la philosophie de la nature et la doctrine morale chez Democrite et Épicure," in Romano, Fracesco (ed.) *Democrito e l'atomismo antico: Atti del convegno internazionale*, Catania: Facoltá di Lettere e Filosofia, Universitá di Catania, 325–51
  1983. "Konstituierung und Verbindlichkeit der Rechtsnormen bei Epikur," in Gigante, Marcelo (ed.) ΣΥΖΗΤΗΣΙΣ: *Studi sull' Epicurismo greco e romano*, Naples: Gaetano Macchiaroli, vol. I, 153–83
  1984. "Die Stellung Demokrits in der antiken Sozialphilosophie," in International Democritean Foundation (ed.) *Proceedings of the 1st International Congress on Democritus*, Xanthi: E. Bouloukos, 423–34
  1985. "Der antike Ursprung der Lehre vom Gesellschaftsvertrag," in Müller, Reimar and Klenner, Hermann (eds.) *Gesellschaftsvertragstheorien von der Antike bis zur Gegenwart*, Berlin: Akademie, 5–29
  1987. "Zu einem Entwicklungsprinzip der epikureischen Anthropologie," in Müller, Reimar (ed.) *Polis und res publica: Studien zum antiken Gesellschafts- und Geschichtsdenken*, Weimar: H. Böhlaus Nachfolger, 233–50
  1991. *Die epikureische Ethik*, Berlin: Akademie
  1997. *Anthropologie und Geschichte*, Berlin: Akademie
Müri, Walter 1976. "ΣΥΜΒΟΛΟΝ: Wort- und sachgeschichtliche Studie," in Vischer, Eduard (ed.) *Griechische Studien: Ausgewählte wort- und sachgeschichtliche Forschungen zur Antike*, Basel: Friedrich Reinhardt, 1–44
Murphy, Mark C. 2007. *Philosophy of Law*, Malden, MA: Blackwell
Nicholson, P. P., and Kerferd, G. B. 1982. "Protagoras on Pre-Political Man: An Exchange," *Polis* 4, no. 2: 18–29
Nussbaum, Martha 1994. *The Therapy of Desire: Theory and Practice in Hellenistic Ethics*, Princeton, NJ: Princeton University Press
Obbink, Dirk 1988. "Hermarchus, Against Empedocles," *Classical Quarterly* 38, no. 2: 428–35

1992. "'What All Men Believe – Must Be True': Common Conceptions and consensio omnium in Aristotle and Hellenistic Philosophy," *Oxford Studies in Ancient Philosophy* 10: 193–231
Obi, Augustine 1993. "Epicurus' Foundation of Knowledge," PhD thesis, Duquesne University
O'Connor, David 1989. "The Invulnerable Pleasure of Epicurean Friendship," *Greek, Roman, and Byzantine Studies* 30: 165–89
O'Keefe, Timothy 1997. "The Ontological Status of Sensible Qualities for Democritus and Epicurus," *Ancient Philosophy* 17, no. 1: 119–34
  2001a. "Would a Community of Wise Epicureans Be Just?," *Ancient Philosophy* 21, no. 1: 133–46
  2001b. "Is Epicurean Friendship Altruistic?," *Apeiron* 34, no. 4: 269–305
  2021. "The Normativity of Nature in Epicurean Ethics and Politics," in Adamson, Peter, and Rapp, Christoff (eds.) *State and Nature: Essays in Ancient Political Philosophy*, Boston: De Gruyter, 181–99
Paganini, Gianni 2020. "Early Modern Epicureanism: Gassendi and Hobbes in Dialogue on Psychology, Ethics, and Politics," in Mitsis, Phillip (ed.) *Oxford Handbook of Epicurus and Epicureanism*, Oxford: Oxford University Press, 671–710
Paneris, Joannis 1977. "Die Staatsphilosophie Demokrits im Hinblick auf die Lehre der älteren Sophisten," PhD thesis, University of Vienna
Pappas, Nickolas 1995. *Plato and the Republic*, London: Routledge
Perelli, Luciano 1967. "La storia dell' umanità nel v libro di Lucrezio," *Atti della Accademia delle scienze di Torino* 101: 117–285
Philippson, Robert 1910. "Die Rechtsphilosophie der Epikureer," *Archiv für Geschichte der Philosophie* 23, no. 3: 289–337
  1923. "Review of Krohn, Der Epikureer Hermarchos," *Philologische Wochenschrift* 43, no. 1: 1–10
Piergiacomi, Enrico 2013. "A che serve venerarlo, se dio non fa nulla? Epicuro e il piacere della preghiera," *Lexicon Philosophicum* 1: 19–28
  2017. *Storia delle antiche teologie atomiste*, Rome: Sapienza Università Editrice
Pigeaud, Maurice Jackie 1984. "Épicure et Lucrèce et la naissance du langage," *Révue des études latines* 61: 122–44
Pohlenz, Max 1953. "Nomos und Physis," *Hermes* 81, no. 4: 418–38
Polansky, Ronald 2014. "Giving Justice Its Due," in Polansky, Ronald (ed.) *Cambridge Companion to Aristotle's Nicomachean Ethics*, Cambridge: Cambridge University Press, 151–79
Pomeroy, Sarah 1975. *Goddesses, Whores, Wives, and Slaves: Women in Classical Antiquity*, New York: Schocken
Porter, James 2002. "Φυσιολογεῖν: Nausiphanes of Teos and the Physics of Rhetoric: A Chapter in the History of Greek Atomism," *Cronache ercolanesi* 32: 137–86
Porter, Mary Packer 1938. *Cicero's Presentation of Epicurean Ethics*, New York: Columbia University Press
Procopé, J. F. 1971. "Democritus the Moralist and His Contemporaries," PhD thesis, Cambridge University

1989. "Democritus on Politics and the Care of the Soul," *Classical Quarterly* 39, no. 2: 307–31

1990. "Democritus on Politics and the Care of the Soul: Appendix," *Classical Quarterly* 40, no. 1: 21–45

Rapp, Christof 2021. "Whose State? Whose Nature? How Aristotle's Polis Is 'Natural,'" in Adamson, Peter, and Rapp, Christof (eds.) *State and Nature: Studies in Ancient and Medieval Philosophy,* Berlin: De Gruyter, 81–118

Rechenauer, Georg 2019. "Kosmos und Polis bei Demokrit: Ordnung des Lebens und der Freiheit," in Riedweg, Christoph (ed.) *Philosophie für die Polis: Akten des 5. Kongress der Gesellschaft für antike Philosophie 2016,* Berlin: De Gruyter

Reinsberg, Carola 1989. *Ehe, Hetärentum und Knabenliebe im antiken Griechenland,* Munich: Beck

Robitzsch, Jan Maximilian 2017. "The Epicureans on Human Nature and Its Social and Political Consequences," *Polis* 34, no. 1: 1–19

2020a. "Epicurus on What There Is," in Arenson, Kelly (ed.) *Routledge Handbook of Hellenistic Philosophy,* London: Routledge, 204–14

2020b. "The Presentation of the Epicurean Virtues," *Apeiron* 53, no. 4: 419–35

2021. "*epibolē tēs dianoias*: Reflections on the Fourth Epicurean Criterion of Truth," *Classical Quarterly* 71, no. 2: 601–16

2022a. "A Functional Reading of the Epicurean Classification of Desires," *Apeiron* 55, no. 2: 193–217

2022b. "Epicurus on Justice 'In Itself' (*kath' heauto*) (Kuria Doxa 33)," *Apeiron* 55, no. 3: 443–53

2023. "Protagoras on How Political Communities Come to Be," *Classical Philology* 118, no. 3: 387–98

forthcoming a. "Democritus on Human Nature and Sociability," *Ancient Philosophy*

forthcoming b. "Epicurean Feelings (*pathē*) as Criteria," *Archiv für Geschichte der Philosophie*

forthcoming c. "Gegen wen ist *Kuria Doxa* 33 gerichtet?," *Mnemosyne*

Rosenbaum, Stuart 1996. "Epicurean Moral Theory," *History of Philosophy Quarterly* 13, no. 4: 389–410

Roskam, Geert 2007. *Live Unnoticed (Λάθε Βιώσας): On the Vicissitudes of an Epicurean Doctrine,* Leiden: Brill

2012. "Will the Epicurean Sage Break the Law if He Is Perfectly Sure That He Will Escape Detection? A Difficult Problem Revisited," *Transactions of the American Philological Association* 142, no. 1 (2012): 23–40

2020. "Politics and Society," in Mitsis, Phillip (ed.) *Oxford Handbook of Epicurus and Epicureanism,* Oxford: Oxford University Press, 284–304

Rossi, Benjamin 2017. "Squaring the Epicurean Circle: Friendship and Happiness in the Garden," *Ancient Philosophy* 37, no. 1: 153–68

Rover, Chiara 2022. "Lucretius' Prolepsis," *Elenchos* 43, no. 2: 279–314

Sallmann, Klaus 1986. "Nunc huc rationis detulit ordo: Noch einmal zum Aufbau der Kulturlehre des Lukrez," in Altheim-Stiehl, Ruth, and

Rosenbach, Manfred (eds.) *Beiträge zur altitalischen Geschichte: Festschrift Gerhard Radke*, Münster: Aschendorff, 245–56
Sandbach, F. H. 1930. "Ennoia and ΠΡΟΛΗΨΙΣ in the Stoic Theory of Knowledge," *Classical Quarterly* 24, no. 1: 44–51
Schmid, Wolfgang 1943. "Nugae herculanenses," *Rheinisches Museum* 92, no. 1: 35–55
Schmidt, Jürgen 1990. *Lukrez, der Kepos und die Stoiker: Untesuchungen zur Schule Epikurs und den Quellen von "De rerum natura,"* Frankfurt: Peter Lang
Schofield, Malcom 1996. "Epilogismos: An Appraisal," in Frede, Michael, and Striker, Gisela (eds.) *Rationality in Greek Thought*, Oxford: Clarendon, 221–37
  2010 [2000]. "Epicurean and Stoic Political Thought," in Rowe, Christopher, and Schofield, Malcom (eds.) *The Cambridge History of Greek and Roman Political Thought*, New York: Cambridge University Press, 435–56
Schrijvers, Piet 1996. "Lucretius on the Origin and Development of Political Life (*De Rerum Natura* 5.1105–1160)," in Algra, Keimpe, et al. (eds.) *Polyhistor: Studies in the History and Historiography of Ancient Philosophy*, Leiden: Brill, 220–30
  1999. *Lucrèce et les sciences de la vie*, Leiden: Brill
Sedley, David 1982. "Two Conceptions of Vacuum," *Phronesis* 27, no. 2: 175–93
  1988. "Epicurean Anti-Reductionism," in Barnes, Jonathan, and Mignucci, Mario (eds.) *Matter and Metaphysics*, Naples: Bibliopolis, 295–327
  1997. "The Ethics of Brutus and Cassius," *Journal of Roman Studies* 87: 41–53
  1998a. "The Inferential Foundations of Epicurean Ethics," in Everson, Stephen (ed.) *Ethics*, New York: Cambridge University Press, 129–50
  1998b. *Lucretius and the Transformation of Greek Wisdom*, Cambridge: Cambridge University Press
  2010 [2009]. "Epicureanism in the Roman Republic," in Warren, James (ed.) *The Cambridge Companion to Epicureanism*, New York: Cambridge University Press, 29–45
  2011. "Epicurus' Theological Innatism," in Fish, Jeffrey, and Sanders, Kirk (eds.) *Epicurus and the Epicurean Tradition*, New York: Cambridge University Press, 29–52
Seel, Gerhard 1996. "Farà il saggio qualcosa che le leggi vietano, sapendo che non sarà scoperto?," in Giannantoni, Gabriele, and Gigante, Marcelo (eds.) *Epicureismo greco e romano*, Naples: Bibliopolis, vol. I, 341–60
Shelton, Jo-Ann 1995. "Contracts with Animals: Lucretius, *De rerum natura,*" *Between the Species* 11: 115–21
Sorabji, Richard 1993. *Animal Minds and Human Morals*, Ithaca, NY: Cornell University Press
Spinelli, Emidio 1991. "*Ploutos ē peniē*: Il pensiero economico di Democrito," *Philologus* 135, no. 2: 290–319
  2019. "Justice, Law, and Friendship: Ethical and Political Topics in Epicurus," in Riedweg, Christoph (ed.) *Philosophie für die Polis: Akten des 5. Kongress der Gesellschaft für antike Philosophie 2016*, Berlin: De Gruyter, 379–408

Spoerri, Walter 1959. *Späthellenistische Berichte über Welt, Kultur und Götter*, Basel: Friedrich Reinhardt
Sprute, Jürgen 1989. *Vertragstheoretische Ansätze in der antiken Rechts- und Staatsphilosophie: Die Konzeptionen der Sophisten und Epikureer*, Göttingen: Vandenhoeck and Ruprecht
Striker, Giesela 1974. "Κριτήριον τῆς ἀληθείας," *Nachrichten der Akademie der Wissenschaften in Göttingen Philologisch-Historische Klasse* 2: 51–110
Struck, Peter 2004. *Birth of the Symbol: Ancient Readers at the Limits of Their Texts*, Princeton, NJ: Princeton University Press.
Sturgeon, Nicholas 2006. "Ethical Naturalism," in Copp, David (ed.) *The Oxford Handbook of Ethical Theory*, New York: Oxford University Press, 91–121
Tanner, Julia 2013. "Contractarianism and Secondary Direct Moral Standing for Marginal Humans and Animals," *Res Publica* 19: 141–56
Taylor, A. E. 1911. *Epicurus*, London: Constable
Taylor, Barnaby 2020. *Lucretius and the Language of Nature*, Oxford: Oxford University Press
Thrasher, John 2013. "Reconciling Justice and Pleasure in Epicurean Contractualism," *Ethical Theory and Moral Practice* 16: 423–36
Tohte, Theodor 1874. *Epikurs Kriterien der Wahrheit*, Clausthal: E. Pieper
Tsouna, Voula 2016. "Epicurean Preconceptions," *Phronesis* 61, no. 2: 160–221
Tutrone, Fabio 2022. "A View from the Garden: Contemplative Isolation and Constitutive Sociability in Lucretius and in the Epicurean Tradition," in Matuszewski, Rafał (ed.) *Being Alone in Antiquity: Greco-Roman Ideas and Experiences of Misanthropy, Isolation and Solitude*, Berlin: De Gruyter, 201–27
Usener, Hermann 1888. "Epikurische Spruchsammlung," *Wiener Studien* 10: 175–201
Valachova, Cassandra 2018. "The Political and Philosophical Strategies of Roman Epicureans in the Late Republic," PhD thesis, University of Edinburgh
Vanderschraaf, Peter 2022. "An Epicurean State of Nature," *Homo Oeconomicus*
Vander Waerdt, Paul 1987. "The Justice of the Epicurean Wise Man," *Classical Quarterly* 37, no. 2: 402–22
  1988. "Hermarchus and the Epicurean Genealogy of Morals," *Transactions of the American Philological Association* 118: 87–106
Verde, Francesco 2016. "Aristotle and the Garden," in Falcon, Andrea (ed.) *Brill's Companion to the Reception of Aristotle in Antiquity*, Leiden: Brill, 35–55
Verlinsky, Alexander 1996. "Do Animals Have Freewill? Epicurus, on Nature, 20 B and 20 j Long-Sedley," *Hyperboreus* 2: 125–38
Vlastos, Gregory 1945. "Ethics and Physics in Democritus," *Philosophical Review* 54, no. 6: 578–92
  1946. "Ethics and Physics in Democritus," *Philosophical Review* 55, no. 1 (1946): 53–64
Voelke, André-Jean 1986. "Santé de l'âme et bonheur de la raison: La fonction thérapeutique de la philosophie dans l'épicurisme," *Études de Lettres* 3: 67–87

Wald, Lucia 1968. "Observations sur l'emploi de animus, anima et mens dans l'oeuvre de Lucrèce," in Harmatta, János (ed.) *Studien zur Geschichte der Philosophie des Altertums*, Amsterdam: Hakkert, 135–44
Warren, James 2002. *Epicurus and Democritean Ethics*, Cambridge: Cambridge University Press
  2006a. "Democritus on Social and Psychological Harm," in Brancacci, Aldo, and Morel, Pierre-Marie (eds.) *Democritus: Science, the Arts, and the Care of the Soul*, Leiden: Brill
  2006b. "Epicureans and the Present Past," *Phronesis* 51, no. 4: 362–87
  2014. "Epicurus and the Unity of the Virtues," in Colette-Ducic, Bernard, and Delcomminette, Sylvain (eds.) *Unité et origine des vertus dans la philosophie anciennce*, Brussels: Ousia, 213–36
Westman, Rolf 1955. *Plutarch gegen Kolotes: Seine Schrift "Adversus Colotem" als philosophiegeschichtliche Quelle*, Helsinki: Akateeminen Kirjakauppa
Westphalen, Klaus 1957. "Die Kulturenstehungslehre des Lukrez," PhD thesis, Ludwig Maximilian University of Munich
White, Nicholas 1979. *A Companion to Plato's Republic*, Indianapolis: Hackett
Wilson, Catherine 2008. *Epicureans at the Origins of Modernity*, Oxford: Oxford University Press
  2019. *How to Be Epicurean: The Ancient Art of Living Well*, New York: Basic Books
Wilson, Jessica 2017. "Determinables and Determinates," in Zalta, Edward (ed.) *The Stanford Encyclopedia of Philosophie* (Spring 2021 edition), https://plato.stanford.edu/archives/spr2021/entries/determinate-determinables
Wolfsdorf, David 2009. "Epicurus on Εὐφροσύνη and Ἐνέργεια (DL 10.136)," *Apeiron* 42, no. 3: 221–58
Woolf, Raphael 2013. "Cicero and Gyges," *Classical Quarterly* 63, no. 2: 801–12
Yona, Sergio, and Davis, Gregson (eds.) 2022. *Epicurus in Rome: Philosophical Perspectives in the Ciceronian Age*, Cambridge: Cambridge University Press
Young, Charles 2006. "Aristotle's Justice," in Kraut, Richard (ed.) *The Blackwell Guide to Aristotle's Nicomachean Ethics*, Malden, MA: Blackwell, 179–97
Zeller, Eduard 2013 [1923]. *Die Philosophie der Griechen in ihrer geschichtlichen Entwicklung*, Darmstadt: Wissenschaftliche Buchgesellschaft
Zinn, Pamela 2015. "Sic hominum genus est: Animals and the Continuum of Life in the De rerum natura of Lucretius," PhD thesis, University of Dublin Trinity College

Index Locorum

Aëtius
  Opinions of the Philosophers IV.11.1–4, 150
Anonymous Iamblichi
  DK 89 B 6, 23
Antiphon
  DK 80 B 44, 4
Aristotle
  Metaphysics I.1.980a20–982a3, 152
  Nicomachean Ethics V.1.1229b25–1130a13, 85
  Nicomachean Ethics V.5.1140a24–31, 84
  Nicomachean Ethics V.7.1134b18–24, 8
  Nicomachean Ethics VI.12–13, 85
  On Interpretation 16a4, 50
  On Interpretation 24b2, 50
  Politics I.2.1253a2–3, 24
  Politics III.9.1280b5–12, 80
  Posterior Analytics II.19.100a3–9, 150

Cicero
  On Duties III.39, 171–4
  On Ends I.30, 20, 56
  On Ends I.31, 156
  On Ends I.44, 102
  On Ends I.45, 102
  On Ends I.50–3, 90–4
  On Ends I.50–4, 103
  On Ends I.52–3, 103
  On Ends I.57, 83, 103
  On Ends I.59, 102
  On Ends I.70, 31
  On Ends II.6–15, 59
  On Ends II.26, 102
  On Ends III.16, 166–7
  On Ends III.62–3, 24
  On Ends III.62–4, 167
  On the Nature of the Gods I.43, 155–6
  On the Nature of the Gods I.93, 33, 108
  On the Nature of the Gods I.105, 153
  On the Orator III.63–4, 63

Demetrius Lacon
  PHerc. 1012, col. LXVI–LXVIII, 28
  PHerc. 1012, col. LXVII, 52
Democritus
  DK 68 A 139, 23
  DK 68 B 5.1, 23
  DK 68 B 174, 104
  DK 68 B 250, 43
  DK 68 B 255, 43
  DK 68 B 264, 104
Diogenes Laërtius
  Lives of Eminent Philosophers VII.85–6, 166
  Lives of Eminent Philosophers X.6, 99, 108
  Lives of Eminent Philosophers X.23, 108
  Lives of Eminent Philosophers X.24, 88
  Lives of Eminent Philosophers X.27, 86
  Lives of Eminent Philosophers X.28, 10, 85, 108, 141
  Lives of Eminent Philosophers X.31, 151
  Lives of Eminent Philosophers X.31–2, 141
  Lives of Eminent Philosophers X.32, 18, 147
  Lives of Eminent Philosophers X.33, 149–51
  Lives of Eminent Philosophers X.39, 18
  Lives of Eminent Philosophers X.117, 42, 63, 88, 92, 108–9, 117
  Lives of Eminent Philosophers X.119, 63
  Lives of Eminent Philosophers X.120, 83, 87, 110–11, 165
  Lives of Eminent Philosophers X.121, 110
  Lives of Eminent Philosophers X.138, 83
Diogenes of Oenoanda
  fr. 2, 63
  fr. 3, 35, 63, 78, 89
  fr. 5, 147
  fr. 9, 152
  fr. 10, 147, 159
  fr. 12, 19
  fr. 14, 58, 138
  fr. 37, 83
  fr. 43, 147, 159
  fr. 56, 94–6
  fr. 119, 89
  fr. 126, 147
  fr. 147, 147
  frr. 167, 44–5

Epicurus
  fr. 24.3.5 Arrighetti, 150
  fr. 24.18.5 Arrighetti, 150
  fr. 24.36.7 Arrighetti, 147
  fr. 24.48.3 Arrighetti, 147
  fr. 26.39.23 Arrighetti, 147
  fr. 26.42.8 Arrighetti, 147
  fr. 30.18 Arrighetti, 147
  fr. 31.5.3 Arrighetti, 147
  fr. 31.7.1 Arrighetti, 147
  fr. 31.8.8–9 Arrighetti, 147
  fr. 34.25 Arrighetti, 68
  fr. 34.28 Arrighetti, 157
  fr. 36.11.4 Arrighetti, 147
  fr. 59.1 Arrighetti, 147
  fr. 8 Usener, 63
  frr. 18–21 Usener, 100
  fr. 28 Usener, 33
  fr. 187 Usener, 62, 147
  fr. 213 Usener, 111
  fr. 226 Usener, 42, 63, 92
  fr. 290 Usener, 131
  fr. 456 Usener, 102
  fr. 504 Usener, 83
  frr. 504–22 Usener, 87
  fr. 509 Usener, 83
  fr. 516 Usener, 87
  fr. 517 Usener, 87
  fr. 519 Usener, 84
  fr. 523 Usener, 24
  fr. 525 Usener, 24, 28
  fr. 527 Usener, 28
  fr. 528 Usener, 28
  fr. 529 Usener, 28
  fr. 530 Usener, 97, 101
  fr. 534 Usener, 101
  fr. 551 Usener, 24, 62
  fr. 555 Usener, 63
  fr. 582 Usener, 102
  KD 1, 46, 82
  KD 2, 82
  KD 3, 82
  KD 5, 83, 88, 103
  KD 6, 38, 62
  KD 7, 20, 38, 51, 62
  KD 13, 61–2
  KD 14, 62
  KD 15, 51, 103
  KD 17, 84
  KD 18, 56
  KD 21, 103
  KD 23, 147
  KD 27, 62
  KD 28, 62
  KD 29, 102
  KD 29 (scholion), 102–3
  KD 30, 102
  KD 31, 31, 49–52, 55, 73, 106, 126
  KD 32, 31, 50, 65–7, 78, 146
  KD 33, 31, 50, 58, 92–3, 95, 138
  KD 34, 173
  KD 35, 31, 50, 173
  KD 36, 26, 50
  KD 37, 26, 50–3, 105, 149, 154, 157
  KD 38, 26, 50, 52–3, 58, 105, 149, 154, 157
  KD 39, 64, 165
  KD 40, 165
  Letter to Herodotus 38, 147
  Letter to Herodotus 39, 147
  Letter to Herodotus 39–41, 130
  Letter to Herodotus 46–53, 141
  Letter to Herodotus 48, 147
  Letter to Herodotus 54, 130
  Letter to Herodotus 55, 147
  Letter to Herodotus 58, 147
  Letter to Herodotus 59, 147
  Letter to Herodotus 62, 147
  Letter to Herodotus 63, 147
  Letter to Herodotus 64, 137, 147
  Letter to Herodotus 65, 147
  Letter to Herodotus 66, 147
  Letter to Herodotus 68, 130, 147
  Letter to Herodotus 68–71, 131
  Letter to Herodotus 69, 139
  Letter to Herodotus 71, 147
  Letter to Herodotus 73, 58, 138
  Letter to Herodotus 75, 17–18
  Letter to Herodotus 76, 17
  Letter to Herodotus 77, 58, 138
  Letter to Herodotus 82, 147
  Letter to Menoeceus 123, 62, 86, 153
  Letter to Menoeceus 124, 62, 147
  Letter to Menoeceus 125, 62
  Letter to Menoeceus 127–8, 102
  Letter to Menoeceus 128, 59
  Letter to Menoeceus 128–9, 20
  Letter to Menoeceus 130–2, 77, 102
  Letter to Menoeceus 131, 87
  Letter to Menoeceus 131–2, 59
  Letter to Menoeceus 132, 82–6, 88, 93, 103
  Letter to Menoeceus 133, 51
  Letter to Menoeceus 134, 62
  Letter to Pythocles 86, 147
  Letter to Pythocles 90, 147
  Letter to Pythocles 91, 147
  SV 1, 82
  SV 2, 82
  SV 3, 82
  SV 4, 82
  SV 5, 83, 88
  SV 7, 173
  SV 21, 102
  SV 23, 88
  SV 25, 51

Epicurus (cont.)
  SV 52, 62
  SV 56–7, 110–11
  SV 61, 165
  SV 66, 111
  SV 70, 173
  SV 78, 62
  SV 81, 102

Gaius
  Institutes I.144, 74

Hesiod
  Histories III.38, 1
Hierocles
  Elements of Ethics, col. XI, 24

Lucretius
  On the Nature of Things I.418–48, 130
  On the Nature of Things I.453–7, 131
  On the Nature of Things I.455–6, 139
  On the Nature of Things I.464–81, 135–6
  On the Nature of Things I.830–920, 130
  On the Nature of Things I.936–50, 15
  On the Nature of Things I.968–83, 173
  On the Nature of Things II.270, 71
  On the Nature of Things II.730–841, 131
  On the Nature of Things III.370–95, 160
  On the Nature of Things III.843–61, 173
  On the Nature of Things III.881, 60
  On the Nature of Things III.950, 32
  On the Nature of Things IV.1–25, 15
  On the Nature of Things IV.26–822, 141
  On the Nature of Things IV.479–521, 141
  On the Nature of Things IV.1018–19, 174
  On the Nature of Things IV.1241, 32
  On the Nature of Things V.182, 156
  On the Nature of Things V.783–836, 22
  On the Nature of Things V.855–72, 72–3
  On the Nature of Things V.855–77, 16
  On the Nature of Things V.861, 73, 170
  On the Nature of Things V.867, 73
  On the Nature of Things V.925–30, 19–20
  On the Nature of Things V.926, 28
  On the Nature of Things V.933–6, 20
  On the Nature of Things V.937–8, 21
  On the Nature of Things V.937–42, 20
  On the Nature of Things V.953–7, 20
  On the Nature of Things V.958, 21
  On the Nature of Things V.958–9, 20, 156
  On the Nature of Things V.960–1, 22
  On the Nature of Things V.962–5, 22, 75
  On the Nature of Things V.966–9, 20
  On the Nature of Things V.988–98, 36, 58
  On the Nature of Things V.1007, 61
  On the Nature of Things V.1007–8, 58
  On the Nature of Things V.1009–10, 61
  On the Nature of Things V.1011, 25
  On the Nature of Things V.1011–18, 15
  On the Nature of Things V.1013, 21, 28–9
  On the Nature of Things V.1014, 28
  On the Nature of Things V.1019, 30
  On the Nature of Things V.1019–23, 60
  On the Nature of Things V.1019–27, 28–37
  On the Nature of Things V.1020, 166
  On the Nature of Things V.1021, 33
  On the Nature of Things V.1021–3, 165, 170
  On the Nature of Things V.1023, 31–4
  On the Nature of Things V.1024, 43
  On the Nature of Things V.1025–7, 36, 60
  On the Nature of Things V.1047–8, 155
  On the Nature of Things V.1105–10, 37–8
  On the Nature of Things V.1107, 38
  On the Nature of Things V.1115–16, 38
  On the Nature of Things V.1136–42, 39
  On the Nature of Things V.1143–50, 39
  On the Nature of Things V.1147, 42
  On the Nature of Things V.1149, 32
  On the Nature of Things V.1151–60, 35, 44
  On the Nature of Things V.1161–240, 44
  On the Nature of Things V.1169–79, 153

PHerc. 16/698
  col. XXX.3–4, 147
PHerc. 1251
  col. XII.4–19, 45, 167
  col. XIV.1–8, 88, 111
Philodemus
  On Anger, col. XXIV.39, 92
  On Anger, col. XLIV.41–XLV.5, 144
  On Death, col. II.14, 147
  On Frank Criticism, fr. 29, 147
  On Methods of Inference, col. VI.3–4, 147
  On Methods of Inference, col. XXIII.9, 147
  On Methods of Inference, fr. I.12, 147
  On Music IV, col. XXVII.6, 147
  On Music IV, col. XXXIV.3–4, 147
  On Music IV, col. XXXIV.17, 147
  On Music IV, col. CXV.29, 147
  On Music IV, col. CXV.45, 147
  On Piety I.138, 147
  On Piety I.413–14, 147
  On Piety I.1379–83, 107
  On Piety I.2149–50, 92
  On Piety I.2150–81, 44
  On Piety I.2260–1, 92
  On Piety I.2263–5, 86
  On Poems I, col. LXXXVIII.21–22, 147
  On Poems I, col. CXXVIII.2, 147
  On Poems II, col. CLIX.6–7, 147
  On Poems II, col. CXCV.17–18, 147
  On Poems V, col. XXIII.25–6, 147
  On Poems V, col. XXVIII.20, 147
  On Poems V, col. XXXIV.3, 92
  On Property Management, col. XXIV.11–19, 91–2

On the Gods I, cols. XIII–XV, 71
On the Gods I, col. XIV.31, 71
On the Gods III, col. I.3–7, 63
On the Gods III, col. XIV.39, 147
On the Good King According to Homer, col. XLIII.16–20, 41
Rhetoric, col. III.12–21 (= I.233 Sudhaus), 105
Rhetoric, col. XIa.2–7 (= II.266 Sudhaus), 157
Rhetoric, col. XX.25–36 (= I.254 Sudhaus), 154
Rhetoric, col. XXIV.26–33 (= I.259 Sudhaus), 51–2
Rhetoric, col XXIV.33–9 (= I.259 Sudhaus), 105
Rhetoric, col. XLII.7–21 (= II.41Sudhaus), 160
Rhetoric, col XLII.21 (= II.41 Sudhaus), 147
Rhetoric, fr. III.6–8 (= II.189 Sudhaus), 157
Rhetoric, fr. IX (= II.282 Sudhaus), 92
To the..., col. V.8–13, 46, 82
Plato
  Euthyphro 11e–12d, 86
  Gorgias 507a9–b4, 86
  Hippias Major 284d, 124–5
  Laws IV.715b2–4, 125
  Parmenides 130a–d, 134
  Phaedo 74a–75b, 5
  Phaedo 100c–e, 5
  Phaedrus 247c, 5
  Phaedrus 247c7, 128
  Protagoras 322b1, 23
  Protagoras 322c3, 30
  Protagoras 329c–e, 86
  Republic II.358e–359b, 3
  Republic II.359c–360d, 3, 171
  Republic V.479e, 5
  Symposium 211b, 5
Plutarch
  Against Colotes 1100d, 147
  Against Colotes 1107e, 41
  Against Colotes 1126c, 108
  Against Colotes 1126e–27c, 63
  Against Colotes 1127d, 98–9, 107
  Brutus 12.3, 109
  On Stoic Self-Contradictions 1038b, 166
  Table Talk VIII.10.2.735a–b, 159
Polystratus
  On Irrational Contempt for Common Conceptions, col. I.2, 69
  On Irrational Contempt for Common Conceptions, col. III.4–5, 69
  On Irrational Contempt for Common Conceptions, col. IV.1–3, 69
  On Irrational Contempt for Common Conceptions, col. VII.1–2, 69
  On Irrational Contempt for Common Conceptions, col. VII.4–5, 69
  On Irrational Contempt for Common Conceptions, col. VII.5–7, 69
  On Irrational Contempt for Common Conceptions, cols. XXI.17–XXIX.1, 1
  On Irrational Contempt for Common Conceptions, cols. XXI.27–XXII.18, 132
  On Irrational Contempt for Common Conceptions, cols. XXIV.8–XXV.15, 133
Porphyry
  On Abstinence I.7–12, 15, 39
  On Abstinence I.7.1–2, 168
  On Abstinence I.7.3, 146
  On Abstinence I.8.1, 42
  On Abstinence I.8.2, 19, 44
  On Abstinence I.8.2–3, 145–6
  On Abstinence I.8.3, 101
  On Abstinence I.8.4, 101
  On Abstinence I.8.4–5, 101
  On Abstinence I.9, 105
  On Abstinence I.9.4, 44
  On Abstinence I.10.1, 58
  On Abstinence I.10.2, 58
  On Abstinence I.10.2–4, 144
  On Abstinence I.10.4, 19
  On Abstinence I.11.1, 59
  On Abstinence I.11.2–5, 57
  On Abstinence I.12.5–6, 70–1, 143
  On Abstinence III.19.2, 169
POxy. 5077
  fr. II, col. II.3–11, 158
Seneca
  Moral Epistles 52.3–4, 96–7, 145
Sextus Empiricus
  Against the Mathematicians IX.45–6, 153
  Against the Mathematicians X.221–3, 131
  Against the Mathematicians X.222, 130
  Against the Mathematicians X.224–7, 136–8
Stobaeus
  Anthology II.63.6–64.12, 86
  Anthology IV.1.40, 43
  Anthology IV.1.46, 43
  Anthology IV.90.7–8, 97, 101
  Anthology IV.671.7–673.11, 24, 166
Zeno of Sidon
  fr. 28 Angeli and Colaizzo, 34

General Index

Anaxagoras, 130
Antiphon, 4–5
Aristotle
  account of justice, 7–8
  on agreements, 80
  on experience, 150
  on friendship, 30
  on human beings as political beings, 24
  on naturalism, 129
  on ontology, 131, 140
  on virtue, 83–6
Austin, 119–20

benefit
  and agreements, 93
  individual vs. group, 55–7, 106–7
  as a natural feature of the world, 53–4
  in relation to harm and security, 55

Callicles, 5
children
  as dependents in agreements, 33–4, 76
  and the loss of self-sufficiency, 27–8
  in the original state, 22–3
Chrysippus, 169
Cicero
  critic of Epicurus, 10, 59, 63, 81
  editor of *On the Nature of Things*, 16
Colotes
  on kingship, 41
common good (*commune bonum*), 20–1, 156–7
community of friends, 25, 62, 165
concord, 35–6, 43, 131
cradle argument, 20

Demetrius Lacon
  on nature, 52
  on properties of properties, 136–8
Democritus
  on being just, 103–4

  on the best form of political order, 40–1
  on concord, 42–3
  on the first human beings, 23
  on moral perception, 159–60
  relationship to Epicurus, 9
desires
  classification of, 56–7, 101–3
  and habituation, 107–8, 114–17
  unnatural and unnecessary, 77
Diogenes of Oenoanda
  on the gods, 44–5
  Golden Age fragment, 94–5
  on foreigners, 78–9, 89
  on law as a divine punishment, 44–5
  on perception, 151–2
Dworkin, Richard, 120

Epictetus, 24–5

family
  and children, 22
  emergence of, 22–30
  structure of, 33
  understood as a community, 22
forms of political order, 40–1
Fourfold Remedy, 46, 82–3
friendship
  amicitia as agreements, 30–1
  as fellowship, 31
  as a means of obtaining security, 62
  reconciling concern for self and others, 56
  saving a friend, 110–12
  saving the institution of, 112
  as a virtue, 88–9
Fuller, Lon, 120

Gassendi, Pierre, 163
Gauthier, David, 65, 164
guardianship, 72–6

Hart, H. L. A., 37, 101, 119–21
Heraclitus, 128
Hermarchus
  on animals, 70–1
  as author of the *KD*, 10
  on moral perception, 143–8
Hobbes, Thomas, 3, 12, 15, 47–8, 65, 80, 163
human beings
  as political beings, 24–5

kingship, 38–41

language
  development of, 17–18
law
  advantages and disadvantages, 43–6
  emergence of, 19–21, 37–42
  in relationship to justice/morality, 94–7, 124–6
  reasons to obey, 101–3, 105–7
Locke, John, 3, 80
Lucretius
  on animals, 71–3
  On the Nature of Things in relation to Epicurus' writings, 15
Lycophron, 80

Metrodorus, 88, 108

nomos-phusis debate, 1–2, 50
  Epicurean view, 9, 14–15, 49–52
  nomos view, 2–5
  phusis view, 5–8

Philodemus
  on animals, 71
  on the gods, 44–5
  on the naturally just, 51–2
pity, 34–5, 60, 76
Plato
  account of justice, 2–3, 5–6, 55
  on the relationship between justice and law, 124–5
  on virtue, 83
pleasure
  aponia and *ataraxia*, 20, 55, 59, 64
  kinetic and katastematic, 20
  vs. virtue, 82–3, 91
Polybius, 40
Polystratus
  on animals, 69–70
  on *nomos* and *phusis*, 126–7
  on properties, 132–4
Porphyry
  as source for Hermarchus, 168

preconceptions
  formation of, 148–52, 155–8
  of justice in relation to the laws, 105
  as lower and higher level concepts, 144–6, 152–5
  as nonrational memories, 144
properties
  determinate and determinable, 139–40
  properties of, 136–8
Protagoras
  on the best form of political order, 40–1
  on the first human beings, 23
  on friendship, 30

rational choice theory, 36, 56
reasoning
  epilogismos, 144–5, 148, 152
  logismos phase of cultural development, 18–19, 37–46
  logismos as reasoning capacity, 18, 69, 71, 84
  logismos as a structuring principle of *On the Nature of Things*, 18
Ring of Gyges, 3, 114–15, 171–4
Rousseau, Jean-Jacques, 12, 15, 48

self-sufficiency
  loss of, 26–8
  of original human beings, 19–25
Seneca, 96–7
Solon, 128
Stobaeus, 97, 101

Themistius, 24
Thrasymachus, 2, 5
Timocrates, 108, 112

violence
  in the original state, 36
  in the state of society, 43–4
virtues
  courage, 83, 86–8
  magnanimity, 88
  moderation, 86–7
  piety, 77, 86–9
  practical wisdom (*phronēsis*), 83–6
  unity of, 85–6
weak, the
  as contracting parties, 34
women
  as contracting parties, 33–4
  in the original state, 22, 75

Xenophon, 41

Zeno of Sidon, 33–4

For EU product safety concerns, contact us at Calle de José Abascal, 56–1°,
28003 Madrid, Spain or eugpsr@cambridge.org.

www.ingramcontent.com/pod-product-compliance
Ingram Content Group UK Ltd.
Pitfield, Milton Keynes, MK11 3LW, UK
UKHW020701060925
462614UK00020B/422